Michael Paterson is the author of *Voices from Dickens' London* (David & Charles, 2006) and of several books on military history. He lives in London.

A BRIEF HISTORY OF

LIFE IN
VICTORIAN BRITAIN

A Social History of
Queen Victoria's Reign

MICHAEL PATERSON

ROBINSON
PHILADELPHIA · LONDON

Cover illustrations from the author's own collection

Constable & Robinson Ltd
3 The Lanchesters
162 Fulham Palace Road
London W6 9ER
www.constablerobinson.com

First published in the UK by Robinson,
an imprint of Constable & Robinson, 2008

A copy of the British Library Cataloguing in Publication data is available
from the British Library

UK ISBN 978-1-84529-707-7

1 3 5 7 9 10 8 6 4 2

First published in the United States in 2008 by
Running Press Book Publishers

US Library of Congress number: 2007941944

US ISBN 978-0-7624-3518-0

3949833I   1/09

Running Press Book Publishers
2300 Chestnut Street
Philadelphia, PA 19103-4371

Visit us on the web!
www.runningpress.com

Printed and bound in the EU

CONTENTS

LIST OF ILLUSTRATIONS

A beach mission at Deal in Kent, 1900
Literature became a serious industry during Victoria's reign
Harrow School football XI
A roller-skating rink in the 1880s
A British 'tommy' as typically drawn for Victorian boys' magazines
Family group, outside their bungalow in Ceylon, 1880s

All illustrations are from the author's own collection

ACKNOWLEDGEMENTS

I would like to express the utmost gratitude to Leo Hollis at Constable for his unfailing patience; to Christopher Feeney for the forbearance, wisdom and humour he has brought to the daunting task of editing the text, and Jessica Cuthbert-Smith for a similar, equally praiseworthy and equally appreciated forbearance; to my sister Carolyn for marrying someone with an encyclopaedic knowledge of both sport and railways – I have been most fortunate in being able to pester my brother-in-law, Mark Rowland-Jones, with questions on these subjects at all hours of the day and night. As usual my debt is immense to Sandy Malcolm for his computing expertise. Lastly, I thank my wife Sarah, whose support has been, as always, invaluable.

To Malcolm Brown
Few are privileged to have a kinder friend

INTRODUCTION: 'A GRAND TRIUMPHAL MARCH' – THE VICTORIAN ERA

When she came to the throne coaches still ran; men wore stocks, shaved their upper lips, ate oysters out of barrels. Women said 'La!,' and owned no property. Wellnigh two generations had slipped by – of steamboats, railways, telegraphs, telephones, bicycles, electric light, and now these motor cars. Morals had changed, manners had changed. The middle class [had been] buttressed, chiselled, polished, till it was almost indistinguishable from the nobility. [It was] an era that had canonised hypocrisy, so that to seem respectable was to be.

> Soames Forsyte, a character in John Galsworthy's
> *The Forsyte Saga*, reflects on Victoria's reign
> in a chapter entitled 'The Passing of an Age'.[1]

Of all the commemorative publications that covered newsagents' stalls in June 1897, none was more lavish than the Diamond Jubilee number of the *Illustrated London News*. An expensive, self-conscious heirloom, it was expected to be treasured for generations to come. The text was bordered in gold, and the colourful and sophisticated chromo-litho illustrations – nowadays almost invariably separated and framed – still attract admiring glances at antique fairs. Among the pictures of the Royal Family, of leading politicians, literary and military heroes and of significant events, space was also devoted to the progress made during the Queen's reign. Gaslight was contrasted with electricity, the sailing vessel with the steamship, the stage-coach with the railway train, bicycle and automobile.

The point was well made. The previous sixty years had been a breathtaking era of change, an unrelenting rush of new technology, new knowledge, new opportunities, new wealth, new politics and new attitudes. Not since the Civil War two and a half centuries earlier had society altered so greatly in so short a time. Never before had the mechanics of living – the ways in which people travelled, communicated, shopped, dealt with sickness, preserved food – undergone such revolutions. To those who originally turned those pages, the lace caps and cutaway coats of the early Victorians, like their conveyances, their manners and their outlook, would have seemed absurdly quaint and distant, evoking the same mixed reactions – impatience, nostalgic longing for a simpler world, amusement ('How could they *wear* those clothes?') – as the 1890s do now.

The accompanying words, a summing-up of the state of the nation and Empire from an end-of-the-century perspective, were written by the novelist Sir Walter Besant. Born the year before the Queen's accession, and much concerned with social improvements – he was a well-known philanthropist – Besant saw his lifetime as a period of consistent and welcome progress. He commented:

> To us, who find it difficult to stand outside and consider events in their true proportion, the period seems like a grand triumphal march. To those of us who can remember English life as it was in the forties, the changes are nothing short of a transformation. And no one regrets the change. During this long period there has arisen in the national mind such a spirit of enterprise, endeavour and achievement as has no parallel in our history except in the reign of Queen Elizabeth. Now, as then, people have been restless: this restlessness has shown itself in colonisation, in emigration, in research, in discovery, in invention – in changes of every kind.[2]

He could not have known that he was capturing the essence of Britain at the high-water mark of its national greatness, and that by the time the Queen died, a few weeks into the year 1901, many of her subjects would consider their country to be in decay. This decline – chiefly caused by the loss of Britain's leading role, as her rivals caught up in wealth and power – would be political and economic, and would of course make no difference to the country's cultural, sporting or scientific achievements. Nevertheless with the passing of the 1890s it was obvious that not just a century but an era had ended, and that Britain could not hope to have such a favoured position in the next one.

With this hindsight any number of later commentators, and writers of memoirs, have referred to the Victorian era, or some part of it, with unabashed sentimentality as a 'golden age', or a 'golden calm', an 'Indian summer' or a 'long afternoon'. It is inaccurate, and misleading, to think of this or any other period in such terms. The Victorian world was not in any sense golden or summery. Epochs only gain allure when seen in retrospect, once their problems are solved or forgotten or – as in the case of Ireland – passed on so that they then belong to another generation. Any age is filled with tension, uncertainty and despair.

Nevertheless while conservatives lamented the erosion of traditional values or practices, to progressive Victorians such as Besant it seemed that there *was* a golden age, not in the past but in the future. Theirs was an era of technological break-through and ever-increasing confidence, in which the efforts of the present were visibly making a better world for their successors. Meanwhile, for all the Victorians' perceived com-placency, no set of practices or assumptions could expect to be left unquestioned, for everything was open to debate, mod-ification, improvement.

Science was solving medical problems, making childbirth easier, infant mortality lower, life expectancy longer; the temperance movement was combating the scourge of drun-kenness; people like Besant were successfully awakening the public conscience to social evils; education was becoming universal and providing opportunities for self-improvement, and a great deal of practical help – most of it the result of private charity and enterprise rather than governmental inter-vention – was being given to the unfortunate, for this was the age of Dr Barnardo and of William Booth's Salvation Army. Many of the savageries that had been unquestioned in earlier generations were being abolished or ameliorated – public executions, animal-baiting, the transportation of convicts, the flogging of soldiers and sailors. Within the sixty-four years between 1837 and 1901 spanned by Victoria's reign – three distinct generations – the British developed into a gentler, more generous, more civilized people than their uncouth Georgian grandfathers had been (by the fifties animal-baiting had been banned; in the following decade transportation and public hangings ceased; and flogging was abolished under Army reforms that began in the seventies). It is in the nature of all ages to disdain – and react against – their immediate predecessors. The Victorians hated the moral laxity of the Georgians as much as they found their architecture and their manners and their ideas passé. The sheer scale of Victorian buildings, ships, bridges or railway networks made everything that had gone before seem small and parochial by comparison. There were of course some setbacks – the disastrous collapse in 1879 of the new railway bridge across the Tay destroyed faith in the invincibility of progress – but there remained a belief that all difficulties could be overcome. Whatever the setbacks, the achievements of former ages were dwarfed by those of the present.

This spirit was already apparent in the early years of the reign, for the adjective 'Victorian' had distinct meaning from the time it first came to be self-consciously applied to the Queen's subjects. It meant belonging to an exciting new generation and a new world. As one historian has remarked, the 1840s were proving to be a time of intense self-scrutiny; newspapers and journals were calling their era 'Victorian', and the term was being associated with 'decency, modernity, a humane and progressive spirit and mechanical advance. To be "Victorian" was to be up to date.'[3] One of the features of the Queen's Diamond Jubilee celebrations was the Victorian Era Exhibition, at which her people could look back at the achievements of their own and their parents' generations. By any measure, they were entitled to feel that the Victorian world had lived up to its initial promise, for in every field it was an age in which giants had roamed the earth. The literature of Dickens, Thackeray, Trollope, the Brontës, Lewis Carroll,

Conan Doyle; the theatre of Kean and Macready, Irving and Ellen Terry; the scientific discoveries of Lister and Faraday; the explorations of Livingstone, Burton and Speke. It almost seemed as if the British Isles might sink under the weight of contemporary genius.

It was reasonable to expect that this process, continuing in the decades to come, would bring about a better society. A character in George Gissing's 1894 novel *In the Year of Jubilee* had remarked of the Queen's fiftieth anniversary celebrations that: 'It's to celebrate the fiftieth year of the reign of Queen Victoria – yes, but at the same time, and far more, it's to celebrate the completion of fifty years of Progress. Compare England now, compare the world, with what it was in 1837. It takes one's breath away!'[4] A commentator who looked at the Queen's reign from the perspective of the 1920s, W. R. Inge, paid tribute to the sense of confident optimism that had guided so much of Victorian achievement: 'The nineteenth century has been called the age of hope, and perhaps only a superstitious belief in the automatic progress of humanity could have carried our fathers and grandfathers through the tremendous difficulties which the rush through the rapids imposed on them.'[5]

People could not imagine where science, and human enterprise, would take them next. Exploration was solving the mysteries of the world – it was Britons who found the source of the Nile and the great African falls named after their Queen. Intellectual and doctrinal Rubicons were crossed by the theories of Darwin. Through the innovations of Lister, surgery became safer and easier, and the operating theatre less like a butcher's shop.

For all the scientific marvels that the era produced, the two most far-reaching and influential innovations were in transport and literacy. Though the railway had been developed before Victoria's accession, it was in her reign that it spread through Britain and the world and became an element in daily life. The advent of the bicycle extended the possibilities for independent travel by enabling even the poor to make journeys cheaply and freely. The Education Act of 1870 (1873 in Scotland), which made basic schooling compulsory, created – within a matter of decades and for the first time in history – a whole population that could read. The implications for literature and the press and for higher education were immense. Both the advent of personal mobility and of access to news and literature changed people's expectations for ever. These things created the world in which we ourselves live.

In more specific respects the world of the Victorians bears a striking resemblance to our own. Like Besant and his contemporaries, the present generation of Britons is ruled by a popular and respected female sovereign who has been on the throne for so long that no one under sixty has known another. Like the Victorians we are constantly in thrall to innovation and to new technology, taking for granted things that only a decade ago seemed like scientific fantasy. The possibility of cloning humans, or carrying a computer in one's pocket, were matched in the nineteenth century by the marvels of having one's image captured through photography or of preserving one's voice by use of the phonograph (it still seems a miracle that we can listen to Tennyson reading his 'Charge of the Light Brigade'). Our generation's fixation with the mobile phone is in some ways an echo of Victorian reverence for its first ancestor, patented in 1876 by Alexander Graham Bell.

Not only the impact of technology but many of the occurrences in their lives show an odd similarity with issues that have preoccupied the present generation. The Victorians feared recession and deplored the prohibitive cost of housing. They were familiar with terrorist bombs at home and with costly, inconclusive wars abroad – not least in Afghanistan. They experienced an outbreak of foot-and-mouth disease (1883) and a collapse of Baring's Bank (1890). They were the victims of an appalling level of crime, and believed that the streets of their cities were not safe after dark. They tutted over scandals within the Royal Family, feeling that while – in terms of personal morality – the Queen had never put a foot wrong, the behaviour of some of her younger relatives caused concern for the future. By the end of the reign, when the cult of respectability had long passed its peak of influence, many believed that standards of behaviour had fallen alarmingly. The Queen herself put the blame for this on the 'fast' element within the aristocracy, which became mired in divorces and public scandals, and set a bad example. Manners and reverence – both for people and for institutions – were in noticeable decline; a great deal of culture was shallow and 'dumbed down'; and a scurrilous tabloid press was obsessed with minor celebrities.

For Victorians – and innumerable historians ever since – their era was perceived as a single entity, but the Queen's reign, which was to last sixty-four years and prove to be the longest to date in British history, could not be categorized so neatly. Indeed the only thing that its disparate decades and generations had in common was the fact that the same head of state presided over them.

As numismatists know, three different portraits of the Queen appeared on Victorian coins. From 1838 until 1887 she was depicted as a young girl, bareheaded and with her hair tied back in the style that was to give 'bun pennies' their name. By the time of her Golden Jubilee, this youthful figure understandably seemed outdated and a new portrait of her, wearing a crown and veil and looking somewhat severe, was struck. This too was replaced, in 1893, by the final image – an elderly woman, still noble, but less austere and perhaps more sympathetic. These are known as Young Head, Jubilee Head and Old Head.

Similarly, her reign might be divided into three phases, though they do not correspond with the dates above. The beginning – effectively a continuation of the Regency – was a time of depression, hardship and frightening social unrest. Her first full decade, the 'Hungry Forties', witnessed further depression at home and the horrors of the potato famine in Ireland, as well as the threat of political upheaval from the Chartists and from the European revolutions.

The hugely successful Great Exhibition of 1851 is seen as ushering in the long middle period – the 'mid-Victorian calm', though there was nothing calm about the Crimean War or the Indian Mutiny, and fear of invasion by the French was so acute that the country's southern coast bristled with fortifications, while volunteer soldiers enlisted in their thousands. In the sixties there were bad harvests and recession once more, as well as the threat of sedition in Ireland. The seventies witnessed a major agricultural depression that resulted from a series of bad harvests. It lasted into the nineties as the price of produce continued to fall, and brought widespread misery throughout rural Britain. For the aristocracy and landed gentry, many of whom now found it impossible to live on the proceeds of their estates, it marked the moment at which it became necessary – and socially acceptable – for their sons to work for a living in the City.

To some observers the eighties were an apogee of British civilization, though there was serious trouble in Ireland, and terrorism, developed in its modern sense by Russian anarchists at this time, spread to Britain; Scotland Yard's Special Branch was founded in 1884 to counter the threat from Irish bombers. The arts became openly decadent in a way that shocked respectable opinion – for the 'naughty nineties' began in the eighties – and led to a number of strident and vigorous campaigns against certain books and plays. In spite of these, the public continued to be shocked. There was thus a feeling among people concerned with moral health that the nation was losing its way and failing to meet its own high standards of civilization. In the event, the backlash against decadence made considerable headway, so that those who advocated freedom in the arts were as frustrated as those who opposed it.

The last phase of the era was seen by many older Victorians as a time of tastelessness, loose morals and unrestrained materialism. Society seemed to have become the preserve of newly titled plutocrats, whose vast and ostentatious wealth – often gleaned from gold and diamond mining or from large-scale trade – offended the sensitivities of traditionalists. Britain was seen as taking its cultural cue from the United States, then in its 'Gilded Age' of vast commercial fortunes, and the possessors of some of these were marrying their daughters into the British aristocracy. Not only had an unapologetic, even boastful attitude to wealth been imported from across the Atlantic, but so had a brash and lowbrow tabloid press ('yellow journalism').

The trial of Oscar Wilde brought into the glare of public scrutiny one aspect of a world of vice that the respectable had preferred to ignore. The traditions of religion had been challenged by Darwinism, religious observance had noticeably lessened, and although society had a structure and a hierarchy, its rules were always changing and its conventions were under constant attack. In addition, Britain was an immensely richer and more advanced country than she had been in 1837, but the sense of steady and unstoppable technological progress that observers had remarked upon was not matched by any feeling that society was much happier or that the worse characteristics of human nature had been subdued.

Speed of travel was eliminating distance and making the world ever smaller. Medicine was conquering pain, saving lives and prolonging life. Machinery was taking the strain out of work. People became richer than their forefathers. They had more money to spend, more choice in the shops, more leisure in which to spend it. The standard of living for millions was continually improving. More people had access to foreign travel, education and culture than had been imaginable a few generations earlier. Mass marketing, mass media and mass culture were all inventions of this time. Predictably, these changes could be seen as negative or dangerous. There was a feeling that with novelty and plenty had come a trivialization and a thoughtless haste that did not represent improvement. In one of his books for boys, the author Talbot Baines Reed remarked on the frantic tempo that had come to characterize people's lives:

It is a common complaint in these degenerate days that we live harder than our fathers did. Whatever we do we rush at. We bolt our food, and run for the train; we jump out of it before it has stopped, and reach the school door just as the bell rings; we 'cram' for our examinations, and 'spurt' for our prizes. We have no time to read books, so we scuttle through the reviews, and consider ourselves up in the subject; we cut short our letters home, and have no patience to hear a long story out. We race off with a chum for a week's holiday, and consider we have dawdled unless we have covered our thirty miles a day, and can name as visited a string of sights, mountains, lakes, and valleys a whole yard long.[6]

The more people *could* do, the more they *sought* to do, and thus the greater the stress under which they put themselves – a notion that is considered equally true of our own time.

The speed of communications was undoubtedly a blessing, but it meant a loss of 'quality of life'. Winston Churchill, writing to his brother in the nineties, lamented this. As an up-to-date young man, Churchill was the very archetype of the thrusting, impatient, indecently ambitious new generation, yet he mourned the loss of good habits that had characterized more leisured days:

> In England, you can in a few hours get an answer to a letter from any part of the country. Hence letter writing becomes short, curt and if I may coin a word 'telegramatic'. A hundred years ago letter writing was an art. In those days pains were taken to avoid slang, to write good English, to spell well and cultivate style: Letters were few and far between & answers long delayed. You may appreciate the present rapidity of correspondence, but you will hardly claim that modern style is an improvement.[7]

It is almost uncanny to compare these remarks with what is said today about the effects of email on the art of letter-writing and of 'texting' on people's ability to spell correctly. When complaining to his mother about the mistakes made in the proof-reading of his first book, Churchill once again blamed the times: 'I might have known that no one could or would take the pains that an author would bestow, a type of the careless slapdash spirit of the age'.[8]

The fact that a multitude of labour-saving domestic devices could now take much of the burden from housewives was expected to make life easier, yet somehow it was not having this effect, as *The Sphere* noted in 1900: 'Every sort of contrivance now lessens labour – carpet sweepers, knife machines, bathrooms, lifts – in spite of these the life of a housewife is one long wrestle and failure to establish order.'[9]

Galsworthy's character Soames Forsyte was right in identi-
fying the emergence of a confident middle class as one of the
most important aspects of the age. The existence of an influential mercantile element in society was, of course, not unique
to the Victorians but was deeply rooted in the culture of
Britain's 'nation of shopkeepers'. Nonetheless it was during
the Queen's reign that this class gradually consolidated its
control over the country's political, financial and cultural
institutions, its power increasing as that of the aristocracy
declined. By the end of the reign it was effectively running the
country (despite the presence in government of aristocratic
figures like Lord Salisbury and Lord Curzon), as it has been
ever since. Writing in 1988, the historian John Lukacs suggested that future generations will refer to our times as 'the
Bourgeois Age'. If so, we will share the label with the Victorians, in whose day this age began.

Britons had, long before 1837, developed the belief that they
had a moral superiority over others, and that this had been
earned by the nation's adherence to (Protestant) Christian
ethics, its pragmatic common sense, its ingenuity and industry,
its enlightened form of government, military skills and superior administrative ability. It was, however, the Victorians who
identified most closely with these attitudes, for a larger Empire
and greater influence made them more evident and more
widespread. It was, they felt, for the British to show the
way to less fortunate peoples, and there were splendid examples of men who did. The best of this breed were superb, and
their achievement in organizing and running a single community that covered a quarter of the globe was undoubtedly
impressive. Whatever faults the British Empire may have had,
it produced a number of significant benefits for its subject
peoples and for the world at large. The greatest of these was
the Pax Britannica – with a major military power to police the

oceans and put down banditry, more people throughout the world probably slept peacefully in their beds than at any time before or since.

Looking at photographs of those who lived during this era, it is often difficult to feel any sense of kinship, even in cases where they are our own ancestors. The outlandish clothes and hair-styles, the awkward-looking hats, the sticks and parasols and the dresses belong to a way of life that is often beyond our under-standing. Their solemn, unsmiling faces seem pompous, hu-mourless, uncomfortable. But it is worth remembering that these images usually bore little resemblance to the sitters' normal lives or personalities. They were positioned uncomfortably in unnatural attitudes that had to be held for several minutes. They were often in their best clothes because people dressed up to have their picture taken, and they were *told* not to smile.

Anyone who thinks they lacked humour should simply read a novel by Jerome K. Jerome, or look through one of the volumes of *Punch* that can still sometimes be found on the shelves of libraries. The cartoons are a triumph of draughts-manship, and the jokes, in a remarkable number of cases, are still funny. This magazine, with the insight it gives into the lighter side of our forebears' world, is another precious legacy of the era and one still appreciated. A member of a later generation, recalling the library at his school, captured the sense of affection the periodical still evokes:

> For the newcomer the bound copies of *Punch* are the most potent drug. I've seen boys work through several volumes in one evening (most of them with the jokes signposted by italics), unsmiling and completely happy.[10]

While they were proud of their nation's accomplishments and of the qualities of leadership that their schools, universities and regiments could produce, the Victorians were never able to feel that the work was finished, for someone was always letting the side down – an aristocrat would bring disgrace on an ancient family by marrying a chorus girl; a colonial administrator in some remote outpost would go mad and shoot himself; a national hero would be found to have a scandalous private life. A small, but revealing, example of this perpetual disappointment that the high-minded were wont to encounter is perhaps worth citing. In descriptions of genteel summer boating parties on the Thames, it is often remarked that the pleasure of ladies and gentlemen in admiring the scenery was marred by the sight of 'savages'. This term refers to small boys, and sometimes men, swimming naked from the banks. The implication was that Britons, who sent missionaries and officials all over the world to clothe the naked and bring civilization to others, should know better than to behave in their own country as if they were no better than natives. In their world there were always 'savages' to mar the beauty.

To deal in a single book with a period so lengthy and crowded is a formidable task. It is also difficult not to generalize about a people so multi-faceted and diverse. Their era was not a solid block of history but a long series of different experiences and a constantly re-forming set of attitudes. The Victorians were not as confident or complacent as we may suppose, and the individuals or organizations that represented particular ideals were not necessarily typical of the populace as a whole.

Inevitably it has been necessary to leave some subjects by the wayside. I have sought to dwell upon, and illustrate, two basic themes: one is that the Victorians' world was created by a set of historical circumstances, unique and unrepeatable, that placed their country in a position of largely unchallenged military and industrial might throughout much of the nineteenth century. The other is that, to a surprising extent, they were very like us. They had a fixation with technology, and were guilty of gross materialism, yet this was balanced – as it is in our generation – by a genuine concern for the less fortunate and a willingness to give charitable aid.

The Victorians are not so far away from us after all. We live in homes and walk streets that they built, eat food that they devised ways of preparing, flush our lavatories into sewers that they created, enjoy pictures and music and buildings that they produced. They bequeathed to our world so many of the things we now use that we would be foolish to regard them as irrelevant museum-pieces. They gave us organized sports, efficient transport and postal systems (the pillar-box was invented by the novelist Anthony Trollope); vigorous, informative and entertaining journalism; cinema; the motor car; electronic communications; modern medicine; and a galaxy of wonderful monuments, museums and art galleries. They built the railways – and most of the docks – that carry people and goods around the world, and many of the hospitals and schools from which we benefit. Our debt to them is enormous.

I

SYMBOL OF AN AGE

By virtue of her long reign over what was then the world's wealthiest, most powerful and influential nation, it was inevitable that Victoria would give her name to the era in which she lived. She had, in fact, two names. The first was Alexandrina (as a child she was known as Drina), in recognition of the fact that her godfather was the Russian Tsar, Alexander I. Had she not abandoned this when she became Queen, the nomenclature of many familiar things – a London railway terminus, a series of waterfalls in Africa, a state in Australia, an award for gallantry, as well as the term for the mid and late nineteenth century – would have been significantly different. 'Victoria' was a French name. Some in government circles felt that both her names sounded too unEnglish, and debated whether, at her coronation, she should adopt the name Charlotte or Elizabeth. Had she taken the latter she would, of course, have been Queen Elizabeth II.

The Nation's Hope

From the moment she succeeded to the throne, at the age of eighteen, in June 1837, it was clear that a new era had begun. There had not been a female sovereign since the death of Queen Anne in 1714, and there had not been one so young since Edward VI almost three centuries earlier. Her immediate predecessors had been two of her uncles, and both had been elderly. The former, George IV, had been highly unpopular with the public, and his death was greeted with indifference or relief. The latter, William IV, had been amiable and conscientious, and had begun the work of restoring public confidence in the monarchy that his niece was to continue. William's large illegitimate family, the Fitzclarences, linked him however with the debauchery and repeated scandal which had latterly made the Hanoverian dynasty a target for hostility and ridicule, and it was refreshing that the new, eighteen-year-old monarch carried no baggage.

At the time of Victoria's birth the elderly, blind and mentally unbalanced George III had still been alive. His eldest son ruled in his name as Prince Regent, and the Royal Family included the King's six other sons: the Dukes of York, Clarence, Kent, Cumberland, Sussex and Cambridge. This large family had not, between them, produced enough legitimate children to ensure the succession. There had been only one heir to the throne: Princess Charlotte, the Regent's daughter. When she died in 1817, the future of the monarchy was placed in doubt.

Since the Prince Regent refused to have any further children by his wife, Parliament was reduced to badgering his brothers to procreate. The Duke of Kent was successful. Abandoning his mistress, he married a German princess, Victoria of Saxe-Coburg-Saalfeld, and went to live with her in the dukedom of Gotha. There the child was conceived. For dynastic reasons, however, it was necessary for the birth to take place in Britain.

In haste and in some confusion, the couple and their entourage travelled to London, where their daughter was born on 24 May 1819.

Unusually for a royal child, Victoria had no siblings. She did not know her father, who died in 1820, and she was brought up in genteel poverty by her mother and a German governess. Though it was in many respects a somewhat dull and lonely childhood, Victoria was a bright and lively girl, gifted at singing and drawing, articulate in her use of words (she spoke well, and kept a journal from 1832 until the end of her life), interested in ballet and passionately keen on opera, and with an immense collection of dolls, to all of whom she gave names and identities.

The personification of the country's future – the 'Nation's Hope' – she was the subject of great public interest from early youth. George IV, as the Regent became in 1820, allowed her to live in Kensington Palace. Parliament voted her an allowance, and William IV tried to befriend her. The increasingly bitter feud between her mother and William, however, kept Victoria away from Court, and she did not attend his coronation in 1831.

The girl's early years were dominated by her mother and the ambitious comptroller of her household, Sir John Conroy, who isolated her from the tainted Hanoverians – a successful move that increased her popularity – but both also wished to exert influence through her once she was Queen, a fact that she was shrewd and strong-minded enough to resent and resist. Nevertheless she gained important qualities from her upbringing – her governess taught her the value of regular and conscientious work; her mother taught her always to be kind and appreciative toward servants, an attitude that she was to display through the whole of her life. As well as excellent manners, she learned from the Duchess to discipline her temper, and to regard her position with relative modesty.

As a child she became increasingly aware of her destiny, famously stating at the age of eleven that, as sovereign, 'I will be good.' By the time she was an adolescent, her training had already begun. She studied history, and was inspired by the personality of Queen Elizabeth. From the age of fourteen she received a thorough grounding in how to rule from her Uncle Leopold, King of the Belgians and husband of the deceased Princess Charlotte, who took a paternal interest in the girl and had a significant influence on her character. To acquaint her with her future realm, she embarked with her mother on a series of annual tours throughout the country, staying at the homes of local aristocracy.

This visibility added to her appeal, and her eighteenth birthday was widely celebrated in May 1837, a significant date because she then came of age (this was the customary age among heirs apparent, or presumptive, rather than twenty-one), and was thus eligible to succeed the ailing William IV. Had he died sooner her mother would have had to act as Regent, and he had been determined to live long enough to prevent this. Victoria reached her majority with impeccable timing, for less than a month later her uncle died. On 19 June she wrote to Leopold that: 'I look forward to the event which must occur soon with calmness and quietness. I am not alarmed at it, and yet I do not suppose myself quite equal to all.'[1] It did occur soon – the following morning she was woken at Kensington Palace with the news that she was Queen.

The great historian Thomas Carlyle wrote at this time: 'Poor little Queen, she is at an age when a girl can hardly be trusted to choose a bonnet for herself, yet a task has been laid upon her from which an archangel might shrink.'[2] She did not shrink from it. Over the succeeding months she proved extremely adept at performing her various duties, for she had not only studied and absorbed much of what was necessary, but clearly loved her role as sovereign. She had a good memory, a flair for languages and a head for figures. A strong-willed, even imperious young woman, on the threshold of adulthood and enjoying the chance to exercise influence, she felt ready to become queen and was undaunted by the challenges involved. She brought youth, vigour, humour and tremendous enthusiasm to an office that had seen none of these things within living memory. She was so naturally regal that, it was said, she never in her life looked behind her before sitting down – someone would always have placed a chair. Another observer commented that: 'Everything goes on as if she had been on the throne six years instead of six days.'[3] Despite her youth and the advanced age of many of the courtiers and politicians who surrounded her, she could deploy her famous temper to effect. The Duchesse de Prasline recorded that: 'Ministers tremble when this young being shows discontent at anything,' for she 'could not hide anger or annoyance.'[4]

Victoria was not considered beautiful. George Eliot said unkindly that her looks were: 'utterly mean in contour and expression . . . worse the more one looks at her.'[5] At just under five feet tall she was somewhat short (she therefore liked to be seen on horseback, and rode frequently in Rotten Row). She had a long nose, slightly prominent teeth, eyes that had a tendency – increasing as she grew older – to protrude, and fair hair that was to darken to brown when she reached adulthood, before turning white in her latter years.

Even as a young woman she was inclined towards plumpness, a trait exacerbated by her love of eating. She was persuaded that this increased girth enhanced the regal aspect of her appearance. Nevertheless she smiled readily, and had beautiful china-blue eyes. Her appearance was regarded as pleasing. Popular prints of the young sovereign, which gave her greater beauty than she possessed, sold briskly and created a horde of admirers. Charles Dickens was one of them. He wrote to a friend that: 'I am sorry to say I have fallen hopelessly in love with the Queen, and wander up and down with vague and dismal thoughts of running away with a maid of honour.'[6] Her voice was much complimented. Lady Lyttelton, who saw her prorogue Parliament in 1839, remembered that it was: 'quite that of a child, a gushing sort of richness with the most sensible, cultivated and gentleman-like accent and emphasis'.[7]

Her coronation took place almost exactly a year after her accession, on 28 June 1838. It marked the beginning of the modern British monarchy, for the new Queen – cheerful, pleasant and simple in her tastes – captured the imagination of the public and the affection of the rising middle class, the sector of society that has provided the most consistent support for the institution ever since. Her coronation was the first for some time to be celebrated with genuine enthusiasm.

Despite her confidence, Victoria would have been lost without the guidance of her Prime Minister, Lord Melbourne. He attended her daily in his official capacity, as well as devoting many afternoons to riding and evenings to dining with her (they became so close that she was jeered in public as 'Mrs Melbourne'). He provided her with a thorough apprenticeship in her craft, as well as being a father figure. She appreciated his wit, experience, wisdom and amiability, but he also strengthened in her an existing – and unconstitutional – bias toward the Whig party, to which he belonged. When he was obliged to resign in 1839 and Victoria was faced with the prospect of the Tory Sir Robert Peel as Prime Minister, she engineered a crisis by refusing to replace any of her Whig court ladies. Peel, seeing this as evidence that she did not have faith in him, refused to form a Government, and Melbourne resumed the premiership – a heady victory for an inexperienced ruler.

'Albert the Good'

The most significant influence in Victoria's life appeared in 1839, when she became engaged. It was considered necessary that she marry as soon as possible and produce an heir. Despite her position and consequent desirability as a bride, her options were limited. She could marry either a cousin within her own family or a foreign prince – so long as he were Protestant. This effectively limited the choice to northern Europe, but a suitable candidate had been unofficially earmarked almost from birth as a future husband. Her uncle, King Leopold, was responsible for the choice of Albert, Prince of Saxe-Coburg-Gotha, and had been preparing the young man since childhood. The younger son of a dissolute minor princeling, Albert was a few months younger than Victoria. He was Leopold's nephew and Victoria's cousin. She had met him once already, when both were seventeen, and had found him pleasant enough. She had recorded in her journal that he was: 'Extremely handsome, his hair is about the same colour as mine; his eyes large and blue, and he has a beautiful nose, and a very sweet mouth with fine teeth; but the charm of his countenance is his expression, which is most delightful.'[8] In what was almost a carbon copy of Victoria's childhood vow to be good, Albert had made a similar youthful commitment: 'I intend to train myself to be a good and useful man.'[9] It was a promise he was resoundingly to fulfil.

Both of them knew of the plan to bring them together, but he was somewhat reluctant. He had heard that she was wilful and short-tempered, and was inclined to withdraw from any putative arrangement. She made clear that she would only marry for love, and insisted that any alliance must wait two or three years, for she had just emerged from an austere and restricted childhood into a life of complete independence, and had no wish to be imprisoned by a husband. Her heroine, Queen Elizabeth, had not married at all, and she toyed with the notion of remaining single. When Albert arrived with his brother at Windsor for a visit, there were no grounds for assuming that the match would win the enthusiasm of either party.

In the event, within a few days they were deeply in love. Victoria was overwhelmed by his handsome appearance, recalling that: 'Albert's beauty is most striking, and he is so amiable and unaffected – in short very fascinating.'[10] She determined to marry him, and Melbourne urged that the arrangements be made at once. The Queen mused whether 'I hadn't better tell Albert of my decision soon . . . for in general such things were done the other way.'[11] Five days after his arrival he was summoned by the Queen for reasons that were obvious. No one could propose to the sovereign, therefore it was she who asked him. He accepted at once. Their engagement lasted only three months, and they married at the Chapel Royal in St James' Palace on 10 February 1840.

The relationship was of great significance for both the monarchy and the nation. Royal families were not known for love matches, and this – one of history's great romances – set the seal of impeccable respectability on Victoria's reign. The couple were mutually devoted, though the Queen's temper and her consort's frequent frustrations made their home-life extremely volatile: Victoria once reputedly tipped a cup of scalding tea on his head, and she frequently followed him, shouting, from room to room (he would control his temper, withdraw, and continue the exchange by letter). Nevertheless he answered a need in her nature for the guidance of a mature masculine figure. As an only child she lacked the security of a large family, and she was always in search of a substitute for the father she never had. Leopold and Melbourne had both provided this, as Disraeli would at a later stage. Albert's intelligence, his wide interests and his devotion to duty – though almost entirely unappreciated by the public during his lifetime – were to prove a gift of inestimable value to his adopted country.

Thanks to Leopold's grooming Albert had arrived in England with a working knowledge of the country's language, laws and customs, yet he found himself unpopular. Among his wife's family – and royalty in general – he was snubbed as a nonentity. The aristocracy – amoral, hedonistic and anti-intellectual – resented his earnest and puritanical nature (even his wife was irritated by his habit of retiring to bed early: if required to stay up late, he might fall asleep in his chair). The British public distrusted him as a foreigner – during the Crimean War there were widely believed rumours that, as a German and therefore presumably pro-Russian, he was to be imprisoned for treason in the Tower of London. They found his poverty in relation to the Queen a source of some amusement. Though he was not – as was widely believed – entirely lacking in humour, this was never obvious outside his family. He had no small-talk and his manner in public – a combination of natural shyness, intellectual snobbery and stiff German etiquette – was seen by many as insufferable. Courtiers were offended that he and Victoria spoke to each other in German at meals, excluding others from the conversation.

Constitutionally, he had no power or position. At first, the sole function he was allowed to fulfil was applying the blotter when the Queen had signed a document, and only gradually did he create a meaningful role for himself. It was, of course, understood that he also had responsibility for providing the country with an heir, and this matter was swiftly addressed. The Queen, who regarded sex as 'a foretaste of heaven' but who was to dread childbearing ('I think of being like a cow or a dog at such moments') was expecting within weeks of marriage, and her first child – a girl, named Victoria but known as Vicky – was born in November 1840. Eight others were to

follow: the Prince of Wales ('Bertie') in 1841, and then Alice
(1843), Alfred (1844), Helena (1846), Louise (1848), Arthur
(1850), Leopold (1853) and Beatrice (1857). There were so
many children that 'the taxpayer groaned', for Buckingham
Palace had to be extended. These frequent, exhausting preg-
nancies were to preoccupy the Queen throughout much of the
first two decades of her reign, and her husband found himself
deputizing for her, in both a ceremonial and a consultative
capacity, increasingly often.

He in any case held a host of titular posts as patron of
societies, chairman of committees or honorary colonel of regiments. Many of these were worthy but dull. The innumerable
addresses he delivered to assorted bodies were summed up by
one biographer in the unkind comment: 'Albert's speeches were
stupefyingly boring.'[12] Nevertheless, he expanded many of his
honorary positions into active roles that enabled him to exert an
important influence, and in doing so he became the prototype of
a figure that would become increasingly familiar in the twentieth
century – the working royal. Under his guidance the Queen, too,
attained a higher visibility in terms of 'good works'. She had
always been a generous donor to the needy (an often-repeated
story that she gave only £5 to relieve hardship after the Irish
potato famine is entirely unfounded). Now she increasingly
took on the patronage of charitable organizations, and was
ultimately connected with over 150 of them.

A talented composer and musician, and a connoisseur of art
with ability of his own, interested equally in arts and sciences,
Albert had much to contribute to British culture. It was Peel
who saw his potential and gave him the opportunity to do so,
for in 1841 he was appointed chairman of a Fine Art Commission to decorate the new Houses of Parliament. He proved an
extremely able administrator, and his other positions, both
honorary and effective, came to him as a result. The Queen

bestowed on him the title 'Prince Consort' in 1857. He was to serve, among other things, as Field Marshal (he declined to become Commander-in-Chief), Colonel of the Grenadier Guards and the Rifle Brigade, Master of Trinity House, Chancellor of Cambridge University, President of the Royal Society, the Society of Arts, the Anti-Slavery Society and the Society for Improving the Conditions of the Labouring Classes.

He introduced the 'Balmoral' tartan still worn by the Royal Family and the helmets worn by the Household Cavalry, as well as the hideous and cumbersome funeral car used at the burial of the Duke of Wellington. He jointly designed the Victoria Cross (with the Queen, who proposed the motto: 'For Valour') and the Italianate Osborne House (with the architect Sir Thomas Cubbitt). He was responsible for the 'model dwellings' for the working class that were shown at the Great Exhibition. In addition, he reorganized the Royal Household, previously a byword for inefficiency, and made the Windsor estates profitable. He created a 'model farm' there, and his livestock competed successfully for prizes at agricultural shows. As a patron of the arts he was undoubtedly important. He built a significant collection of paintings that was later acquired for the nation, and he and Victoria took it upon themselves to rescue English theatre from the doldrums by having frequent performances staged at Windsor.

'Dual Monarchy'

While he filled his diary with cultural and philanthropic activity, he also assumed an increasing significance in the conduct of royal business, becoming *de facto* his wife's private secretary. She recorded that, 'Albert grows daily fonder and fonder of politics and business, while I grow daily to dislike them more and more.'[13] He had, since their marriage, exerted an important influence on the Queen's outlook (he even helped her choose her bonnets). She had already begun to leave behind her youthful frivolity, but his example encouraged her to develop the serious and dutiful side of her nature, and she became increasingly dependent on his advice. He read state papers, condensing complex issues for her perusal, and he normally dictated her letters. Though she might sometimes alter the tone of a sentence or a paragraph, she almost invariably followed his advice. How closely they worked together can be appreciated by present-day visitors to Osborne, who are shown their side-by-side desks. Albert sat to the left of the Queen, reading documents, adding comments and passing them to her for approval and signature. As Laurence Housman observed: 'Without the Prince Consort to train her, she would not have been a good Queen.'[14]

Albert wanted Victoria to claim foreign policy as a personal sphere. It was to her that ambassadors presented their credentials, and he therefore saw the Queen as legitimately entitled to exert influence. This was, he considered, necessary because Lord Palmerston, who was Foreign Secretary or Prime Minister during much of her first two decades, was reckless and confrontational. It was also obvious that Victoria could deal directly with other monarchs in a way that her Government could not. It was the Queen who, by making a private visit to King Louis-Philippe in 1843, began to develop cordial official relations with France for the first time in centuries. This friendship survived a change of dynasty, for in 1855 she journeyed to Paris to see Napoleon III, and both French monarchs reciprocated by coming to England. These connections (interestingly, both monarchs settled in England after being overthrown) set a precedent in Anglo-French friendship that was to be significant in the following century.

While Victoria appreciated Albert's assistance, it increased his unpopularity in the country at large. In Parliament, the press and the public, there was considerable resentment of his perceived interference in affairs of state. The period between his marriage in 1840 and his death in 1861 has been dubbed 'the dual monarchy'. He did not lack defenders, however, on the grounds that his advice was given without political bias. Lord Malmesbury wrote that: 'No sovereign could have at his side a better counsellor, removed as he is from all personal disputes of parties.'[15]

He also persuaded Victoria to adopt a more politically neutral stance. In the volatile political climate of the 1840s it was vital that extremes be avoided. Though this period of instability passed without mishap, the lesson was never adequately taken to heart, for throughout her life she would display both personal and political favouritism towards governments and prime ministers. He persuaded her, however, to abandon her reservations regarding Peel and to work with the Tory Government. By doing so she increased public respect, for her Whig loyalties had been much discussed in the press. This show of impartiality would not last, and in the latter part of her reign it would be the Tory party with whose policies and outlook she would openly sympathize.

Needing privacy for their growing family – for at Windsor the public could come close enough to peer through the castle windows – Victoria and Albert sought homes of their own that were more suited to bringing up children. The result was the creation of two personal retreats. The first was at Osborne on the Isle of Wight, where, between 1845 and 1849, they had an existing house converted into a rambling Italianate villa. Here they spent idyllic summers, though it also provided a refuge when in 1848 a mass demonstration by Chartists made London seem too dangerous.

Their other sanctuary was at Balmoral in Scotland. In 1842 they had visited the Queen's northern realm and had fallen in love with the Highlands, which bore a passing resemblance to the Germany of Albert's youth. They found the local people – forthright in speech and behaviour – a pleasing contrast to the deference and backbiting of London. Between 1853 and 1855, a Scottish baronial castle was built for them. Here they lived, for months at a time, in a world of kilts and pipers and stalking and fishing. As at Osborne, Albert's influence on the building and its interiors was noticeable. With its tartan wallpaper and deer-antler furniture it was a fantasy almost worthy of the Bavarian king, Ludwig II.

Such was Victoria's pleasure in these surroundings that she published two books about her life in Scotland. *Leaves from a Journal of Our Life in the Highlands* sold well, spawning a sequel – if only because it was unprecedented for a reigning monarch to publish a work about her life (she presented Dickens with a copy of the first book inscribed: 'From the humblest of writers to one of the greatest.'). The fact that her subjects could read about her summer holidays and family picnics was symptomatic of the monarchy as it had developed under Victoria. Previously, the private life of the Royal Family had been a subject for scurrilous mockery. Depictions of it in popular prints had been disrespectful and often vicious. Now the monarch and her consort were a model of respectability whose example the public were encouraged to follow. The fact that Albert did not gamble, keep a mistress or waste his time in idleness, and that Victoria was a doting wife and mother as well as a queen, meant that their private life fitted – entirely unintentionally – with the ideals of an evangelical element in public opinion that was at its most powerful around the mid-century. Their earnestness, together with a climate of piety, were a marked influence on the Victorian era and have been seen by later generations as defining its character. Pictures, which sold well in cheap coloured editions, showed them enjoying simple pleasures in cosy domestic settings – gathering around a Christmas tree (Albert was credited with introducing this custom to Britain, though in fact it was probably Queen Charlotte, the German wife of George III, who did so) or romping on the carpet. One such image, entitled 'The Queen and Prince Albert at Home', shows the Prince on all fours while his children pretend he is a horse.

Albert and Victoria were untypical parents, as they were atypical of many things that characterized their era. They were not punctilious churchgoers, for instance, and did not believe in the keeping of the Sabbath as rigorously as many of Victoria's subjects did. Though their children were naturally put in the care of nurses and tutors, they were not in the least neglected, and a great deal of attention was paid to them – especially remarkable considering the commitments of both parents. Their education was meticulously planned, but was not without pleasures. At Osborne they each had garden plots to look after. In the grounds can be seen their toy blockhouse and the miniature Swiss chalet in which they learned housekeeping and entertained their parents to tea. One of its features was a little grocer's shop called Spratt's, in which they learned the value of money. The Queen described how, on one occasion she: 'went with the children – Alice and I driving – to the Swiss Cottage, which was all decked out with flags in honour of [Prince] Alfred's birthday. A band played and after dinner we danced, with the three boys and three girls and the company, a merry country dance on the terrace.'[16] The Queen had no fondness for babies (she thought they looked like 'frogs') and found it difficult to talk to her children, of whom she and Albert made considerable demands. Yet their sons and daughters were given a childhood that was often idyllic, and on which in later years they would look back with immense nostalgia.

Royals in Public

Two new developments meant that some of this family life could be shared with the public. The first was the railway. A royal train enabled the Queen and her family to travel swiftly all over the realm and permitted vast numbers of people to see them. The other was the invention of photography, which had coincided with the Queen's accession. In 1841 the first photographic portrait studio opened in London. Albert was photographed the following year and Victoria in 1845. By the 1850s it was possible to make numerous copies of a single photograph, and the result was the *carte de visite*, a visiting-card-sized image. A widespread and long-lasting fashion developed for collecting pictures of celebrities, and this brought the Queen's family into the public eye in a way never before possible. Numerous, young and attractive, the Royal Family was an obvious subject for photographs. Before Victoria's reign, very few people had seen the monarch other than as an image on coins. Now millions of subjects knew what she, her husband, her children and her homes looked like. The clothes they wore could be imitated, and, in two cases, quickly set fashions for children's dress: the kilts and bonnets worn by the boys were adopted in thousands of middle-class households. The sailor suit made for Bertie in 1846 by a tailor aboard the royal yacht – and recorded in a portrait by Winterhalter – was so enchanting that it was also adapted for girls and set a worldwide trend that lasted until the Second World War (the original is in the National Maritime Museum). The Royal Family had become – to use a modern phrase – accessible. As a result of new technology (the mass-printed illustrated newspaper as well as photography) they became part of everyday life in precisely the way that television documentaries have demystified the Royal Family in our own time. These things made a cult of Victoria and Albert.

The Queen had a sharp eye for detail and sometimes her foibles took on the nature of commands. When visiting France in 1855, she recorded in her sketchbook the uniforms of the soldiers who lined the route or guarded her residences – these were, after all, the allies of her own troops in the Crimea. She was especially taken with the Zouaves – infantrymen dressed in a North African uniform of turbans, short jackets and immensely baggy trousers. On her return she expressed a desire to see some of her own soldiers outfitted in this manner. Englishmen would have looked ridiculous in such clothing, so War Office officials were obliged to study maps of the Empire in search of somewhere in which it could be introduced. They chose the Caribbean, and it became the distinctive uniform of black troops of the West India Regiment. It was seen in London when a contingent participated in the Queen's Diamond Jubilee, and it is still worn by bandsmen of the Barbados Defence Force.

A notable characteristic of the Royal Family was its seeming ordinariness. The Queen, when not in robes of state, had a dress-sense that was much commented upon, and not favourably. When she made her visits to France, in 1843 and 1855, the crowds were astonished at her appearance. Charlotte Brontë happened to see her on the former occasion, and described her as 'a little, stout, vivacious lady, very plainly dressed, not much dignity or pretension about her'.[17] On the latter visit the public – accustomed to their own Empress, the statuesque and beautiful Eugénie – were surprised to see Victoria in an unremarkable dress, carrying a large green umbrella and an ugly handbag decorated with a parrot that had been embroidered by one of her children. It was also noticed that she wore rings on every finger and even on both thumbs (though this habit was an attempt to conceal her somewhat unsightly hands rather than to show off wealth

or taste in jewellery). She could easily have been mistaken for
the wife of a bourgeois Englishman, and this too enabled her
subjects to identify with her.

As well as their irreproachable family life, Victoria and
Albert won admiration by their enthusiasm for progress. In
an era of self-conscious modernity, they clearly enjoyed and
made use of the conveniences and pleasures that technology
provided, and whatever was done by the Queen and her family
was inevitably going to be emulated by others. They travelled
extensively by rail. They became patrons of the Photographic
Society. Most significantly, the Queen agreed to have chloroform when giving birth to her eighth child, Prince Leopold, in
1853. At the time this caused considerable controversy. The
practice of giving this anaesthetic to women during childbirth
had been introduced only in 1847, and its dangers and possible
side-effects were not well understood. Attempting to avoid the
pain of labour was also seen in devout circles as proof of a lack
of trust in the divine will. The Queen ignored these criticisms,
and was profoundly grateful for the benefits. As Elizabeth
Longford has written, it could be argued that Victoria's greatest gift to her people 'was a refusal to accept pain in childbirth
as woman's divinely appointed destiny'.[18]

Despite the Royal Family's perceived goodness and empathy, Albert was still widely disliked. Yet his achievements were
considerable. Among other things, he had the Cambridge
curriculum modernized, rescuing the university from a state
of moribund complacency and putting it on a par with those
on the Continent. He guaranteed the success of the Great
Exhibition. It was he, as president of the Royal Commission
that organized it, who decided on its name and approved the
design for the revolutionary glass building that became its
symbol. He also defied opposition and had it built in Hyde
Park, increasing its accessibility. By insisting that foreign

manufactures be displayed beside those of the United Kingdom, he ensured that the exhibition had international, rather than merely national appeal. The resulting success owed more to him than to any other individual, and the considerable profit – £185,437 – was sufficient to purchase 70 acres of nearby land and ultimately to build the great museums that have given the district the nickname 'Albertopolis'.

These things were achieved, however, at considerable personal cost. As the 1850s wore on Albert aged prematurely, becoming increasingly stout and bald, and his health was in visible decline. He was worn out with stress and overwork, and with worry. The decade witnessed two outbreaks of conflict: the Crimean War and the Indian Mutiny. Both were traumatic for Britain, but Victoria, extremely proud of being 'a soldier's daughter' (the Duke of Kent had been a much-hated Commander-in-Chief), discovered a new role as a symbolic war leader, for she had perhaps seen an opportunity to emulate Queen Elizabeth. Her statement that she had never regretted more that she was a 'poor woman and not a man', for she would love to have gone to war herself, has about it a conscious echo of Elizabeth's speech at Tilbury. The country indulged in a frenzy of war fever and the Queen, showing a pugnacious side of her nature that was at odds with her more customary shyness, was carried away by it. She watched the departure of troops and ships, visited the wounded and knitted woollen garments for the army (but was annoyed to find that the things she had made were distributed among officers rather than given to the common soldiery).

Albert, a reluctant field marshal with an antipathy to militarism, acted as a restraining influence on his wife's enthusiasm. Nevertheless his idea for a gallantry medal named after the Queen proved highly popular, and she took great pleasure in awarding the first Victoria Crosses in Hyde Park in June 1857.

During the Crimean War, press and public criticism of him had risen to such heights of hysteria and absurdity that eventually a reaction had set in. Since he had not – as anticipated – sided with Russia and had worked tirelessly in support of Britain's war effort his critics were to a large extent silenced. He would not suffer as greatly at their hands thereafter.

Four years later, during the final weeks of his life, he also single-handedly prevented hostilities from breaking out between Britain and the United States, which at that time was involved its own civil war. In November 1861 a British mail packet, the SS *Trent*, was boarded in the Caribbean by US Marines, who apprehended two Confederate commissioners bound for the United Kingdom. Whitehall reacted with outrage, and Palmerston, the combative Prime Minister, drafted an aggressive ultimatum to Washington. Albert, who saw the document before it was sent, rewrote it on his sickbed, toning down its bellicosity and allowing the US government an honourable way out of the crisis by affecting to be convinced that the vessel's captain had acted on his own initiative and not at the behest of his government.

Less than a month later he was dead. He died at Windsor on 14 December 1861 of, it was believed, typhoid, though more recent research has suggested that he suffered from cancer of the bowel or stomach. Whatever the immediate medical cause, there can be no doubt that other factors affected him. Abroad, his hopes that a united and liberal Germany would emerge to dominate Europe were being crushed by the rise of an increasingly aggressive Prussia, while at home his eldest son had been involved in a (minor and unimportant) sex scandal while serving in the army in Ireland. He had frankly lost the will to live.

Only a few months earlier, the Duchess of Kent had died. Mother and daughter had not been close since Victoria's accession, and the loss was more symbolic than significant.

Nevertheless the Queen, who was dependent by nature, felt suddenly and entirely abandoned by this double bereavement. She had a nervous breakdown, and for a time it was believed she had gone insane. She withdrew into mourning, as was expected, but she never came out of it. There is some truth in the perception that she shut herself away for decades afterwards and lived as a sort of Miss Havisham, though this strict purdah lasted only a few years. She famously had Albert's shaving water brought and his clothes laid out every day as if he were still alive. She also dressed in black for the rest of her life, though by the conventions of the time this was normal. She never changed the style of her dresses from that of the 1860s (only forty-one when Albert died, she immediately looked much older) and created the image of herself in black dress and white cap – 'the Widow of Windsor' – that has remained in the public mind ever since. Since her loss was also the nation's, she expected the public to share, and sympathize with, her grief. She could not understand that by absenting herself from her people she was courting unpopularity.

The Widow of Windsor

She continued to participate in the business of government, though, for a time, when the Privy Council met she did not attend in person but sat in an adjoining room, receiving questions and conveying answers through a secretary. She effectively abandoned Buckingham Palace, living at Windsor, Osborne and Balmoral. She became deeply involved in the creation of monuments to her husband, having a mausoleum built for him at Frogmore and an ostentatious memorial unveiled in Hyde Park, as well as the huge concert hall next to it named in his honour. She did not appear on ceremonial occasions and she did not welcome foreign dignitaries (though she did, in the sixties, establish the annual garden parties that have continued to be held). There were no 'walkabouts', and it was not expected that the Queen should open Parliament or attend the Trooping the Colour every year. As time passed, resentment grew at her continued absence from public life. In 1864 she resumed travelling in an open carriage, and she opened Parliament (as well as attending a dance at Windsor) two years later. In 1868 she went privately to Switzerland, the first of many European holidays that were to add considerable pleasure to her life, though her loyalties would transfer to the French Riviera. Her seclusion was not as great as is perhaps imagined.

These forays into the outside world were not enough to convince sections of her people that she was an effective head of state, and republicanism enjoyed a brief vogue. In 1871, after the overthrow of Napoleon III in France, there was growing criticism in Britain of the cost of a large Royal Family with an all-but-invisible head. A pamphlet by G. O. Trevelyan entitled 'What Does She Do with It?' estimated that the Queen accumulated £200,000 a year. A speech by Sir Charles Dilke, the MP for Chelsea, received wide applause – and publicity – for suggesting that the monarchy was a 'cumbersome fiction' and an unnecessary expense. Though she had no intention of changing her habits, Victoria was greatly upset.

The Crown was saved by suffering. That summer, the Queen became seriously ill at Balmoral, and before she was fully recovered the Prince of Wales caught typhoid. For a few anxious days, as the tenth anniversary of his father's death from the same disease approached, he remained in danger. When these twin crises passed, the enthusiasm of her people began to revive. When Victoria and her son drove through London to a thanksgiving service at St Paul's, she was overwhelmed by the adulation of the crowds. An attempt to

assassinate her a few days later added to the wave of public
sympathy, and republicanism became a dead letter. Dilke was
shouted down in the Commons, and subsequently abandoned
his views. A fellow-traveller, Joseph Chamberlain, went on to
promote the Queen's near-apotheosis in the Diamond Jubilee
celebrations.

Following her husband's death, her greatest need had been
for a strong male influence, and she had found it, from 1864,
in a most unlikely place. John Brown had been one of Albert's
ghillies at Balmoral. A blunt-spoken and uncouth Highlander
somewhat given to drink (the Queen's toleration of this excess
in others was further evidence that she was an atypical
'Victorian'), he was the antithesis of a polished courtier. She
had always cherished loyal servants, and Brown was solicitous
and efficient. He spoke to her without a hint of deference,
lecturing her on her dress and behaviour, and – surrounded as
she usually was by flattery – she responded to this treatment.
He induced her to take up riding again, and his rough sense of
humour made her laugh. He quickly became her confidant,
and she created for him the title 'the Queen's Highland
Servant'. Not the least of his services would be saving the
Queen from an attempted assassination. His privileges, and his
manner, irritated Victoria's family and officials, none of whom
could criticize him in front of her. He also bemused the public,
for he accompanied her everywhere, becoming so much a part
of her life that she was nicknamed 'Mrs Brown'. There were
rumours that they were secretly married, though such a thing
would have been unthinkable to the Queen.

The void in her life was filled by busying herself with her
family. Her eldest daughter, Vicky, had married Prince Frederick of Prussia in 1858. The Queen had greatly regretted the
loss of this personable and intelligent young woman, who was
seen as the ablest of her children, and compensated for it with

an exhaustive correspondence that often involved writing to her three or four times a day. As her other children began to marry and the number of her grandchildren increased (there were to be thirty altogether) she found herself at the head of an extensive network of dynastic connections that ultimately embraced not only German states but Spain, Sweden, Greece, Russia and Romania. This brought no political power, merely a series of ties of blood and sentiment, but it greatly enhanced Victoria's status as 'Grandmother of Europe'.

'The Kindest of Mistresses'

She developed another valuable friendship. No Prime Minister since Melbourne had endeared himself to Victoria, and one of them – Palmerston – she had clearly hated. Benjamin Disraeli, who briefly became premier in 1868, was a florid and effusive personality, more theatrical than political. His excessive flattery towards the Queen, who described him as 'full of poetry, romance and chivalry', was in stark contrast to Brown's manner, but she again responded with intense loyalty. During his second term in office (1874–80), he successfully coaxed her further into the light of day. Their remarkable rapport owed much to the manner in which he ostentatiously sought her advice and valued her opinions, and to the fact that he treated her as a woman and not as an institution. She admired his wit, his considerate courtesy and his political opinions, for her conservative outlook and that of the Tory party were now in harmony.

Disraeli was keen to promote the idea of Empire, a subject in which the Queen had previously shown comparatively little interest, but he successfully made her an imperial figurehead – a role that was to become increasingly important in the decades ahead – by persuading Parliament to grant her the style Empress of India. This title, which she adopted as of 1 January 1877, had been considered absurdly pompous and foreign-sounding, both unsuited to and unnecessary for a British monarch. Victoria, however, was delighted, not least because her eldest daughter, married to the Prussian Crown Prince, was expected to become German Empress and would therefore have taken precedence over her. She in turn bestowed a title on Disraeli, creating him Earl of Beaconsfield, and paid him the unprecedented honour of calling upon him at his home. She was deeply grieved by his death in 1880. On his death-bed he was asked if he would welcome a visit from the Queen, but he declined. 'She would only want me to convey some message to Albert,' he said.

With Disraeli's rival, William Gladstone, the Queen's relations were somewhat chilly. She felt little empathy with the austere and intellectual Liberal leader, who spoke to her – she famously observed – as if he were addressing a public meeting. She was horrified by his proposals for Irish Home Rule, regarded his party as taking the country to the dogs, openly sided with his opponents and did whatever came within her power to obstruct its policies. The only thing they had in common was an extreme aversion to women's emancipation, which Victoria referred to as 'this mad folly'. When in 1885 General Gordon died at Khartoum because Gladstone's government had dithered and delayed too long before sending a relief expedition, she was incandescent with anger and administered a blistering rebuke: 'To think all this might have been prevented and many precious lives saved by earlier action is too frightful.'[19]

This notwithstanding, the gulf between them – another of the clichés of Victoria's reign – should not be exaggerated. The Queen was pleasanter in person than her letters to him suggest. Gladstone genuinely regretted that he could not befriend her and, though he sympathized with critics of her reclusive life-style and the cost of the Civil List, he refused to attack her in the Commons. When republicanism briefly flourished in 1871, he could – like his successor Blair in 1997 – have destroyed the monarchy had he not chosen to defend it, gaining some unpopularity in his party as a result.

Though she met, in the course of her life, all sorts and conditions of people from emperors to the Highland tenants at Balmoral, Victoria was never able to rid herself of a painful shyness. She was not gifted at small talk and had difficulty initiating conversations. As a result, some who came in contact with her considered her aloof. As she grew older, she in any case became increasingly averse to new faces – indeed, to any change in her surroundings – and preferred the company of women, unless they were family members or old family friends. When with those who were familiar, she had a surprisingly adroit sense of humour, and loved to be enter-tained by good conversation. She was even known to laugh at risqué stories, though she preferred that these should not be told in the company of impressionable young court ladies. Her most famous utterance – 'we are not amused' – was, unlike many supposed sayings of famous people, entirely authentic, and was doubtless deployed on more than one occasion.

Yet its implication that she was a priggish and humourless matron is entirely inaccurate, and her journals bear witness that, on many occasions, she was '*Very Much Amused*' or even '*Very Much Amused Indeed*'. It was known, as one courtier put it, that 'H.M. don't like being bored', and that she expected wit and diversion from those around her. Just as she did not abandon her sense of humour when widowed, so she did not give up other pleasures. As time passed, there were once again dances and concerts and theatrical performances at Windsor and Balmoral. She enjoyed circuses, and saw Buffalo

Bill's Wild West Show when it toured England. Victoria possessed a very fine singing voice (she could boast: 'I was taught to sing by Mendelssohn') and sometimes surprised those around her by rendering airs from Gilbert and Sullivan. During her annual visits to the south of France she attended the 'Battle of Flowers' in Grasse, and entered into the spirit of the event with noticeable enthusiasm. The image of this elderly sovereign pelting the revellers with blooms does not, of course, tally with any notion of a perpetually grieving widow. As one of her companions recalled: 'The Queen demanded more and more flowers, until at last we had to resort to the trick of having them picked up and brought back from the street below to be flung down again.'[20]

The austere image of Victoria hid a lighter side, as well as an intellectual curiosity. She embraced the scientific developments of the age. She had earlier sat for photographs, allowed chloroform to be administered and made extensive use of the telegraph. Now she had electric lighting installed at Osborne, became a habitual user of the telephone, made a gramophone recording (it was sent to the Emperor of Ethiopia, who stood to attention while listening to her message) and took an interest in the early cinema as both subject and spectator. She viewed a film of the Lord Mayor's Show in 1896, remarking that she found it 'very tiring for the eyes, but worth it to have seen such a marvel'.[21]

Gladstone's successor, the patrician Tory Lord Salisbury, observed that if he knew what the Queen thought about an issue, he knew what the middle classes would think. This implies a narrowness of outlook of which she was certainly guilty, yet the painter Landseer was to describe her as having the finest intellect of any woman in Europe, and another observer, Charles Greville, went even further by saying that she had the most interesting mind and character in the world.

In spite of this, she was distinctly uncomfortable in the company of intellectuals for, having had a limited education, she felt overawed by the very people – scientists, thinkers, academics – whose company Albert had enjoyed. Her tastes and abilities were more practical. Studying, and advising on, national and international issues was something she did with unflagging determination to the end of her life.

A modern biographer, Giles St Aubyn, has written that: 'Never before had an English sovereign proved so assiduous a correspondent, or so dedicated a bureaucrat. During the course of her reign she wrote, on average, two and a half thousand words a day.' He cites as example the fact that during the Tel-el-Kebir crisis in 1882 she wrote to the Secretary of War seventeen times in a twenty-four-hour period.[22] Laurence Housman summed up the Queen as having: 'a wonderful, contradictious character – not highly intellectual, but highly intelligent, narrow in its opinions and prejudices, yet extraordinarily shrewd and sensible in its use of a long experience and a retentive memory, obstinate and self-willed, but to the guiding star of her life devoted, and wholly adoring.'[23]

Mother of the Nation

Throughout the three decades between the nadir of her fortunes in 1871 and her death, Victoria's popularity increased. In the sixties she had been consumed with self-pity at her loss, had expected soon to die and had threatened to abdicate. Now her gifts of tireless energy and sense of duty were coming back into play. Her long years of service had, of course, caused her to be seen as a national treasure, and this feeling became especially acute when, on 23 September 1896, she overtook George III as the longest-reigning monarch in British history. Her subjects realized how extraordinary it was that, through all the upheavals of the past decades, this same small woman had overseen the fortunes of the nation and the Empire. Though memory of her less admirable forebears had faded, the example of her eldest son, who was involved in recurrent scandals (it was widely said that 'God will not permit such an evil man to become King'), gave rise to a feeling that Britain was fortunate to have a moderate and moral ruler, whose reign would be looked back upon with affection when less worthy sovereigns had taken her place.

As the ebullient, noisy patriotism known as 'new imperialism' or 'jingoism' became, increasingly, the dominant national mood in the 1890s, the Queen was swept along on the tide of popular feeling, and she came largely to share these sentiments. In her latter years she became almost obsessively interested in things Indian. She was no longer merely a symbol of Britain but of a vast, wealthy and powerful Empire, the existence of which was not simply taken for granted but celebrated as parallel with the glories of Ancient Rome. Though she had, since the days of Disraeli's premiership, come increasingly to embrace the outlook of imperialism, she took a view of her subject peoples that was not widely shared at the time and which would fit well with current political correctness. She was to describe 'Her very strong feeling (and she has few stronger) that the natives and coloured races should be treated with every kindness and affection, as brothers, not – as, alas! Englishmen too often do – as totally different beings to ourselves, fit only to be crushed and shot down!'[24] Victoria's Golden Jubilee in 1887 was a major event, but by the time her Diamond Jubilee was marked ten years later, imperial pride had been brought to fever pitch and imperial pomp – in the form of contingents of colonial troops and of visiting Indian princelings – made this single day, 22 June 1897, a celebration of everything that Britain had achieved in the nineteenth century.

The sun was to set with remarkable swiftness on this splendour. Within two years Britain was involved in an expensive and humiliating war in South Africa. It would last until 1902, and Victoria would therefore not live to see the end of it. Despite dimming eyesight and rapidly failing health – she found it necessary to be pushed in what she called a 'rolling chair' – she rediscovered some aspects of the role she had adopted in the Crimean conflict, that of war leader. As then, she made herself responsible for aspects of her soldiers' welfare, knitting garments ('The Queen,' wrote one observer, 'turns out khaki comforters as if her life depended on it),[25] and had 100,000 tins of chocolate despatched to the seat of war. She pored over casualty lists and – unusually for that era – felt genuine concern for the black South Africans caught up in the conflict. She visited military hospitals – as she had done almost half a century earlier – and said: 'I like to think I am doing something for my soldiers, although it is so little.'[26] Her statement to Arthur Balfour, after the British defeats of 'Black Week' in December 1899, that 'Please understand that there is no one depressed in this house. We are not interested in the possibilities of defeat; they do not exist'[27] was worthy of Winston Churchill. Her last official action, a few days before her death, was to receive Lord Roberts, who commanded her forces in South Africa, for a private visit at Osborne.

Victoria died there on 22 January 1901, aged eighty-one. Her body had simply worn out. She suffered from rheumatism and was almost blind, but like her husband forty years earlier her condition was made worse by stress and depression. The war, with its reverses and blunders and disappointments, grieved her, as did the loss of so many young men. Her second son, Prince Alfred, also died during 1900 and her eldest daughter, Vicky, whose life in Germany had been one of frustration and misery, was terminally ill with cancer. The

Queen had a stroke, possibly two, and sank gradually into unconsciousness while members of her family – including Kaiser Wilhelm, who hurried from Berlin to be at her bedside – were summoned. Her subjects gathered outside telegraph offices and at strategic places, such as London's Mansion House, for the news that the Victorian era had ended. It came just after half-past six in the evening.

There was, of course, a widespread sense that an era was over. Typical of the outpourings was this one in the *Daily Telegraph* lamenting that:

> The golden reign has closed. The supreme woman of the world, best of the good, is gone. The Victorian age is over. Never, never was loss like this, so inward and profound that only the slow years can reveal its true reality. The Queen is dead.[28]

Laurence Housman was a writer of a later generation, who produced in 1934 a dramatization of her life, *Victoria Regina*. Though he was often guilty of artistic licence, his observations on the Queen were valid. He wrote:

> By no act of her own, but merely by the course of events, the virtue of age, and the glamour of a long reign with the splendid finish of a double jubilee, she became the tutelary deity of the whole nation, and died in an odour of sanctity unapproached by any previous British monarch since the Norman conquest.[29]

He added:

> Queen Victoria, in her capacity as reigning sovereign, lived too long. Yet though she outstayed posterity's welcome from a political point of view, from the human she remains extra-ordinarily interesting and attractive.

2

THE MASSES

The Court of King Cholera

The majority of Queen Victoria's subjects were poor. Though her realm saw a vast increase in wealth during the course of her reign, with the already-comfortable becoming better off and social mobility greater than it had ever been – the middle class quintupled in size – this still left many millions who were impoverished, barely able to earn a living or destitute.

The problem of mass poverty was exacerbated by the steady increase in numbers of people (the population of London, for instance, increased fourfold between 1800 and 1900; Manchester, Sheffield, Leeds and Birmingham all doubled in size during the century's first decades) and the strain this put on resources. The supply of housing could not keep up with the demand, and led to intense overcrowding in the cities, which in turn brought higher mortality from disease. Funding from charities and from local authorities had to be stretched further. The workhouses that provided relief for the homeless and workless might be overwhelmed if there were a succession of bad harvests or some equivalent disaster. The sheer scale of the task faced by those who wished to help the poor was unprecedented in history, and there was no single body – governmental, religious or social – whose responsibility it was to address these issues.

Most town-dwellers of the labouring class lived in lodging-houses, crammed together in rooms without privacy, or in rooms or cellars of larger houses, often built around a court, in which whole families – together with their own lodgers – might occupy a single room. One such place was described by a Dr Lethaby, the compiler of a report on living conditions for the Commissioner of Sewers in London. He spoke of:

> The too frequent occurrence of necessitous overcrowding, where the husband, the wife, and young family of four or five children are cramped into a miserably small and ill-conditioned room . . . there are numerous instances where adults of both sexes, belonging to different families, are lodged in the same room, regardless of all the common decencies of life, and where from three to five adults, men and women, besides a train or two of children, are accustomed to herd together like brute beasts or savages. I have seen grown persons of both sexes sleeping in common with their parents, brothers and sisters, and cousins, and even the casual acquaintance of a day's tramp, occupying the same bed of filthy rags or straw; a woman suffering in travail, in the midst of males and females of different families; where birth and death go hand in hand; where the child but newly born, the patient cast down with fever, and the corpse waiting for interment, have no separation from each other, or from the rest of the inmates.

He gave an example, in case it should be thought that he was exaggerating:

> I visited the back room on the ground floor of No 5. I found it occupied by one man, two women, and two children; and in it was the dead body of a poor girl who had died in childbirth a few days before. The body was stretched out on the bare floor, without shroud or coffin. There it lay in the midst of the living.[1]

Though the doctor, and those who commissioned his report, may have been shocked by these conditions, there was nothing in the least unusual about them, for millions lived this way. The rooms he described would have had no furniture, the inhabitants sleeping on straw and rags, which might not necessarily be uncomfortable (the Russian tsar, Nicholas I, chose to sleep the same way!) but which was a breeding-ground for lice and other vermin. There would be no running water, as a consequence of which neither bodies nor clothing could be kept clean. There would be no means of removing sewage, with the result that the bodily waste of a building's inmates would be left in corners and on staircases. Even to those who knew no other way of life these must have seemed difficult circumstances. It was some compensation that they would be off the premises for much of the twenty-four hours, at work or in the streets. In homes where no one possessed cooking skills, and where there were in any case few facilities, there would be no incentive even for the womenfolk to stay indoors.

The homes of the poor often occupied the centre of cities, while the better off moved to the edges or to the burgeoning suburbs. In central London the great rookeries – as slum districts were then known – around Drury Lane, Seven Dials and Westminster Abbey were so complex, and so dangerous to outsiders, that even in daytime the police did not venture into them except in numbers. When large building projects, such as the creation of Victoria Street in Westminster or Holborn Viaduct, were undertaken, scores of homes were demolished – without any attempt at rehousing their occupants – and thousands left to crowd into tenements elsewhere. Proud attempts at civic improvement could exacerbate the problem.

The Streets and the Workhouse

It would be a mistake to imagine that the Victorians were complacent about conditions like these. For a host of reasons there was considerable anxiety regarding the rookeries. There were innumerable visits, numerous reports, frequent meetings of committees and commissions, and several schemes for alleviation of overcrowding. One motive was the danger from illness, for there were outbreaks of cholera in the forties and fifties – a disease previously not known in Britain, and therefore a symptom of a worsening situation. Another reason was fear, on the part of the property-owning classes, of social unrest. The thirties and forties were decades of serious depression and disturbance. In neighbouring countries there were outbreaks of revolution (France experienced these in 1830 and 1848). The broad mass of the poor was regarded as a potential threat to order, and it was in the interests of the state to see that they were not driven to extremism. More significantly, there was a realization that industrialization had created intolerable conditions and that these must be improved. One of the many attractive qualities of comfortably-off Victorians was their sincere concern for the unfortunate. There was a genuine desire, in an age that saw itself as enlightened and progressive, to better the lot of the destitute. Prominent among those concerned with the problem of housing the poor was Prince

Albert, who designed a set of 'model dwellings' that were exhibited at the Great Exhibition (an example of this is preserved). Another was George Peabody, an American philanthropist who in 1862 donated a sum of money large enough to build eight entire housing estates during the following two decades. Though these may strike modern observers as having a barrack-like austerity, they were a very considerable step forward in urban planning, and the original buildings – estates can be seen near Covent Garden and Westminster Abbey, among other places – are still doing duty today. His efforts were, of course, welcomed by the Government (both official and public opinion favoured private enterprise as a means of solving social ills); the Queen offered him a knighthood, though he was unable to accept it without giving up his United States citizenship, something he was unwilling to do.

For those who were destitute, and who lacked the means even to rent bed space on a floor, there were the streets. Today we are used to seeing people sleeping rough in the streets of cities, but there are comparatively few of them. In the nineteenth century there were thousands, just as – in an age when poverty was greater than we can comprehend – there were thousands, not dozens, of beggars. At dusk in London the benches on the Embankment began to fill with rough-sleepers, while Hyde Park, Green Park and St James' Park housed swarms of them. Naturally it was easier to live in the open during summer, and each autumn numbers of homeless – most commonly the elderly – committed suicide to avoid the rigours of winter. Many others in any case died from exposure, their bodies found huddled in doorways by patrolling policemen.

The alternative to living rough was to apply for admission to a workhouse, for despite widespread instances of crushing poverty, Victorian society made provision for the destitute. The system had been in place since the reign of James I, and was organized on a parish basis. Anyone who could prove themselves out of work, or otherwise in want, would be granted admission, and it is worth remembering that inmates were not confined indefinitely. One might be there for only a few days or weeks. It was possible – and commonplace – to sit out a severe winter in the workhouse, and this was done by men such as builders' labourers whose outdoor work was seasonal. While some of those who lived there were no doubt habitual idlers, many others were unfortunates of all classes who had fallen on hard times. One observer described the range of humanity that could be encountered there as:

> people of every clime. As regards their past history, the inmates are as promiscuous an assemblage as it were possible to get together. Those who were born in splendid mansions are there reduced to the same level as those who first drew their breath in the most wretched hovel; it lays the axe at the root of all the conventional differences which exist in society.[2]

Life in the workhouse was not as grim as readers of *Oliver Twist* might imagine, for the institution depicted by Dickens was a deliberate exaggeration. These establishments were, however, not intended to be comfortable. They divided their inhabitants between the sick and the healthy. Like many schemes for assisting the unfortunate, they were designed to get able-bodied inmates back on their feet as soon as possible, and this would be difficult if life inside was made too easy. Men and women were segregated – regardless of whether they were related – and lived in barrack-like wards. They were also required to perform some form of work – tending garden plots, picking oakum (unravelling old rope), assisting in the kitchen or infirmary – depending on their age and strength. The workhouse was often the destination of those too infirm to live on their own, and it has entered mythology as a heartless separator of aged married couples. While it is true that facilities were too limited, and rules too inflexible, to allow families to live together (children usually went with their mother, and saw their father only on Sunday afternoons at 'visiting time') it is important to remember that parishes also provided 'outdoor relief' which enabled recipients to stay at home. This practice was officially stopped in 1830, but carried on anyway. Recipients were given, at the beginning of the reign, between one and three shillings a week, and a loaf.

Victorians, whatever their means or their social class, hated the workhouse. To have to call upon public charity either alive or dead (those who could not afford a funeral were buried at parish expense) was a spectre that haunted millions. The cult of self-help and respectability meant that this public admission of failure was, in a sense, worse than death. Henry Mayhew, during his researches into the poor, interviewed a woman whose husband was terminally ill. His one fixation, in the last days of his life, was that after he was gone he would suffer the humiliation of a 'parish funeral'. Those who succeeded in swallowing their pride and entering the workhouse often found themselves adequately fed – paupers had meat dinners up to three times a week, which must have been considerably more than many of them were accustomed to – and were relatively comfortable. These institutions survived the Victorian era, and finally became extinct only after the Second World War when the welfare state was set up.

Child Labour

Those at the bottom of society began their working lives early. Children were likely to start earning as soon as they were able, and this usually meant about the age of five or six. There were always coppers to be made by running errands, or by holding horses while their owners went about some piece of business. In financially desperate families, tailoring work might be undertaken at home by the parents, and children, from the moment they could first hold a needle, would be set to work helping make up garments. More specialized jobs – selling matches or watercress, blacking shoes or sweeping a crossing – required not only equipment but access to a 'pitch', and there might be stiff competition for this. Crossing-sweepers, once they had a particular place of work, guarded it jealously and might remain there for the rest of their lives. Victorian memoirs often refer to men or women who have stood at the same kerbside for decades (there was, for instance, a black man who swept the crossing at the bottom of Ludgate Hill), becoming part of the urban landscape.

By the age of thirteen, boys and girls would be launched in the adult world of work. If they were fortunate they might be apprenticed at that age to some trade. Their parents, or any other well-disposed relative or adult, would pay for them to spend a period of five years or so in learning a profession, after which they would be qualified to practise it. Apothecaries, butchers, carpenters and a host of others were organized in this way, as they had been since the Middle Ages. To become an apprentice was the first step on the road towards respectability and financial security, and it did not always require private means to make this move, for parish authorities often paid for pauper boys to be apprenticed as tailors or shoemakers. For girls there was effectively only one apprenticeship – that of milliner. This involved little more than learning the basic skills of sewing, and then working at making dresses or bonnets for as long as one's health and eyesight lasted. It was both dull and tiring work, and it was not constant – demand for clothes fluctuated according to the time of year and changes of circumstance (a death in the Royal Family would mean the adoption of mourning black by Society). Whether in London or elsewhere, the demand for new dresses was dictated by the social season, which meant frantic periods of overwork to get costumes ready in time. The conscience of the Victorian middle and upper classes was often pricked by *Punch* and other periodicals that published drawings of exhausted milliners collapsed over their sewing as they worked through the night.

The Road to Ruin

For women there were many possibilities for earning a living in small and insecure ways. They could sell things – flowers, foodstuffs or other commodities – in the streets. They could 'take in washing' or look after other people's children ('baby-farming'). Many thousands of them pursued an older profession, and this had the 'advantage' that it could be a part-time activity. Milliners and servant girls often supplemented their incomes in this way.

However deplorable this may be from a moral point of view, it is worth remembering that such an activity gave them a certain independence. Female servants, especially if they were young and pretty, had often been 'ruined' by male counterparts or by employers, and thus fallen off the ladder to respectability. With nothing left to lose – and possibly having been dismissed from their position – they worked on the streets, but by doing so they were able to earn much more than they could in their former occupation, and they could also choose their hours and dress as they liked (respectable ladies sometimes met their former maids in the street, and were scandalized by their expensive and fashionable dress, for it would have been obvious at a glance how it had been obtained). If they were successful they would consort, on more or less equal terms, with men of their employers' class. The most fortunate of them might well be set up as 'kept women', and for a few years have their own household. As a result many of them found 'ruination' a positive, even desirable state, and moral campaigners lamented that many young women actually looked forward to it. Ironically – at least for the few short years before disease, imprisonment or the loss of beauty ended their careers – it made them freer and more self-respecting than they had been as part of the official world of work. The temptations of this way of life were described by Superintendent James Dunlap of the Metropolitan Police. In his evidence to the Select Committee on the Protection of Young Girls in 1881, he related how servants 'get small wages; they come out on errands; they see these girls walking about the streets, their equal in social standing; they see them dressed in silks and satins; they say: "You can go and dress in silks and satins, while I am slaving"; they talk to the girls, and they are influenced.'

Factory work claimed large numbers of young women, especially in the North and Midlands. This too was repetitive and exhausting, frequently involving long hours standing at machinery. It might also be highly dangerous, not only because unprotected machinery could be lethal, but because the constant breathing of fumes could kill by degrees those who worked in confined or unventilated spaces. Reports into working conditions refer incessantly to this:

The duties of the powder-packer consist of filling casks with bleaching powder. To do that he has to enter the chamber, which for several days has been filled with chlorine gas. The heat is sometimes tremendous, especially as the poor wretch who has to endure it is swathed about the head in a way that would protect him from arctic cold. With the muzzle on, the effort of breathing appears to be most painful even in the open air. The chest heaves like that of a man struggling for breath in the violent stages of lung disease. The appearance of the face gives you an impression that he is being suffocated; the eyes seem distended as they stare through the goggles.

Even with dry-cleaning, or 'French cleaning' as it was called, there was danger of:

Giddiness, nausea, vomiting, and headaches, sometimes of tasting the spirit, and usually loss of appetite, intoxication with hysterical symptoms, sleepiness and, in the more severe cases, of loss of consciousness.[3]

The girls and young women who worked at Bryant and May's match factory in London's East End were the subject of public interest when they went on strike in 1888 under the leadership of the socialist Annie Besant. She reported that:

One girl was fined 1 shilling for letting the web twist round a machine in the endeavour to save her fingers from being cut, and was sharply told to take care of the machine, 'never mind your fingers'. Another, who carried out the instructions and lost a finger thereby, was left unsupported while she was helpless.[4]

While these conditions – created by unregulated industrialization – are shocking to us, we must remember that they were also shocking to contemporaries. The mere fact that they were recorded indicated that there was concern and that something was being done about them. To the Victorians' credit there were constant enquiries, reports – and Factory Acts. The improvement of conditions was gradual, piecemeal and un-finished by the end of the reign, but it was nevertheless being pursued. It must also be remembered that nineteenth-century workers did not simply exist in pathetic misery. There were trade unions – the movement had been particularly active in the early part of the century – and a host of societies had been formed by these men and women, supported by modest regular subscriptions to pay the costs of sickness and other distress.

We would also be mistaken in imagining young factory workers merely as sunk in exploitation and misery. A con-temporary description shows them to have had, in spite of the awful hardship of their lives, a certain spirit and sense of fun:

Factory girls are often the daughters of dock labourers or other irregularly employed workmen, frequently of drunkards. They have been brought up in stifling rooms, with scanty food, in the midst of births ands deaths, year after year. They have been accustomed to ups and downs; one week they have been on the verge of starvation, another they have shared in a 'blow-out'. They have learnt to hate monotony, to love drink, to use bad language as their mother tongue, and to be true to a friend in distress. They care nothing for appearances, and have no desire to mix with any but their equals.

On the whole these girls, outside their homes, lead a healthy, active life. They do not over-exert themselves at the factory. They rise early and have plenty of open-air exercise, both on their way to and from the factory and in their evening walks. They are rough, boisterous, outspoken, warm-hearted, honest working girls. Their standard of morality is very low, so low that to many they may seem to have none at all.

Their great enemy is drink; the love of it is the curse they have inherited, which, later on, when they are no longer factory girls, but dock labourers' wives, will drag them down to the lowest level, and will be transmitted to the few of their children who survive. They are nearly all destined to be mothers, and they are almost all entirely ignorant of any domestic accomplishments.[5]

Below Stairs

The brothers of the Bryant and May match-girls might well have been employed as casual labour at the London docks. They would earn considerably less than the four shillings or so that were paid, in a good week, to their sisters, for they would make threepence a day. They had no guarantee of getting work loading and unloading cargoes, and each morning had to wait for the dock gates to be opened – the signal for a stampede to get in first and be taken on. The same scene would have taken place in Liverpool or Glasgow.

Given working conditions like these – and that agriculture was in a state of depression for much of the nineteenth century – it was fortunate that another possibility existed. Domestic service was a huge field of employment. In a wealthy age in which the property-owning classes were expanding, there was a constant need for servants (it was estimated that a third of the population of London was made up of servants, though in other towns this would have been less). They worked both indoors and outside. In large households there would be a hierarchy, reaching from the butler at the top through the footmen to the 'boots' – a boy, doubtless destined to be a footman once he was big enough to fit a livery, who cleaned the shoes. Among the women the housekeeper was at the top, with below her a cook and a range of ladies' maids, chambermaids and kitchen maids. Outside there would be a head gardener and a number of helpers, varying in expertise down to young boys who gave general assistance. The keeping of a carriage would require further staff – a coachman and at least one groom. Naturally, comparatively few households could run to this number of servants (though the 1881 census shows a moderately wealthy Kent doctor to have had a 'page' as well as a maid. The young man's job would have been to run errands.). It was more common, further down the social scale, to have only a maid, and even the most modest lower-middle-class household would usually have a single servant – a young girl of thirteen or so from the local board school or work-house. Such labour was very cheap, and at a time when domestic appliances were still expensive it would have been extremely difficult to run a home without it.

Most servants began this life in their early teens. Those who worked in cities frequently came from the country, having been recommended or found places through a network of acquaintances or previous employers. In larger households they might be more or less anonymous, their names unknown to their employers. In smaller establishments they could well be treated as one of the family, confided in or trusted with money for shopping. The hours they worked were usually long, for they had to be up very early to light the stove, heat water and prepare breakfast. They could not go to bed until the day's work was over, which might mean clearing up after a dinner-party in the small hours of the following day. They lived in whatever accommodation was available – typically they occupied small bedrooms on the top floor of a house and took their meals in the basement kitchen, the bottom floor being regarded as their domain. They would usually have only one afternoon off each week, and therefore had little oppor-tunity to explore their surroundings or increase their circle of friends. Females were often recruited on the understanding that they had 'no followers', and if a servant married she would be expected to leave. Otherwise, domestics could spend decades – their entire working lives – with the same employer. In the best instances, being a servant in such a household gave men and women a sense of belonging to a close-knit, family-like group. It could provide security, shelter and enough to eat until they were too old to continue. Once they reached that age, it was possible that their grateful employers would make provision for them.

The stereotypical image of Victorian servants is of dumbly obedient, resigned men and women, loyal enough to their masters to spend years in menial work. The reality was less straightforward. Good servants were extremely difficult to find, and would-be employers often despaired of the appli-cants they interviewed. Their domestics were frequently lazy or insolent. Middle-class books and periodicals – *Punch* is, as ever, an invaluable reflection of this – lament their propensity to pilfer, to break ornaments, to dawdle on errands, to help themselves to the wine-cellar and to mock their betters. It was so difficult to find good ones that often a certain amount of leeway had to be granted in order not to lose them. Servants did not necessarily feel any loyalty to a household, and might leave at very short notice if offered better prospects elsewhere. They might also flounce out if they took offence at the hours or the tasks expected of them. Cooks were notorious for this, for they knew they could blackmail their mistress by threatening to leave just before a dinner-party.

Darkest England

The Victorians, who believed themselves to be civilizing the wider world, cared with equal passion for the disadvantaged at home. The scale of social problems had no parallel in history. There was no quick remedy. Nevertheless a great deal of work was done, by individuals and societies, to alleviate specific evils, and by the middle decades of the reign there were more than five hundred organizations devoted to charity, an effort that was maintained throughout the Victorian era. Contemporaries were horrified by the observation of the commentator Charles Booth that a third of the British population lived in want, and in 1890 the seminal study *In Darkest England* by his near-namesake William Booth coined the phrase 'the Submerged Tenth' to describe the estimated 3 million people who were 'living in such conditions of misery and destitution, vice and crime, as put them outside the limits of civilised society'[6] He himself founded one of the principal bodies that sought to help this group – the Salvation Army. It was an immediate success, spread all over the world and is still doing very valuable work.

Since alcoholism was the single greatest scourge, the temperance movement came into being. Rather than simply disapproving of drink, it offered wherever possible practical solutions – establishing reading rooms and coffee rooms to give workmen more wholesome places of resort than public houses, awarding temperance medals to soldiers who abstained and persuading many thousands to 'sign the pledge' – a promise that was often taken seriously for years or decades afterwards by those who did so.

The Ragged School movement, another instance of tackling a social evil head-on, sought to educate street children who had neither the time nor the means to attend school. Lessons were taught to them by volunteers, using whatever premises could be cheaply rented, and classes were held in the evenings to enable them to continue earning their livings during the daytime. Because they often arrived hungry, meals began to be provided for them. Because they suffered from the usual urban lack of fresh air, annual holidays were arranged for them.

Because many of them had no prospects of useful employment, numbers of them were trained as shoe-blacks and deployed in the streets as a smartly uniformed, distinctive body. This movement opened new vistas for entire generations of the poor.

The fact that some people today smile at this Victorian earnestness – and at the outlandish names of charitable societies ('The Society for Returning Young Women to Their Friends in the Country', the 'Ladies' Association for the Benefit of Gentlewomen of Good Family, Reduced in Fortune Below the State of Comfort to Which They Have Been Accustomed', and the painful-sounding 'National Truss Society for the Relief of the Ruptured Poor') – does not detract from the importance of the work that was done by organizations of this sort.

It says much about the climate of the times that philanthropists should have become national celebrities, but this was true of Dr Barnardo, who devoted his life to helping the 'waifs and strays' of London, of Quentin Hogg, who devoted *his* life to the betterment of boys through the London Polytechnic, and of Lord Shaftesbury, the greatest friend to the poor that the era produced – a man so popular for the legislation he brought before Parliament (the Mines Bill of 1842 and the Ten Hours Act of 1847) and for his personal commitment to a host of charitable initiatives that, at his funeral in 1885, the streets were lined with thousands of paupers. Philanthropy was one of the major preoccupations of the Victorian era, and one of its greatest achievements.

Garrotters and Hooligans

Nor should we imagine that Victorian streets were safer than ours: quite the contrary. There had been anarchy before the advent of modern law enforcement (beginning with the founding of the Metropolitan Police in 1829), and it took several decades to bring both manpower and methods to a level of efficiency that made them effective. Cities abounded – as readers of Dickens will know – with pickpockets, kidnappers, confidence tricksters and assorted criminals who made it their business to prey on the gullible, the young and the weak. The struggle to live was so desperate for the poorest that anything might be stolen from those who were not careful. There was a practice, for instance, of luring lone children off the streets and stripping them of their clothes to sell – there were, in other words, entire sub-species of criminal that have thankfully since become extinct. In the centre of cities there were whole districts that it would be dangerous to enter in daylight and suicidal at night. Anyone leaving London's Drury Lane Theatre late in the evening would have to hail a cab at once. The surrounding alleys teemed with men waiting to rob those who set out to walk the few yards to the Strand.

The suburbs were not necessarily safer. Street lighting was poor, and there were numerous opportunities for attackers to lurk in shrubbery or on waste ground. In 1862 – during what was perhaps the decade of greatest elegance, and therefore the one that most typifies the 'mid-Victorian calm' – there was a much-publicized outbreak of suburban mugging known as 'Garrotting'. This was carried out by groups of three. Two would surround a victim, pinioning his limbs while a third – known as 'the nasty man' – applied pressure to prevent resistance. A magazine article described the process:

The third ruffian flings his arm around the victim, striking him smartly on the forehead. Instinctively he throws his head back, and in that moment loses every chance of escape. His throat is fully offered to his assailant, who instantly embraces it with his left arm, the bone just above the wrist being pressed against the

'apple' of the throat. At the same moment the garrotter,
dropping his right hand, seizes the other's wrist, and draws
his back upon his breast and there holds him. His burden is
helpless from the first moment, and speedily becomes insen-
sible.[7]

Though this probably occurred less frequently than the newspapers implied, it still represented a notably vicious outbreak
of premeditated crime, and for a time brought fear to the
comfortably off. In 1898, during another decade that is
popularly associated with confident complacency, there was
a rash of gang violence so severe that a new term – 'hooligan' –
was invented to describe those responsible. Like the skinheads,
'hoodies' and similar groupings of a later century, hooligans
were instantly recognizable by their dress. It was described by
a newspaper:

> No hat, collar or tie is to be seen. All of them have a peculiar
> muffler twisted around the neck, a cap set rakishly forward,
> well over the eyes, and trousers very tight at the knee and very
> loose at the foot [what would later be called 'flares']. The most
> characteristic part of their uniform is the substantial leather
> belt heavily mounted with metal. It is not ornamental, but then
> it is not intended for ornament.[8]

The response to this was a penal system that was both harsh
and humane. It included transportation to Australia (until
1867), flogging in prison (though a doctor was present, and
could stop the punishment if the victim were suffering too
much) and the wearing of masks by prisoners to prevent them
recognizing each other. Child criminals were incarcerated with
adults and given the same punishments. In some sample cases
seen at Wandsworth Prison in 1872, fourteen-year-old Wil-

liam Trimmer was sentenced to ten days' hard labour and five years in a reformatory for stealing two bottles of lemonade. James Hempson, a year younger, received four days' hard labour and ten strokes of the birch for purloining a box of figs. James Leadbeater was given a whipping and four days' labour for the theft of celery worth a shilling, and John Morrells twenty-one days' hard labour for stealing a glass worth sixpence.[9] It was widely felt that sentences for serious criminals were not sufficiently harsh, and the return to the streets of paroled ('ticket-of-leave') prisoners was seen as dangerous folly. The 'ticket-of-leave man' was a particular bogey.

The Victorians were as afraid of crime as any people before or since. One reason for their preoccupation was – as we have found in our own age – that better communications mean more incidents are reported. A climate of fear, fed, in their case, by journals of the *Police Gazette* variety, could create periodic hysteria. In fact, Victorian law enforcement was highly effective. Prior to the Queen's accession the Army had been used as a matter of course to quell civil unrest. That this became extremely rare during her reign indicates how successful the police were in maintaining order.

Serious crime was no better or worse than was to be expected among a crowded and expanding population that experienced both frequent recessions and the temptations of flaunted wealth.

WHAT THEY ATE

Beef and Beer

The British had always prided themselves on their diet. While Frenchmen, Italians and assorted foreigners lived on pastries, fricasees and all manner of fripperies, and the other inhabitants of the British Isles on a basic diet of oats and mutton (the Scots), toasted cheese (the Welsh) and potatoes (literally the only thing eaten by large numbers of Irish peasants), the English dined on beef. This was, at least, the stereotype, for the beefsteak was as much an emblem of their country as it would later be of the United States. This meat, which gave them their nickname among the French – *les rosbifs* – symbolized the nation's prosperity, and implied that their solid and nutritious feeding made the English happier and more successful – at winning wars or undertaking trade or running a parliamentary democracy – than the wretched inhabitants of other nations. In caricatures from the Napoleonic Wars the English, whether personified by the comfortably paunched John Bull or the brawny, cutlass-wielding Jack Tar, were shown as well fed. Despite the famine and depression that followed these wars, this image was perpetuated throughout the century. *Punch* and other publications continued to symbolize England in the same way after the Second World War.

Tea and Margarine

The reality was, as always, very different. A modern observer looking at the people in a Victorian street would be struck by the thin, wizened and unhealthy appearance of large numbers of them. Throughout the century, the very poor lived principally on a diet of bread and tea, the latter being drunk without milk or sugar. A possible addition to this diet was margarine (originally called 'butterine'), invented in the sixties and widely sold by the mid-seventies. Not only did this lack of vitamins – and 'vitamins' were a concept discovered and named at the end of the Victorian era – make them vulnerable to diseases like scurvy and rickets, it also meant that comparatively few of them achieved even a modest robustness; when men volunteered for service in the Boer War, many had to be rejected as failing to meet even the minimum fitness requirements, and the situation had not greatly improved half a generation later in 1914. Friedrich Engels, observing in 1844 conditions in the industrial cities of the north, recorded that the only meat that many saw was:

> A small bit of bacon cut up with the potatoes; lower still even this disappears, and there remain only bread, cheese, porridge and potatoes, until on the lowest round of the ladder, among the Irish, potatoes form the sole food.[1]

Slightly higher up the social scale, among those who had regular work and were therefore free from absolute want, it was possible with careful management to live on basic but wholesome food. A Scottish artisan with a wife and four children, earning just over £2 a week, listed the dinners in his household for a typical week in February 1892:

Sunday – Apple tart and tea (no meat as a rule, partly to leave the mother leisure for church, etc.)

Monday – Soup, meat and potatoes; half pound of boiling meat.

Tuesday – Stewed meat and vegetables and potatoes; three-quarters lb. stewing meat.

Wednesday – Soup made with bone, and remainder of apple tart left from Sunday.

Thursday – Collops, vegetables and potatoes; three-quarters lb. stewing meat.

Friday – Soup and semolina pudding.

Saturday – Stewing meat and potatoes; three-quarters lb. meat.[2]

He added that 'Children get no butcher's meat; they get the sauce and potatoes, and a piece of bread after, and mother and I have always a cup of coffee after dinner.' Their weekly outlay on food was thirty-seven shillings. Though they were able to eat healthily, the amounts they consumed were probably less than a modern nutrition expert would prescribe.

Adulteration

This family was fortunate in having a garden to grow vege-tables. Millions of others among the poor and moderately well off could do the same, and therefore ensure a supply of essential vitamins. The absence of 'quality control' for food-stuffs during the early part of the reign in many cases meant that adulteration was commonplace. Any commodity could be made more profitable for those selling it by making it go further. Milk was therefore watered down as a matter of course. It would also sell more readily if it looked attractive, so it was whitened by adding chalk. This was at least prefer-able to the traditional means of whitening bread – which was done with ground bones – though alum and even plaster of Paris were also used. Coffee was adulterated with acorns, sugar with sand, pepper with pea-flour, cocoa with brick-dust. The froth on beer might be the result of adding green vitriol. Tea, whether China or India, was one of the things most commonly interfered with. The former, which was green, was often counterfeited by using thorn leaves treated with verdi-gris. For the latter, which was dark in colour, black lead could be used. It was in any case possible to 'recycle' tea by obtaining used leaves – or floor sweepings – from commercial premises and repackaging them. The results of adulteration could be unpleasant at best and lethal at worst.

The public was aware of these abuses, some of which were caused by the fact that a commodity – such as tea – might simply be too expensive in its original form, and that sub-stitutes brought it within reach of millions who would not otherwise have been able to afford the genuine article. Never-theless, efforts were made to address the issue. A publication by a German chemist in 1820 had drawn public attention to the worst abuses. In 1850 an Analytical and Sanitary Com-mission was set up, and over the next three years its findings were also published. Parliament eventually brought in legisla-tion, with the Food and Drugs Act 1860, extended twelve years later. Though the quality of foodstuffs therefore gradu-ally improved, there was no adequate means of checking the

goods sold by thousands of street vendors, and abuses continued throughout the century.

Tinned and Frozen

By the time the railway had become an established part of life, its
implications for feeding the population had already become
obvious. It was possible, for instance, to send fish inland from
coastal ports within a matter of hours (fish could be frozen
aboard the trawlers that caught it), thus providing a new source
of relatively cheap protein to people throughout the country,
not least through the proliferation of fish and chip shops. Even
more importantly, the railway could carry vastly more food
than the lumbering wagons that had preceded it, and this in itself
helped to bring down the price of many things. Livestock
had always been herded to the towns by drovers and slaughtered
in the shambles once it arrived. Now it could be killed at home
and sent as prepared carcasses even from the farthest-flung
regions. Milk was one commodity that was not easily transpor-
table, for it could not be kept fresh even on short journeys, and it
was not until the sixties that the development of a mechanical
cooler, and of metal churns, solved this difficulty.

From the seventies – a decade when bad harvests were
ruining agriculture in Britain – grain imported from the United
States and Canada was a godsend. These territories had
experienced their own railway revolution, enabling the vast
granaries of the western prairies to send their produce east-
ward to Atlantic ports for shipment. Australia was to join
these suppliers by the end of the century. The availability of
this grain effectively meant that, for the first time in history,
Britain was free from the danger of famine. Although the
population was increasing alarmingly, the availability of food
kept pace and shortages could be avoided.

The other part of this process concerned the shipping of meat, and this was an even greater breakthrough. The preservation of food, first in sealed glass jars and then in metal cans, had been achieved by the second decade of the century, though food packed in this way was initially too expensive to command wide sales. Gradually a canned-meat industry developed (from 1868 cans were made by machine and not by hand, enabling huge 'canneries' to operate) and the cost fell, but because manufacturers came only slowly to understand how the canning process killed bacteria, the contents of tins were often rancid when they were opened. Not only meat but fruit and vegetables were preserved and shipped in these containers, but there might be hidden dangers: it is thought that members of Sir John Franklin's Arctic expedition were poisoned by the lead used to seal their canned supplies. Canned meat initially came from Australia, and was so unappetizing that only its cheapness made it acceptable. By the seventies, when America began seriously to compete in supplying Britain, the killing of bacteria had been perfected and canned food was part of everyday life – though no one could pretend that it tasted like the fresh variety. Tinned mutton was derisively known as 'Fanny Adams' in reference to a young woman murdered – and chopped up – by her lover in 1867.

Even this was not the end of developments, however. In 1877, for the first time, a cargo of frozen meat was brought to England from Australia, three months after a similar cargo had crossed the Atlantic from Argentina to France. Shortly afterwards, New Zealand lamb also arrived by sea. By that time the ice machine was already known throughout the world, and there were ice-making factories. The use of refrigeration on ships was a new venture, and one that was successful from the beginning. Though the transport of carcasses from the Antipodes represented a tremendous achievement, it was more expensive than American meat, which therefore gained a greater share of the market. Fruit and vegetables could come by the same means, and for the first time pineapples and bananas could be bought cheaply, when earlier only hothouse specimens would have been available. Steadily, gradually, more and better food was becoming available to a greater number of people.

New kitchen equipment also made a noticeable difference. Stoves had begun to replace the open fireplace with its range of spits. A British diplomat, Benjamin Rumford, used his observations of artillery – which grew hot after sustained firing – to formulate a theory of heat conservation that enabled him, in 1795, to design a stove for cooking. Over sixty years later stoves, or 'ranges', were cheap enough to be widely available to householders, and to become an essential part of kitchen equipment. In the eighties gas cookers began to be used, and in the following decade the electric version arrived, though its use was extremely limited until the next century.

By this time yet another revolution had taken place. The rising middle class was interested in food because of the social rituals that surrounded it. The giving of dinners was not simply a matter of impressing one's neighbours with the skill of the cook – who was often hired only for the occasion – but of showing off the sophistication of one's kitchen and dining-room and one's knowledge of correct form. Since, as always, many members of this class were unsure about such matters, there was an opportunity for qualified authors to assist them. The result was the bestselling cookery books that not only told readers what to offer their families and their guests, but also gave information about how to entertain. Two of the best-known appeared in quick succession. One of them, *Modern Cookery for Private Families* (1845) by Eliza Acton, made a household name out of a lady whose original desire had been to be published as a poet. *The Modern Cook* by Charles Francatelli (1846) commanded respect because the author was employed by Queen Victoria (though he was dismissed for hitting one of the maids!). The third seminal work on the subject of middle-class entertaining – and the one that eclipsed all others – was Mrs Isabella Beeton's *Book of Household Management*, published in 1861. This, as its title suggests, was not simply a cookbook (Mrs Beeton championed simple English cooking rather than French) but a veritable bible for housewives, including as it did a great deal of information on the mechanics and finances of running a home. She listed, for instance, thirty-seven 'articles required for the kitchen of a family in the middle class of life', including one pair of brass candlesticks, one cinder-shifter, one bread-grater and six spoons. She tells readers where to buy them (Messrs Richard & John Slack, 336, Strand) and exactly how much it should all cost: £8 11s 1d. She also informed her audience of what meat, fish, fruit and vegetables were in season during every month: in January, dace, eels, flounders and lampreys were among the fish that could be offered to guests, while in February 'cod may be bought, but it is not so good as in January'. She warned that 'in very cold weather, meat and vegetables touched by the frost should be brought into the kitchen early in the morning and soaked in cold water.' Armed with such a wealth of detailed advice, what young wife could go wrong? Not all of her advice would seem to us sound, or necessary. She cautions, for instance, that ices, a standard finale to a dinner, should not – because their coldness may be a shock to the system after several hot courses – be eaten by elderly people, children (!) or those of delicate constitution.

One book of this type that was *not* aimed at a bourgeois audience came from an unusual source. Alexis Soyer, a Frenchman (which automatically conferred gravitas on anyone in the world of cookery), was head chef at the Reform Club. He had shown a compassionate nature by opening soup kitchens for the London poor, and ran similar facilities for soldiers in the Crimea, using a field kitchen of his own design. In 1855 he published a book of sensible and nutritious recipes, *A Shilling Cookery for the People*. It offered no touch of clubland – or indeed French – glamour, for both ingredients and recipes were basic and somewhat lacklustre, but it provided a sound basis for healthy eating on a small budget. It sold almost a quarter of a million copies.

The propertied classes did not stint themselves when it came to eating. It would give a modern reader indigestion just to examine some of their menus. A typical breakfast might involve bacon and scrambled eggs, chops, kedgeree, snipe and woodcock, often devoured in such quantities that one wonders how they could even get up from the table. Domestic staff in a grand house might have much the same breakfast in the servants' hall, and at least one account describes how the footmen, having consumed a massive repast, were in the habit of filling the pockets of their livery coats with boiled eggs – to see them through to luncheon.

The result of such consistent indulgence was, unsurprisingly, a great deal of illness and early death; many otherwise healthy young men did not survive even into their mid-forties because of a diet that was too rich and too extensive. Both ladies and gentlemen wore such tight-fitting clothes that the effects were exacerbated. Their unhealthy eating habits explain the immense and enduring popularity among Victorians of health spas and all manner of 'cures', for it is ironic that a people so given to sport and exercise should also have suffered from such excesses.

Dinners in mid-Victorian households had traditionally been served in the French style, which meant that the components of the meal were all placed on the table together, cluttering its surface with tureens and serving-dishes. Meat was carved by the host at the table, and the plates passed to his guests. Gradually, this habit was replaced by what was known as *à la russe* dining, in which the dishes were all prepared on a sideboard and then handed to guests by the servants. This meant that the table itself was given over to ornamentation: silver set-piece ornaments, complex flower arrangements, elaborate place-settings with folded napkins and desserts on stands that were admired by the guests before being demolished.

Menus were commonly in French. A sample one, from a dinner at a wealthy private house in London, gives some indication of how many courses there were and what they comprised:

87 Eaton Place, Diner, du 30 mars, 1878

Potages
Consommé à la Doria
Crème d'Asperges Faubonne

Poissons
Suprème de Saumon Richelieu
Turbot sauce Crevette

Entrées
Cotelettes Hasseur aux Pointes
Mousselines à la Princesse

Relèves
Quartier d'Agneau sauce Menthe
Jambon à la Gelée et Mirabelles
Salade assortie

Punch au thé

Rôts
Ramier de Bordeaux
Asperges d'Argenteuil sauce Maltaise

Entremets
St. Honore aux Pistachio
Abricots à l'Almedorine
Corbeilles de Glaces[3]

The accompanying of each course with an appropriate wine was an important part of the ritual. A contemporary book described the rules governing this:

Sherry is always drunk after soup, hock either with oysters before the soup or with fish after the soup, and Chablis sometimes takes the place of hock. Champagne is drunk immediately after the first entrée has been served, and so during the remainder of dinner until dessert. Claret, sherry, port, and Madeira are the wines drunk at dessert.[4]

These rigid conventions were eminently risible. Thackeray, in his *Book of Snobs*, pokes gentle fun at them:

Everybody has the same dinner in London, and the same soup, saddle of mutton, boiled fowls and tongue, entrees, champagne, and so forth. I own myself to being no better than my neighbours in this respect, and rush off to the pastrycook's for sweets, &c.; hire sham butlers and attendants, have a fellow going round the table with still and dry champagne, as if I knew his name, and it was my custom to drink those wines every day of my life. I am as bad as my neighbours; but why are we so bad, I ask? – why are we not more reasonable?

If we receive great men or ladies at our houses, I will lay a wager that they will select mutton and gooseberry tart for their dinner; forsaking the entrees which the men in Berlin white gloves are handing round on the Birmingham plated dishes. Asking lords and ladies who have great establishments of their own, to French dinners and delicacies, is like inviting a grocer to a meal of figs, or a pastrycook to a banquet of raspberry tarts. They have had enough of them. And great folks, if they can, take no count of your feasts, and grand preparations, and can but eat mutton like men.[5]

Herbs and Spices

Something very familiar to us appeared at Victorian tables, and that was curry. The British connection with India dated back more than two hundred years to the founding of the East India Company, and many thousands of families had members or acquaintances who had been to the sub-continent. They brought back with them some of the eating habits they had acquired, and one was the use of spicy powder to sharpen the taste of meat or vegetables. As with so many imported foods ('chop suey' is another example), the 'curry' consumed in Britain would not have been recognized in its place of origin. The term itself is thought to have been a corruption of the Tamil word *karbi*, meaning sauce, and it came to be a general term for any Indian food that was prepared with sauces. Curry powder – a blending of more or less whatever spices were available in an Indian kitchen – was a British invention, and is likely to have horrified Indian cooks. Curries had been an accepted part of the national diet in the eighteenth century, and by the 1860s commercially produced powder, as well as curry paste, was widely available in the shops. A New York chef described how the powder should be made:

One ounce of coriander seeds, two ounces of cayenne, a quarter ounce of cardoman seeds, one ounce salt, two ounces of turmeric, one ounce ginger, half an ounce of mace and a third of an ounce of saffron.[6]

And Mrs Beeton advised on how to prepare the dish:

Put all the ingredients in a cool oven, where they should remain one night; then pound them in a mortar, rub them through a sieve, and mix thoroughly together; keep the powder in a bottle, from which the air should be completely excluded.[7]

Another cookbook then recommended:

Two tablespoons of meat curry paste, a tablespoon of curry powder, and as much flour as may be required to thicken the quantity of sauce needed.[8]

A similar national institution was chutney. This means of preserving fruit or vegetables by a form of pickling (the difference was that in chutney the ingredients were pounded rather than left in large pieces, and that sweet ingredients were included) was actually used by Indians, although the British took it home and made it their own. Once again, British firms quickly produced a range of these products (and at least one such Victorian firm, Sharwood's, is still in business), which became a familiar sight on the shelves of grocers.

Many other products also became familiar, for with developments in printing the possibilities for producing, at small cost, colourful and elaborate packaging greatly increased. Whether on paper bags, cardboard packets or tins, eye-catching slogans, detailed pictures (showing the product itself or some other image) and striking lettering began to command the attention of shoppers. Some products – such as Lea and Perrin's Sauce or Lyle's Golden Syrup – have kept their Victorian labelling to this day. Many items that we still consume had their origins in the Victorian era, as did some of the places from which we buy them (Sainsbury's, for instance, began trading in 1869). A glance at any picture of a nineteenth-century streetscape will show, through a wealth of placards and posters on walls and on the sides of buses, the power of advertising and the extent to which products were thrust into public awareness: Fry's Chocolate, Keen's Mustard, Keiller's Dundee Marmalade, Bovril and Oxo. The era of mass advertising, as well as the world of standardized food products in which we ourselves unquestionably live, began with the Victorians.

Ready Meals

'Convenience food' was as much a characteristic of Victorian times as of our own. There were both sit-down dining-rooms in which quick meals could be consumed, and kerbside stalls at which refreshment could be taken standing. These were hugely popular, not just because they were fast and cheap but because for many thousands of the poor there was no alternative way to eat.

A great proportion of the urban poor had no cooking facilities, and in the cramped, highly inflammable buildings in which they lived the risk of accident would outweigh the benefits of lighting a cooking fire. Vegetables could be had cheaply, but could not easily be prepared. Thus people bought hot or cold food in the streets or bought ingredients and paid someone else to prepare them. Because whole generations had grown up in this way, there were numerous families in which not even the mother possessed basic cooking skills.

Street Food

To serve the needs of this vast group of customers, there were
thousands of street vendors selling both food and drink, luxuries
and necessities. The men and women who dealt in comestibles
might walk through a city, selling as they went, or set up a stall, a
barrow or a pitch at some strategic place and wait for custom.
Sellers of fruit or watercress (the latter were usually little girls)
would need only a tray or a basket, while those who sold pies,
gingerbread, chestnuts or potatoes would have to carry not only
the viands themselves but the means – usually a charcoal oven –
of preparing them. There was a hierarchy among street-traders,
and those who merely carried a basket were at the bottom of it.
The owners of stalls and complex equipment, who might be
helped by family members or even paid assistants, were at the
top. Some of these tradesmen had followed their specialist
calling for a considerable time; Charles Spurgeon photographed
in 1884 a 'champion pie-maker' whose sign claimed that he had
been in business for 'upwards of 50 years'. Henry Mayhew, who
made a study of these itinerant vendors in the London streets of
the 1850s, described how:

> Men and women, and most especially boys, purchase their meals
> day after day in the streets. The coffee-stall supplies a warm
> breakfast; shell-fish of many kinds tempt to a luncheon; hot eels
> or pea soup, flanked by a potato 'all hot', serve for a dinner; and
> cakes and tarts, or nuts and oranges, with many varieties of pastry,
> confectionery, and fruit, woo to indulgence in a dessert; while for
> supper there is a sandwich, a meat pudding or a 'trotter'.[9]

Coffee stalls were everywhere. Mayhew estimated that the
capital contained over three hundred in the forties, and in the
following decade he made the calculation that they sold about

550,000 gallons a year – far more than stalls that sold chocolate or tea. Both coffee and tea stalls remained open all day. Some were not so much money-making ventures as attempts to reform social habits: the temperance movement sponsored a number of them to ensure that alternatives to strong drink were available. They were doing business at roadsides from early morning, for many people depended on them for sustenance on their way to work. The coffee, costing a halfpenny a cup, was made in large cans over a charcoal burner, and would be drunk on the spot from a china cup and saucer that would be returned and – it is to be hoped – rinsed before it was offered to the next customer. The drink itself might well be adulterated, containing more acorn or carrot than coffee beans. Piled on the stall would also be hard-boiled eggs, perhaps hot or cold bacon, rolls and bread and butter. The latter was a staple that Victorians seem to have appreciated more than we do, for it was always popular.

Another item that to us seems somewhat bland was the ham sandwich. There were stalls that dealt in nothing else, and Mayhew computed that almost half a million of them were sold in London every year. They were eaten for breakfast, but were also much in demand outside theatres in the evenings. These would not, of course, have been the thin and neatly triangular affairs that are found in supermarkets today, but made with thick 'doorsteps' of bread and with meat that would have been cut from joints in front of the customers.

Fish and chips is often considered to be the most traditional of British 'convenience foods', but it does not have a long pedigree. Strips or chunks of fried potato were introduced from the Low Countries (where they remain an emblematic national dish to this day), and it was a Belgian who first sold them from a street barrow, in the 1850s, at Dundee in Scotland. Initially they were served with peas, and it was only later that the notion of combining them with fried fish was tried. Potatoes already had a place on the streets, though the trade in them dated only from the 1830s. Roast potatoes were sold in paper bags or twists of newspaper, baked ones could be bought individually for a halfpenny. Heated at a bakehouse, they were carried in, and sold from, metal cans, although as the trade developed it became more common to use portable ovens. Once ready, the potatoes were impaled on metal spikes attached to the top of the oven, where their aroma would tempt passers-by. After years of eclipse, the baked potato has re-emerged as a popular snack, though the Victorians did not, as we do, stuff them with assorted fillings. Saveloys, a type of spicy sausage still found in chip shops, were also warmed in these ovens and sold by dealers in potatoes.

Pies were the traditional British fast food, and numerous varieties could be bought both from stalls and from 'pie-men' who carried trays on their heads. Ham, beef, mutton, veal and eel pies cost about a penny. With no procedures for testing the authenticity of the contents, meat might well not be what it pretended to be, and it was widely suspected that dogs and cats ended up in some of them. Pies were also filled with whatever fruit was in season – apple, gooseberry, rhubarb, plum, cherry.

Oysters were such a staple of the nineteenth century poor that in Mayhew's time they could be had for a penny a dozen. By the later years of Victoria's reign they were more than a penny each, though still within reach of the poor. They were sold from barrels at stalls and eaten, standing up, from the shell. They were on sale from 25 July, the beginning of the oyster season, and this was celebrated by children, who sought to collect coppers from passing adults by holding out empty shells.

A number of other items were also sold from trays carried about the streets. The muffin man, who traditionally bore his wares on his head, and the signal of whose approach – the ringing of a handbell – was one of the most joyous sounds in a

Victorian childhood, continued in business until the Second World War. Cakes, pastries and puddings, such as bread pudding and 'spotted dick', were also sold in this manner.

Ice-cream was something of a latecomer to the streets. Although it was available by the time of the Great Exhibition, it became common only in the eighties, when portable freezing equipment was invented by Agnes Bertha Marshall, the principal of a London cookery school. The author of books on the subject of ice-cream, she made it with a mixture of cream, egg yolks and caster sugar. Placed in an aluminium and wooden drum, these ingredients were mixed and frozen by rotating a handle, a process that took about ten minutes. It was she who invented the cone in the late eighties. Prior to that, ice-cream had often been frozen onto metal rods that had to be returned after it had been licked off!

The streets were fairly flowing with drink, then as now. Gin was favoured as the cheapest narcotic, but beer was the universal thirst quencher and was highly useful, given that water was often unsafe to drink. Lemonade and ginger beer were the most popular in hot weather. Both were sold by vendors from barrels on a stall or from portable cans that were simply put down at a kerbside. Before there were such things as disposable cups, the customers drank on the spot and returned the glass.

Though the Victorians, as a whole, may have been less fastidious than we are regarding both hygiene and ingredients (Mrs Marshall, of ice-cream machine fame, called the items proffered by vendors 'poisonous filth'), we can only conclude that the taste-buds of our nineteenth-century ancestors functioned differently from ours. Mrs Marshall herself included in a cookery book the recipe for a Parmesan ice flavoured with Leibig's meat extract, and the peckish could find themselves tempted by frozen curries in cups of aspic.[10] Though we have much to learn from the Victorians, their eating habits are not worthy of our admiration.

4

TASTE

Georgian Afterglow

In the nineteenth century Britain was able to enjoy the benefits of the Industrial Revolution on a grand scale. Despite an economy that often veered between boom and bust, this meant a steadily rising standard of living for the middle classes as well as a huge rise in their numbers. It also meant a vast increase in technology. Not only did domestic conveniences – such as piped water – make houses more comfortable, ornaments and furnishings became far more inexpensive and readily available. 'Taste' therefore became something that many millions could afford to exercise for the first time.

In the Georgian era, items such as wallpaper, carpets and furniture had been extremely costly, and beyond the reach of most. It had also been a matter of taste to devote attention to the outside of a house rather than the interiors in order to make a good impression on others. Inside, even in the homes of the wealthy, decoration was simple and even severe. Since the Greeks and Romans, the inspiration for all things Classical, were perceived as having lived in sparse surroundings, this fashion was blessed by historical precedent. When Victoria came to the throne there was no sudden alteration in the way things were designed or laid out. Regency taste continued to dominate architecture and interiors for well over a decade after her accession.

Clutter

By then, however, technology had made it possible to produce more elaborate décor, and to do so without enormous cost. It became a sign of moving with the times to cram one's home with the marvels, fripperies and luxuries created by industry, and people began to seek status symbols that could be displayed *inside* their homes. Victorians filled their parlours with ornament and utilities not only to enjoy these things but to show visitors that they possessed the currently modish objects and styles. The simplicity of the Georgians was turned on its head, for a room with empty stretches of wall, or corners bereft of tables and ornaments, was considered poor taste – a classic example of one generation reacting against the outlook of the last.

The desire for a wealth of ornament reached its apogee in the fifties, for the Great Exhibition at the start of that decade acted as a huge market-place for domestic furnishings, showing the public what was available not only from British manufacturers – who constituted by far the largest element – but from overseas. However, this taste for heavy, elaborate, machine-made furniture and ornament had scarcely begun to make an impact when it was challenged by designers and thinkers, most notably John Ruskin and William Morris.

Though cluttered homes continued to be characteristic of Victorian living right to the end of the era, the accepted notions of popular taste were under constant, often spirited attack, and alternatives were found. No sooner, in other words, had the industrial era reached its high point than a reaction against it began. The Queen Anne revival later in the century led the way to styles of building and furnishing that were a direct repudiation of those which dominated the mid-Victorian years. Taste went from simple to elaborate and back to simple.

Because it was there that status and wealth were displayed, the home became the focus of unprecedented and increasing attention. As opportunities expanded for planning, decorating and furnishing houses, these matters developed into a national preoccupation, somewhat similar in scale to the present-day interest in do-it-yourself and renovation. The trend was reflected in the number of books and periodicals produced throughout the reign. The best-known was Charles Eastlake's *Hints on Household Taste*, which was first published in 1868. Other titles that sold well included Shirley Hibberd's *Rustic Adornments for Homes of Taste* (1857), Robert Edis' *Decoration and Furniture of Town Houses* (1881) – which became a standard text for the Queen Anne movement – Mrs Mary Haweis' *The Art of Decoration* (1881), and Mrs Lucy Orrinsmith's *The Drawing-Room, its Decoration and Furniture* (1877). In addition there were multi-volume reference works such as *Cassell's Household Guide* (1869 onwards) and *The Cabinet-Maker, a Journal of Designs* (1868). By the end of the century there were influential periodicals such as *The Artist* and, most famously, *The Studio*, which, instead of setting out the mores of taste for readers to follow, offered through their articles continuous and updated information about developments in Britain and abroad. Decorative ideas in vogue in Germany, Scandinavia or Russia, for instance, could be disseminated through text and illustrations, and thus quickly incorporated into British homes. It is worth noticing, incidentally, given our notions of how little scope Victorian ladies had for earning income or following careers, that much of this material was written by women. As with the equally lucrative books on etiquette, household management and domestic economy, ladies were seen as the natural repository of wisdom in this area. Some of them made considerable names, as well as incomes, from their pens, though none of them matched the degree of fame achieved by Mrs Beeton.

The home was not only a showplace for one's taste and possessions but a contrast to the violence and uncertainty outside. The Victorian wealthy, and middle classes, saw themselves as surrounded by a sea of poverty, crime and disturbance. There was always the threat of robbery, but during the unrest of the thirties and the upheavals of the forties, there was an additional likelihood of civil disorder and they felt physically endangered by political mobs. The Duke of Wellington, despite being a national hero, had felt sufficiently at risk during the Reform Bill riots to have the windows of his town house in Piccadilly fitted with bulletproof iron shutters (thus gaining his nickname 'the Iron Duke'). In the following decade the Queen and her family fled London before the Chartist rally on Kennington Common in expectation of widespread violence.

Fortress and Sanctuary

In the comfortably off, these circumstances perhaps induced a siege mentality. The home, or at least the notion of home life, became more important in this era than at any time before or since. It was becoming sanctified in Victorian mythology as a place of refuge from the world and its troubles, and as such it became a fortress. Sometimes, it even looked like one. The very streets in which the wealthy had their homes were often segregated from the surrounding area by hefty, though elegant, barriers. Even fairly modest homes that were built in terraces were commonly set back from the pavement behind a set of sharp-pointed railings and a ten- or fifteen-foot 'moat' that could only be crossed by a stone 'drawbridge'. Arthur Schlesinger was greatly amused by what he saw as domestic premises bristling with defences, and remarked that: 'Every English house has its fence, its iron stockade and its doorway bridge. It is exactly as if Louis Napoleon was expected to effect a landing daily between luncheon and dinner, while every individual Englishman is prepared to defend his household gods to the last drop of porter.'[1] Whether they were expecting to sit out a revolution or were merely protecting their privacy, British people of the property-owning sort appeared to be suspicious and fearful of everything beyond their own fireside.

Town houses designed in this way were not a Victorian invention. Their predecessors the Georgians had created this type of townscape in the previous century, as can be seen by any visitor to Bath. The nineteenth century expanded it – as befitted an era in which there were far more people wealthy enough to live in grand town houses – and the Victorians made it their own with a number of architectural touches and innovations. In London, the covering of facades with a coat of off-white stucco, which looks especially attractive when lit by evening sun, was first seen in the Grosvenor Estate, the building of which began in 1824 but continued well into Victoria's reign. Instead of the comparatively simple fan-lighted Georgian doors, the builders of later generations created more imposing entrances, the doors themselves sheltered by balustraded balconies that were supported by pairs of Corinthian columns. A street uniformly filled with this architecture, such as those on either side of Eaton

Square, presents a prospect of striking beauty and magnificence, an undeniable achievement of architects and builders. This style was imitated, in many thousands of smaller houses, throughout London and beyond. The spacious, ordered facades, pillared entrances and Italianate balustrades, which were in essence a continuation of eighteenth-century Classical styles and which had been refined in the Regency period, became characteristic of the Victorian era because houses of this sort continued to be built throughout the early and middle decades of that epoch. Buckingham Palace characterized this heavy Classical style, though it was not a product of the Queen's reign. It had been begun by John Nash in about 1825 and he himself had died two years before she came to the throne, yet it became associated with Victoria because she was the first monarch to live there, moving in a month after her coronation in 1838. This type of architecture was seen as stately as well as familiar. It suggested to both natives and foreign visitors that in terms of national greatness Britons were the heirs to Ancient Rome. It also reflected the Mediterranean taste developed by architects who had either been on the Grand Tour or had studied under others who had. The fashion for Italianate buildings would continue throughout the reign. It would be seen not only in the design of private houses (the square campanile, two of which were such a feature of Osborne House, was much copied in suburban villas) but in communal and public buildings. Anyone walking through St James' Park and Pall Mall in London will not fail to notice that the back of the Foreign Office looks as if it would be more suitable in Rome, and several of the gentlemen's clubs seem to have been lifted directly from medieval Florence – as their designs largely were.

Though the huge town houses of Belgravia might represent the heights of urban domestic architecture, most Victorians who needed a home belonged to social strata that could not dream of affording such splendour. Scaled-down versions of the classic town house were therefore built in vast numbers on the edges of cities. The terrace was a space-saving option which – as the architects of Bath had discovered a century earlier – enabled a whole group of dwellings to increase their elegance by being joined together in a uniform row that had a pleasing harmony and balance. Speculators who built such houses (one of them was 'Superior Dosset', the founder of the Forsyte dynasty in Galsworthy's novels) threw up these rows of houses in fields and at roadsides, where they might remain as truncated eyesores until the arrival of neighbouring – and perhaps unsympathetic – buildings joined them together to form streets. The houses of lower-middle-class families might have half-stuccoed facades in imitation of Nash's great projects, and even these were likely to have areas (the railing-enclosed open space at basement level in front of a house) and servants' attics, for anyone belonging to the class of small householder was likely to have a servant, even if it were only a single young girl from the local orphanage. The houses were also likely to have touches of gentility in the form of fanlights over the door or pairs of columns or pilasters framing it. In the case of especially pretentious builders there could even be niches, Classical urns or pseudo-Greek statuary on the pediment of a terrace. All of these things, like the genteel or aristocratic names often given to streets and squares by developers in bourgeois neighbourhoods, appealed to the aspirations of a society that took its cue entirely from the top and which delighted in being able to display its own modest expressions of taste and status. The advent of the railway meant that building materials could be more widely, and rapidly, distributed around the country, and therefore that Welsh slate – to name one major example – could be used to build houses in Newcastle or Brighton.

Artisan Dwellings

For housing the working class there was a new development, the tenement. This word, which we tend to associate with slums, was in fact precisely the opposite. It offered a comparatively hygienic and spacious living unit in which a number of families could dwell. Though largely unknown in England, the tenement had a long and honourable history in Scotland, where families lived for generations on single floors in a building that was served by a 'close' or communal entrance. These continue to function, and a Victorian example is preserved in Glasgow by the National Trust for Scotland. The English versions, whether they were erected for the Guinness Trust or the Great Exhibition (Prince Albert's 'Model Dwellings', a sample unit of workmen's housing, can still be seen in London's Kennington Park) tended to consist of blocks of single-storey dwellings that opened onto communal balconies and were reached by outside staircases. Many of them are still in use, and they often display pleasant decorative touches in the form of wrought-iron railings or patterned brick.

The pseudo-Georgian, vaguely Classical townhouse of the lower middle class, with its cube-shape and shallow roof and stucco coat, represents an important Victorian legacy. It was popular in its day in part because it was so simple in design and appearance that it was cheap to build and cheap to buy or rent, and its usefulness has been proved by the number of such houses still inhabited. A more complex style, and one that by its very nature made little appeal to builders of mass housing, had also emerged in the Regency and early Victorian eras. This was Gothic revival. It had had its beginnings, in the eighteenth century, in the garden follies and sham-temples of country-house parks. In the latter decades there had been two major and influential private buildings employing this style throughout.

One was Horace Walpole's Strawberry Hill (1750–63), the other was William Beckford's Fonthill Abbey, a structure entirely inspired by medieval models but which was so over-ambitious that its immense tower collapsed and it had to be abandoned. Gothic styles attracted a core of devoted, but often eccentric, adherents even when they were out of general fashion.

Gothic Revival

The nineteenth century's greatest proponent of Gothic architecture was Augustus Welby Northmore Pugin (1812–52), the son of a French émigré who was an expert on medieval architecture and the author of several volumes on the subject. The younger Pugin was already, by the age of fifteen, helping his father with the restoration of Windsor Castle by designing Gothic fixtures. He subsequently became a convert to Catholicism, and thus added to his technical ability a sense of passionate nostalgia for a lost age of faith. He found a crucial outlet for his ideas when, in 1835, he was invited by the architect Charles Barry to work on the new Palace of Westminster. Following its destruction by fire in 1834, it had been decided to rebuild it in Gothic style in order to match its neighbours – King Henry VII's Chapel at Westminster Abbey, and the fourteenth-century Westminster Hall. The project was to occupy most of Pugin's life. He was placed in charge of the palace interiors, and personally designed virtually every detail – carpets, wallpaper, woodwork, tiles, stained glass, furniture and lightfittings. In order to carry out these designs he assembled an army of craftsmen and apprentices who were kept busy for over a quarter of a century, for the Houses of Parliament were not completed until 1860. The project represented a flowering of individual craftsmanship that was in sharp contrast to the spirit of the times, for industrial mass-production was creating a culture of furnishing and decoration that was filling both private homes and public buildings with factory-made ornament. Pugin's influence on the later Arts and Crafts movement, which similarly sought a return to the values of the pre-industrial world, was profound. The mass-production of furniture and *objets d'art* against which he and others fought was not entirely to be despised, however. The cheapness of these items brought at least a hint of beauty and elegance within reach of millions of households that could not have afforded anything created by hand. An imitation Roman statue, fashioned by machinery, on the mantelpiece of a lower-middle-class household looked, at least from a distance, much like the one displayed in a country house as a relic of the Grand Tour. Machine-made floor tiles and cheaper, factory-produced wallpaper brought colour and a certain (arguably vulgar) splendour to the homes of the clerical classes.

The influence of Pugin was enormous. When the Lords' chamber was opened to public inspection in 1847 it caused a sensation, and brought Pugin a host of imitators. His style provoked further interest when he organized the Medieval Court at the Great Exhibition. The fact that this work coincided with a revival of both Roman Catholic church-building and increased ceremony within the Anglican Church meant that medieval-revival architecture and interiors became immensely fashionable. Not only places of worship but institutions such as schools, hospitals and almshouses came to be built in this style, which was considered particularly appropriate for seats of learning (even down to infant schools), and for which the genuine buildings of the late middle ages – such as many of the Oxbridge colleges – provided a wide range of models. Pugin also created private houses. As early as 1837 he designed Scarisbrick Hall in Lancashire, but while his great achievement will always be considered his interiors in

Parliament, his most extensive work was that which he did with
the 16th Earl of Shrewsbury – the most powerful Catholic
layman of the time – to create a series of Roman Catholic
churches throughout the north Staffordshire countryside and
elsewhere, building what are perhaps the most beautiful church
interiors seen in Britain since the Reformation. He also altered
the Earl's home, Alton Towers, between 1839 and 1852 into a
magnificent showpiece of neo-Gothic architecture and decoration. Pugin's output was so prodigious that the stress proved
fatal. He died after a breakdown in September 1852, though his
son Edward continued his work into a third generation.

Further Heights

One of Pugin's most able successors in what was to be dubbed
'High Victorian' taste was William Burges (1827–81). He too had
grown up with a passion for medieval workmanship, and he had
honed his knowledge of building and design with extensive travel
abroad. All English architects with a bent toward the gothic were
highly influenced by the Frenchman Eugène Viollet-le-Duc
(1814–79), who had successfully remodelled a number of medieval French buildings. Like Pugin, Burges had a wealthy patron –
in his case the Marquess of Bute – and therefore the opportunity
to work on large and costly projects. His most significant
commission was the renovation of Cardiff Castle, beginning in
1868. The buildings were originally medieval, and Burges transformed them into an almost absurd Victorian fantasy, as he did
with a further commission at nearby Castell Coch. Anyone seeing
the charming fireplace in the Castle's banqueting hall, with its
plaster turrets and colourful trumpeters, would realize that he
had introduced, in place of Pugin's high-minded religiosity, a
lively humour and a quirkiness that are very endearing. Like
Pugin, he died suddenly and relatively young.

Burges' contemporary, George Gilbert Scott (1811–78), also made his name through the restoration of medieval buildings. He sought to make Gothic revival architecture less purist and more adaptable to the needs of the age. Unmotivated by religion or by strict adherence to accuracy, he developed a looser style that unashamedly made use of modern technology such as iron girders, and he employed to great effect the revived Renaissance decorative material terracotta. He was responsible for two of London's best-known buildings – the Albert Monument (1862–72) and the vast and conspicuous Midland Grand Hotel at St Pancras station (1868–77). Another architect who worked in the Gothic tradition and has left conspicuous monuments was William Butterfield (1814–1900). In some of his major projects – and the two most outstanding are the quadrangle and chapel at Keble College, Oxford (1868–76) and the chapel and New Quad at Rugby School (1872 and 1885) – use of brick in contrasting colours has led him to be seen as an extreme exponent of the style, and his work requires, even among those who share a taste for it, some getting used to. For those who are not admirers, it is nerve-janglingly offensive.

Another exponent of this style, who admired its combination of high-mindedness and technical skill, was John Ruskin (1819–1900). The most important artistic figure of the Victorian era, Ruskin was not an architect but an artist, writer and critic (he in fact created art criticism as a discipline), as well as a philosopher and philanthropist. His exhaustive six-volume work *Modern Painters* (1843–60) gave him a national reputation as an authority on art. *The Seven Lamps of Architecture* (1849) extended the reach of his expertise into the field of architecture. Even more of an impact was made by his next work, *The Stones of Venice* (1853), which used the architecture of that city to celebrate the virtues of individualist medieval craftsmanship and added to the gothic a moral element – in other words, he championed the notion that this was not simply a decorative style copied from the past but a statement of idealism and faith that had relevance in the present. Ruskin became a symbol of resistance to the industrial society that had come to maturity in the Victorian era and found its expression in the artefacts at the Great Exhibition. His influence was vast, and spread so far that it could become almost a caricature. He was to lament that: 'There is scarcely a public house near the Crystal Palace that does not sell its gin and bitters under pseudo-Venetian capitals.'[2] Despite the trivialization that sometimes followed in the wake of his ideas, he was to be a guiding spirit for much of the design that characterized the later Victorian period.

The Terrace

Most town dwellings were terraced houses, whether this meant the vast and opulent five- and six-storey versions that can be seen in London's Belgravia and Bayswater or the 'two-up, two-down' that is such a feature of the industrial north and Midlands. Houses were vertical, and the arrangement of the rooms followed a particular pattern that dictated, to a large extent, the lives of those who inhabited them. In the larger town houses – whether they were in London, Edinburgh, Glasgow, Manchester or Birmingham – the usage of the rooms was much the same and reflected a lifestyle that has now almost entirely vanished, both because of a lack of the servants that made it viable and because the prohibitive cost of property means that few can afford to run such establishments. The Victorians would not, in most cases, have *owned* these houses. They lived in a 'rental culture' similar to that which is still found on the Continent today. Nevertheless the cost of leasing a large town house and paying the servants who ran it would be beyond the means of most. Looking today at the overwhelming stuccoed, Italianate terraces that were put up around Hyde Park at the time of the Great Exhibition, almost all of them now occupied by embassies or institutions, we may be intrigued to know who would have lived in them in the years after they were built. The contemporary journalist George Augustus Sala similarly wondered about their occupants. When walking one day he observed that:

> magnificent lines of stately mansions, towering park gates, bring us to the two gigantic many-storeyed edifices at Albert Gate, which we have long-since christened 'Gibraltar', because they were for a long time supposed to be impregnable, no tenant having been found rich or bold enough to take them.[3]

Many houses of this type were set in terraces or culs-de-sac that were not accessible to the general public. To an extent that barely still exists, the Victorian wealthy lived in streets that were defended by railings and liveried gate-keepers. One example of this remains in fashionable London: Kensington Palace Gardens, a street of massive detached houses at the west end of the Gardens, looks much as it did when built in the 1850s. Because it houses the embassies of countries – such as Russia – with whom relations have been sensitive, its private character has deliberately been maintained. Today it is a curiosity; then it was merely one of many.

Inside a town house, whether as grand as those in the gated streets or more modest, like those in Bloomsbury, the layout followed the same general plan. Max Schlesinger, a German writer and traveller visiting London, gave this description of the interior and the uses of the various rooms:

> The small space between the street-door and the stairs, hardly sufficient in length and breadth to deserve the pompous name

of a 'hall', is usually furnished with a couple of mahogany chairs or, in the wealthier houses, with flower-pots, statuettes, and now and then a sixth- or seventh-rate picture. The floor is covered with oil-cloth, and this again is covered with a breadth of carpet. The English houses are like chimneys turned inside-out; on the outside all is soot and dirt, in the inside everything is clean and bright.[4]

From the hall we make our way to the parlour – the refectory of the house. The parlour is the common sitting room of the family, the centre-point of the domestic state. It is here that many eat their dinners, and some say their prayers; in this room does the lady of the house arrange her household affairs and issue her commands. Large folding doors, which occupy nearly the whole breadth of the back wall, separate the front from the back parlour either to the purposes of a library for the master, the son, or the daughters of the house, or convert it to a boudoir, office, or breakfast room. Frequently, it serves no purpose in particular, and all in turn. These two rooms occupy the whole depth of the house.[5]

All the other apartments are above, so that there are from two to four rooms in each storey. Hence each storey has its particular destination in the family geographical dictionary. In the first floor are the reception rooms; in the second the bedrooms, with their large four-posters and marble-topped wash-stands; in the third storey are the nurseries and servants' rooms; and in the fourth, if a fourth there be, you will find a couple of low garrets, for the occasional accommodation of some bachelor friend of the family.[6]

What also intrigued Schlesinger, as an outsider, was the servants' territory in the basement. Unique to Britain, but found throughout the United Kingdom from Belgravia to Dublin and to Edinburgh's New Town, was the area. As has been described,

each house was set back from the street with a narrow open
space in front of it paved at basement level, and crossed at street
level by a bridge. The area, which had a stairway leading down
to it, allowed light into the basement. It accommodated the coal
cellar and other storage space. It enabled servants and tradesmen access to the building through a separate entrance without
disturbing the occupants.

Inside this basement was the kitchen, which with its range
and table and shelves of pans, would be the centre of the
servants' world. Schlesinger examined this too:

> In the place of the carpets which cover the floors of the upper
> rooms, we walk here on strong, solid oilcloths which, swept
> and washed, look like marble. Add to this, bright dish-covers of
> gigantic dimensions fixed to the wall, plated dishes, and sundry
> others utensils of queer shapes and silvery aspect, interspersed
> with copper saucepans and pots and china, the windows
> curtained, with a couple of flower-pots on the sill, and a
> branch of evergreens growing on the wall around them. A
> large fire is always kept burning; such is the English kitchen in
> its modest glory. Several doors open into sundry other sub-
> terraneous compartments. There is a back kitchen, whither the
> servants of the house retire for the most important part of their
> daily labours – the talking of scandal apropos the whole
> neighbourhood. There is also a small room for the washing-
> up of plates and dishes, the cleaning of knives and forks, of
> clothes and shoes. Other compartments are devoted to stores of
> provisions, of coals, and wine and beer.[7]

The fittings in such a house might well be extremely up to date,
though this did not mean that the home was pleasant to live in.
George Sala, who like Schlesinger was writing in the fifties,
described what would be found inside:

This is the sort of house that is neatly solidly furnished from top to toe, with every modern convenience and improvement: with bathrooms, conservatories, ice-cellars, with patent grates, patent door-handles, dish-lifts, asbestos stoves, gas cooking ranges, and excruciatingly complicated ventilatory contrivances; and this is also the sort of house where, with all the conveniences I have mentioned, every living soul who inhabits it is uncomfortable.[8]

Early Victorian

The exterior of a typical early Victorian terraced house, of the type lived in by lower-middle-class families, would be brick-built (though in Scotland or the north of England stone might actually be a cheaper material) and of a style that was almost entirely a continuation of Georgian. It would be three or four storeys, with the walls becoming thinner the higher it went. It would often have a ground-floor façade that was contrived to look like blocks of stone and covered in stucco, and the surrounds of the sash windows might also be painted white. The door would have a Georgian fanlight above it, and there would be a basement area. The roof would have a parapet, behind which there would be a 'valley gutter' – the roof would not be pointed but v-shaped, so that rainwater would run to the back of the building and could be channelled into a drainpipe. In London, such houses were required to have an 'upstand' – another brick parapet running front-to-rear and through the chimney-stacks that divided the roof of every individual house from its neighbours. The purpose of this was to prevent fire from spreading through a whole terrace via the roofs. Inside, the stairs were often at the back of the house, lit by a tall window that was ten or twelve feet high and bisected by the stairs. The servants' quarters and kitchen would be in the basement, though a kitchen below the family rooms had the disadvantage that smells would drift upward, and the kitchen was therefore often built at the back of the house instead.

The interiors of an early Victorian middle class house retained much of the simplicity associated with the Regency, for it was only with the Great Exhibition in 1851 that the notion of fussiness and ornament was to become fashionable. Another element that was missing in the early part of the reign was the nocturnal gloom that filled many later Victorian rooms, crowded – as they often were – with unnecessarily large amounts of dark furniture and protected from daylight by heavy curtains. The early Victorians lived amid a brightness and colour that would perhaps surprise us.

One reason for the increase in light was the advent at this time of plate glass. Since it was no longer necessary to have one's view obstructed by wooden glazing-bars, the windows in new houses were made bigger. This was a highly noticeable symbol of technological advance and thus a feature to be shown off rather than obscured with curtains. The result was that more daylight entered the interiors of houses than had previously been possible or would shortly be considered necessary.

The house in Doughty Street, London, in which Charles Dickens lived between 1837 and 1839 is preserved as a museum, and a number of the rooms are furnished as they were at that time. The building – a modest five-storey terraced dwelling – was typical of thousands of such homes. On its ground floor was the dining-room (at the front) and morning-room (rear). On the floor above, the drawing-room ran the whole width of the house, with Dickens' study behind it. The second floor contained two bedrooms, one larger than the other, and a dressing-room. The attic floor would have contained servants' bedrooms and a nursery for the Dickens children. In the basement was the kitchen (at the front, with its own entrance from the area). Behind it, the still-room was used for the storage of food but was probably also the room in which the servants relaxed. At the rear of this floor were the scullery and a wash house, as well as a small wine cellar. There was no bathroom. In the house lived Dickens, his wife, his sister-in-law and his children, together with four staff – a normal number for a family that size – a manservant, a cook, a maid and the children's nurse.

The furniture is heavy and substantial, with machine-made ornamentation in the form of curlicues and turned legs. The mantels and fireplaces are painted white and are Greek in inspiration. Some details are extremely plain, such as the banister or the black-and-white-tiled hall floor. The drawing-room is the centrepiece of the house, and the colours in which it is decorated tell us something about the taste of the time, which the guidebook concedes may strike visitors as gaudy. The wallpaper is mauve and white. The curtains, with their heavy pelmets, are raspberry-red. The chairs and sofa are upholstered in dark green, and the fitted carpet is in a floral pattern of greens, with touches of blue, yellow, pink and red. The solid wooden furniture is dark mahogany, and there are elaborate rococo-style mirrors. Shades of green and red are found throughout the house. Even the less formal rooms look uncomfortable.

Furniture was still influenced, as it had been in the Regency, by Greek designs, but these years witnessed the so-called 'battle of the styles', for though Classical interior design was to remain influential, Gothic had made inroads. This trend had begun in 1818 when the novelist Sir Walter Scott commissioned furniture for Abbotsford, his neo-medieval house in the Scottish borders. Scott died in 1832, five years before Victoria came to the throne, but his historical novels exerted an immense influence on the imagination – and therefore the taste – of a whole generation, not only in Britain but throughout the world. By the 1830s the homes of even the most modest members of the affluent classes might contain baronial touches in the form of chairs, tables, sideboards and fireplaces of at least approximately medieval or Tudor design. Chair backs, for instance, often boasted medieval tracery, and table supports might have spandrels or other medieval touches. Though these items would recall a world of draughty and uncomfortable manor houses, they were expected also to allow for modern comfort. The increasing demand for upholstery and horsehair stuffing in chairs and sofas was evidence of a developing desire for furniture that was restful as well as merely elegant.

Wealth of Ornament

These fashions aside, most furniture was simple and functional. It began, however, to lose a good deal of its elegance. The slim-legged and fragile-looking chairs of the Regency were being superseded by heavier styles. The turned leg – a feature of tables, chairs and pianos that would come to be seen as archetypally Victorian – began to appear. Ornamentation became less refined. Rosewood had been favoured for furniture-making, but this began to give way to mahogany, and the progression toward interiors dominated by dark wood began. It would have been normal practice for chairs and sofas to have fitted cloth slip-covers – often in bright patterns – that were only ever removed when important entertaining made it necessary. As a result a great many items of this sort survived the Victorian era intact. Another novelty was furniture made from papier mâché. This unlikely material – pressed paper – was strong enough for chairs on which people could sit and tables at which they could dine, but it could not by its very nature become more solid as was increasingly the case with its wooden counterparts. It was normally black in colour, though it would be decorated with gay designs of painted flowers, and was much used for the making of occasional tables and other small pieces.

The invention of coil springs led to a fashion for deep, upholstered chairs and sofas that became characteristic of the forties, fifties and sixties, stuffed with horsehair and with their surfaces punctuated by buttons. This style is now so out of favour that it is difficult to imagine any young bride aspiring to have her home filled with such pieces, but it was admired for its modernity and for the technical achievement it represented.

If they lived in London, the middle classes found the furniture they coveted in Tottenham Court Road. There the firms of Maple and Heal began trading in 1841 and 1843 respectively, and were then joined by similar businesses. Though disdained by the snobbish as epitomizing the taste of the would-be sophisticated, both firms enjoyed considerable success (Maple's were to furnish apartments for the Empress of Russia) and are still flourishing today.

The lengths to which love of display could go are illustrated by the reference, in an official report, to the making of shoddy articles. The compiler of this, recalling an interview he conducted, describes how in furniture manufacturing:

> there are things done which make the article cheap, using Alga marina instead of hair, and using this cotton wool instead of hair, and using leather which is called Russian leather when it is not, and all those things that make up so that the eye is deceived and you cannot tell what the goods are. People buy them, and after a time find it out.
>
> Let me give you an example of this; a man told me he was a chair-maker; a lady came to him and bought some chairs. His price was 10s. 6d. each chair; so after a time the woman comes back to him and said, 'Did I not buy half-a-dozen chairs from you for 10s. 6d. each?' 'Yes, you did.' 'But do you know that

they are all in pieces?' 'What, all in pieces; how is that?' 'Well, a short time after I had them home, and we began to sit upon them, and they all fell abroad.' 'But,' he said, 'do you mean to tell me that you sat upon them?' 'Of course I sat upon them; what else?' He said, 'These ten-and-sixpenny chairs were made to be looked at, not to sit upon. If you had told me that you wanted chairs to sit upon I would have charged you 5s. a chair more for them.'[9]

Explosion of Colour

Although colours were comparatively muted in the early years of the reign, by the fifties they had become bolder and louder. One reason for this trend was the development of artificial dyes. In 1856 a chemistry student called William Perkin discovered a process for creating mauveine, the first such dye. The result was an explosion of noisy and often incompatible tones that characterized people's clothing as well as their homes. At about the same time, the development of power-loom weaving made carpets more cheaply available, and the machine-printing of wallpapers had the same effect on another aspect of interior decoration. Improvements in the production of wallpaper meant that patterns became more elaborate, involving highly complex shapes, colours and patterns. Many designs were floral, and sought to look as three-dimensional as possible. The effect was beautiful to contemporary eyes, but extremely fussy.

Plaids were much in vogue, both in tribute to the influence of Scott's sentimental view of the Highlands and, from the 1850s, in imitation of the Queen's Scottish tastes. These interior colours could well be reflected outside the house, where the iron railings in front of the area would have been painted in whatever colours the occupier desired. There might, for instance, be an attempt to render in realistic shades the iron flowers, leaves and bunches of grapes that decorated them. The story that these railings were all painted black in mourning for Prince Albert is untrue. A gradual desire for uniformity was responsible.

The Gothic revival also led to the greater prominence of colour in interior design. Medieval design had involved a wealth of complex patterns and bold colours, as shown in surviving stained glass or in the pages of illuminated manuscripts. The revival of this style therefore sought a similar richness in colour, making use of bright reds, blue, greens and golds, as well as a return to complexity in tracery and other ornament, a reaction against the severe lines and simplicity of the Regency. In 1856 what was to become perhaps the most influential document on the subject of design to be published in the nineteenth century appeared: Owen Jones' *The Grammar of Ornament*. This was an exhaustive collection of decorative details taken from the great, and lesser known, civilizations of the past – Classical and Egyptian as well as medieval and Renaissance. Its lavish illustrations were rendered in colour, thanks to recent advances in printing technology. Artists and architects had never previously had the opportunity to evaluate so vast an assemblage of styles, or to gain such a clear idea of the extent to which they had made use of bold colour. Jones' work became a bible for architects, painters, interior decorators and the makers of furniture, ceramics and tapestry.

Knick-knacks

Ornament was often fussy because what Victorians valued were skill, dexterity and cleverness. A thin glass dome that contained highly realistic flowers or fruit would be seen not only as a thing of beauty but as a triumph of craftsmanship, and the same notion would apply to displays, similarly under glass, of stuffed kittens, squirrels or other animals dressed in miniature costumes and posed as if attending a wedding, sitting in a schoolroom or involved in a battle. Though these do not appeal to modern sensitivities, the people for whom they were made thought them amusing as well as clever.

Interior Landscape

By the start of Victoria's reign gas lighting was beginning to become widespread. It had first been introduced as early as 1805, but it was not until 1840 that it became more readily available to London houses with the formation of the Gas Light and Coke Company, though it was to be more than a decade before other cities were able to follow. Gas was piped into the house from the street and channelled into a – usually elaborate – ornamental lightfitting that would be either in the middle of the ceiling or in imitation candle sconces above the fireplace, perhaps flanking a painting or mirror. It gave a pleasant and constant light, creating a sense of greater cosiness than had been possible even with candlelight, and was accompanied by a gentle hissing sound.

A newly introduced amenity that has lasted to our own day was the conservatory. The notion of attaching a greenhouse to an urban or suburban dwelling was something quite new. These conservatories were small-scale imitations of the plant-houses and orangeries that could be found on country estates. They were often very cramped, as befitted the modest homes to which they were added, but they gave a pseudo-aristocratic flourish to many thousands of humble suburban dwellings, and fitted well with the love of gardening that has always been characteristic of the British. In larger houses, conservatories often grew to monstrous size as they became a setting for summer entertaining. The Victorians, at all stages of the reign, had a passion for indoor plants – the potted aspidistra in lower-middle-class parlours became something of a cliché – and as well as placing these in drawing rooms they filled conservatories with showy, exotic and often expensive specimens: potted palms, orange trees and varieties of fern (the collecting of which was in particular vogue in the decades after the mid-century). The keeping of these would involve piped heating that made the conservatory into an actual 'winter garden'. The plants might represent the Empire in metaphor, gathered for their associations with particular overseas territories, but would more often simply reflect individual preference. In addition to this flora there might be fauna, represented by a hanging cage containing a tame parrot or some songbirds, and there could be sculpture – a tinkling fountain with perhaps a Classical statue or a pair of urns. If space allowed, there might even be diversion in the shape of a two-seater swing. A well-stocked conservatory, with its trees and shrubs, would provide opportunities for flirtation and offer courting couples momentary privacy. The overall effect was sometimes charming, often overwhelming and – to modern taste – as cluttered and overdone as we expect a Victorian interior to be. To Victorians the conservatory was a place of escape, recreation and refuge as well as a badge of wealth and position in an age obsessed with status and its symbols. James Tissot, whose paintings of fashionable life in the seventies and eighties have given us a vivid if somewhat idealized picture of life at that time, set several of his pictures in an opulent conservatory. It was the one at his own home in St John's Wood.

Late Victorian

A late Victorian terraced or semi-detached house is such a commonplace in any urban landscape that it is scarcely noticed.

It was in essence the same shape as its Georgian-type predecessor – though the staircases might now be at the side rather than in the rear – but was a good deal more elaborate. In many cases there would be a front garden, even if this were only three or four feet deep. By now unashamedly of brick and not hiding behind pseudo-stone or stucco, it might be decorated with courses of contrasting coloured brick, and would have mass-produced cornices and other decorative touches to add a hint of architectural grandeur. Tiles could be attached to front walls, and were commonly used to floor a front path, a doorstep or the walls of a recessed front porch. It had lost the semi-basement, for most such houses had now sprouted a narrow extension at the back in which the kitchen and scullery and the lavatory (if there was one inside) were situated, and any basement was used simply for storing coal. Though lower-middle-class house-holders still had servants, these were increasingly unlikely to 'live in' and required no quarters. Roofs were now higher and pointed, sloping either to front and back or – especially in the case of semi-detached dwellings – to the sides, thus creating attics that were large enough to use for storage.

The greatest interior difference between an early and a late Victorian house would be the existence of a bathroom and of plumbing. Prior to this development, washing would have been done with a jug and basin kept beside the bed. A bath would have been portable, kept hanging in the scullery or wash house and brought indoors to be filled with hot water in front of the bedroom fire. As attempts were made to improve domestic comfort, a gas-heated bath was invented in 1871. This involved bathing with gas flames burning underneath the tub and, as the water began to boil and the bath itself became unbearably hot, must have been like sitting in a giant sauce-pan. As boiler-heated piped water arrived in the late seventies, however, even a modest-sized bathroom could develop into a temple of beauty and comfort. Baths with a shower fitting became more common. The use of – usually blue – decorated china gave unexpected elegance to everyday activities, and transformed ablution from a necessity into a pleasure. The arrival of running water also enabled those fortunate enough to have these facilities to keep themselves a good deal cleaner than had previously been possible, changing – gradually though permanently – people's notions of personal cleanliness.

Without the necessary pipes to bring water in and carry waste out, people had not had a separate room in which to relieve themselves. The back yard was a suitable place for the privy, and in dining-rooms there was often a chamber-pot in a cupboard for the gentlemen to use after dinner, once the ladies had retired. Otherwise, these facilities were in the bedroom. The chamber-pot has a long and honourable history, and is doubtless still in use in some quarters. Before the advent of modern plumbing, people made use throughout the day and night of pots or commodes, the clearing of which ('emptying slops') was an entirely routine – if thoroughly unpleasant – part of a housemaid's or manservant's duty. The most extraordinary of these arrangements, perhaps, was the 'night table'. This was a desk with a sloping top and three drawers underneath. The top drawer was for papers, the one below it for linen. The bottom drawer, when pulled out, had struts to support the weight of a person sitting on it, for it contained a china receptacle and was used as a lavatory. After use, the drawer would be shut until a servant could deal with the contents. While this may sound to us distasteful in the extreme, there was nothing unusual about it at the time. Indeed, there were those who resisted the notion of change. When the elderly King of Prussia was told that it was possible, for the first time, to equip his palace with flush lavatories, he harrumphed irritably: 'We're having none of that new-fangled nonsense around *here*!'

Facilities

The water closet revolutionized all that. This useful device had been in existence, in various forms, for centuries (Queen Anne had one at Windsor) but without an efficient sewage system they could not be efficiently installed or used *en masse*. Public concern in this area was galvanized by the outbreaks of cholera that occurred from the thirties onward, and by the death in 1861 of Prince Albert, allegedly as a result of typhoid contracted from the drains at Windsor Castle. In 1858, the same year that on a summer's day the Thames virtually solidified with raw sewage and assorted industrial waste, the Metropolitan Board of Works was established, and within twelve months work had begun on creating an efficient disposal system. The massive diggings, which produced two parallel pipes running eastwards, on either side of the river, to treatment plants, were completed by 1865. Other towns and cities followed this example, and thus created a network for sewage removal and treatment upon which we still rely.

By 1844 a water closet was available consisting of a boxed-in seat that contained a cistern. Fourteen years later a clergyman, the Reverend Mr Moule, created the 'earth closet'. This used dry, sifted earth instead of water, but was similarly activated by pulling a handle. Moule's reasoning was that the earth not only acted as a deodorizer but broke down the sewage. His invention worked, and enjoyed a popularity that has revived in recent years among the ecologically-minded. Water, however, remained the favoured option. The Optimus, a water closet produced by the firm of Dent and Hellyer, immediately went into extensive use and, whatever the Prussian king may have thought of them, was installed for the British monarch at Buckingham Palace. In 1875 the 'wash-out' closet was perfected and became standard, and in the eighties

the cistern came into general use. For the first time the type of
sanitary facilities we use ourselves and regard as essential had
come into being. Toilet bowls appeared in a vast range of
styles, shapes and colours that suddenly made this very basic
object a pleasure to look at.

Lavatory paper was introduced in the eighties. Prior to that,
and indeed for a long time afterwards for those who saw it as a
luxury, people made their own. Any paper that came into the
home – newspapers, calendars, advertising handbills – was
liable to be used in this way when it was no longer needed. One
of the chores performed in even upper-middle-class households was the cutting or tearing of paper into squares, which
were then threaded with string and hung on the back of the
lavatory door.

Pocket Paradise

The Laurels, Brickfield Terrace, Holloway, the small north
London villa that is the home of the Pooter family in George
and Weedon Grossmith's novel *The Diary of a Nobody*, is
surely one of the most famous of late Victorian addresses. It
was entirely typical of the houses in which lower-middle-class
families lived. Though the book was published in 1892, the
building is clearly not up-to-date, and belongs rather to the
world of half a century earlier. Pooter describes his domain:

> A nice six-roomed residence, not counting basement, with a
> front breakfast-parlour. We have a little front garden; and
> there is a flight of ten steps up to the front door which, by-the-
> by, we keep locked with the chain up. Our intimate friends
> come to the little side entrance, which saves the servant the
> trouble of going up to the front door, thereby taking her away
> from her work. We have a nice little back garden which runs

down to the railway. We were rather afraid of the noise of the trains at first, but the landlord said we should not notice them after a bit, and took £2 off the rent. He was certainly right; and beyond the cracking of the garden wall at the bottom, we have suffered no inconvenience.[10]

Eclectic

Higher up the scale of affluence and gentility, though certainly not among the grandest dwellings, is Linley Sambourne House, 18 Stafford Terrace, Kensington. It was the home of a well-known *Punch* cartoonist from 1874 until his death in 1910. It has been preserved in what is more or less its original condition and is open to the public. Though it seems spacious, compared with the homes in which many city-dwelling families live today, the Sambournes could host only small dinner-parties, for their dining-room was not large enough to accommodate many guests. They shared their house with two children and four servants.

The house is typical of the brick-and-white-stucco terraces that were built all over the area in the mid-Victorian decades (in this case 1868–74). It is five storeys high and has a small garden at the back. The kitchen, wine cellar and coal-bunkers were on the bottom floor, which is a semi-basement, and were connected with the upstairs rooms by bells and speaking-tubes that still exist. Rather than a porticoed entrance there are two pilasters framing the front door. The house is therefore of the Classical-influenced type that continued to be built throughout the century.

Inside, the hall was originally floored with coloured tiles, and the stairs are at the rear. The walls are hung with groups of pictures whose frames almost touch, but the wallpaper behind them is a Morris design. The effect when seen today is dark, but this is because the colours have faded with time. On the ground floor, the front of the house is occupied by the dining-room. This has a plate-glass bay window, but with lace curtains, fabric curtains and blinds there is little direct daylight. There is Morris wallpaper and there are multitudes of pictures that form an eclectic mixture of original works and reproductions, paintings and photographs (framed photographs of famous paintings seem not to have been considered bad taste). A hexagonal table has Gothic, Puginesque legs, while one of the mirrors is Regency in style. There is a shelf at 'frieze level' – about ten feet above the floor – on which blue and white porcelain is displayed, and there are brass plates hung as wall decorations. There is also a large sideboard with painted panels. One feature that would strike visitors as distinctively Victorian is the use of curtains to cover doorways. These were often hung from a brass rail and, when not needed, were pulled to one side and secured. Before the advent of central heating they were extremely necessary for protection from draughts.

The furnishings are therefore – to use a term that is frequently applied to both architecture and interiors of the period – eclectic. The phases of developing taste in the Victorian era naturally often overlapped. This house has a combination of old and new, fashionable and passé that is not uncommon, or unexpected. The ground floor morning-room has Regency furniture that was inherited. It also has stained glass leaded windows. The staircase and upstairs drawing-room have these too. The latter fills both the width and the length of the first floor. It has embossed wallpaper in red and gold, and a gold ceiling. There are two fireplaces and a number of chests and tables whose tops seem almost invisible beneath the array of ornaments – plates, bowls, vases, statuettes, photograph frames. Again there is a high shelf running along the wall on which plates are displayed.

The householders of the middle and later Victorian era did not, as we often do, feel that large areas of blank wall are 'restful'. It would simply not have occurred to them to leave space empty. Where they did not hang pictures, they hung shelves filled with ornaments or photographs, creating a clutter that to them represented comfort and taste. On an inventory made at 18 Stafford Terrace are the following: 'Right of fireplace 1 drawing in oak frame, 3 engravings in ditto, 7 photographs in ditto, 1 photograph in gilt ditto. Left of fireplace 13 photographs in oak frames, 2 engravings in ditto,'[11] and this was only one wall in one room!

Upstairs are the family bedrooms, and above them the day nursery, night nursery and the maid's room. On one landing there is a bathroom with a coffin-shaped marble bath and there is a separate lavatory with tiled walls, a marble floor and a basin. Most unmistakably Victorian, perhaps, is the 'water garden' on the first-floor landing. This comprises a glass tank into which piped water flows, trickling over a number of stones so that their colours will be brought out. This may not sound very exciting, but it was typical of the interest which people of the era felt in minerals, plants, fish and birds – all of which could be incorporated into the home through such small displays. It was fashionable to have aviaries or fish tanks, or to keep a collection of ferns in a miniature greenhouse. In *Our Mutual Friend* Dickens refers to one of these displays. Ascending a staircase 'tastefully ornamented' with flowers, his characters:

> came to a charming aviary, in which a number of tropical birds, more gorgeous in colour than the flowers, were flying about; and among these birds were gold and silver fish, and mosses, and water-lilies, and a fountain, and all manner of wonders.[12]

Further Revival

In the middle decades, design found another direction in the Queen Anne style (the phrase was first used in 1862 in reference to furniture, but it was from the seventies that it picked up momentum as an architectural movement). This was not, in any sense, a simple nostalgic reference to the reign of Queen Anne (1702–14), for it involved few features that belonged to that era. Rather it was an attempt to rediscover the beauties of traditional English vernacular architecture and amalgamate them into modern buildings. In doing so, a quintessentially English style was created, and one that is still followed, to some extent, today. Many features found in regional English building traditions – tall brick chimney-stacks, weather-boarding, half-timbering, tile-hung walls, oriel windows, pargetting and emphasis on (often white-painted) gables – were incorporated and thus given a national, even international usage. Though the term 'Queen Anne' is a misnomer, for the work of architects in this style drew much more heavily on Tudor and earlier Stuart styles, one thing that their Victorian buildings had in common with the early eighteenth century was the use of red brick. In southern and eastern England, houses had largely been created from pale-grey, tan or yellow brick, and this was frequently hidden by stucco. The use of orange-coloured brick gave an entirely new look to townscapes in these regions, especially given that the scale of apartment buildings, for instance, became so much grander by the end of the century. The style was adapted for offices, libraries, fire stations, public houses and shops as well as numerous types of dwelling, and became such a pervasive influence that its tiles and gables and chimneys are still used in the design of houses and even housing estates.

The most notable instance of this style is to be found in Bedford Park, a suburb set between Acton and Chiswick in west London that was built between 1877 and 1881. It was deliberately planned as a rural village for middle-class aesthetes. It had a church, a school, a pub and some five hundred houses of different sizes and types. This was the first 'garden suburb' to be created, and its rural aspect, together with the overall harmony of its buildings – which has survived – give it a character that is distinctly English and entirely of its time.

Within houses like those in Bedford Park, the colours tended to be muted. The Queen Anne style sought to escape from the garish and artificial shades of earlier decades, which in any case would not have complemented the architecture. Simplicity was not, however, a keynote, for two elements created a taste for knick-knacks. One was the fashion for collecting antiques. These commonly included porcelain and pottery, so that surfaces – such as the now-inevitable frieze shelf – might be covered with an array of vases, bowls and dishes. Another was the growing awareness of other cultures. African and Asian objects became conspicuous as ornaments in British drawing-rooms, and this was especially true of Japanese items. The country had been out of bounds to foreigners for centuries when, in 1853, an American mission succeeded in persuading its rulers to establish trading and diplomatic relations with the wider world. In the years that followed, imported artefacts proved a major influence on the aesthetic movement. Japanese furniture, fabrics, ceramics and prints became immensely popular in Western homes. Lacquered furniture (the process of applying this was called 'japanning'), screens, fire-guards, fans – often stuck behind the corners of mirrors – and lacquered paper umbrellas joined the potted palms, fish tanks and porcelain vases that filled the interiors of middle-class homes. The fad became so all-pervading that it provoked the tribute of a Gilbert and Sullivan operetta – *The Mikado* – in 1885.

Arts and Crafts

After Ruskin, the most important artistic influence of the century was one of his numerous admirers, William Morris (1834–96). Morris shared Ruskin's veneration for craftsmanship, seeing it – in an attitude by now familiar among the thoughtful and creative – as an important expression of individuality in an era that had forgotten the value of work done by hand. He, like Ruskin, developed a socialist outlook that married neatly with his idealized view of the dignity of labour, though it was only because both men inherited sufficient wealth that they could afford to devote their lives to the pursuit of artistic integrity.

Morris was as much in love with the Middle Ages as Pugin was, and claimed to have read all the novels of Sir Walter Scott by the age of seven. While at Oxford he formed lifelong friendships with several like-minded young men (they were known as the Brotherhood), began writing poetry, tried painting (he worked for Dante Gabriel Rossetti on neo-medieval decorations for the Oxford Union) and decided to become an architect. When he married, he commissioned another architect, Philip Webb, to create a home for him. The Red House, at Bexleyheath, was completed in 1860, and Morris designed all its furnishings and interiors. The house became a showpiece for his vision and a definition of the Arts and Crafts movement that was to form under his influence. As a history of the building states:

> Webb and Morris were young, idealistic and reformist. Their house was more than just a home. It was a statement, in three dimensions, of their beliefs, a challenge to the tyranny of the machine. It was formed and shaped in simplicity from traditional materials – brick and tile, robust walls and massive barn-like roofs.[13]

Though it is original in appearance and design, it did not represent a revolution in domestic practices:

> Not all the architectural conventions of the mid nineteenth century were challenged in the design, which like other middle class homes at that time relied firmly on a ready supply of cheap domestic labour. The house was heated by coal fire-places, and hot water by a 'copper' in the scullery; there were no bathrooms; and the servants slept in a dormitory.[14]

Morris became not an architect but a general craftsman. He designed decorative tiles, woodwork, tapestries and carpets, wallpaper and stained glass. Though he himself worked on the carving, printing, weaving or production of all these items – for he believed in learning the processes of making things before designing them – he had the assistance of a workforce. He founded a business – Morris and Co. – to produce artefacts commercially. The firm was established at Merton Abbey Mills in Surrey, where its weaving-looms were operated exclusively by women. Perhaps the most famous of Morris' products was his wallpaper. The plant themes of his patterns became an easily recognized trademark and they sold well. They were, however, highly complicated to make. To produce his Acanthus design in 1876, for instance, the firm of Jeffrey and Co. had to use thirty blocks to print the intricate patterns and the fifteen colours involved. Later in life he added to his fields of activity an interest in manuscript illumination and printing. He established the Kelmscott Press at a manor house of that name in Oxfordshire in which he was by then living. The press created a number of fine bindings and beautiful printings that included a work of surpassing excellence – an edition of Chaucer (1896), printed and bound as if it were a medieval book and illustrated by his friend Edward Burne-Jones. Morris died before it was completed.

Unlike much that was created by the Victorians and reflected their taste, Morris' designs, like those of the Arts and Crafts movement that he inspired, have never gone out of fashion. In every subsequent generation there have been admirers who have reprinted the patterns, reproduced the furnishings and written – or read – books about them. However, his notion of combining socialist principles with traditional craftsmanship was hopelessly impractical. The things made by his workshops used such expensive materials, and required so many man-hours to produce, that no one below the level of the wealthy middle class could afford to buy them. The artisan class could not directly enjoy their beauty and artistry, which *de facto* became the property of an elite, and it was only in the century after his death that a wider public could enjoy them through exhibitions, publications and better reproduction techniques.

In Arts and Crafts houses the textures were very different from what had preceded them. Wooden surfaces – whether doors, tables or cupboards – were often not waxed or polished, and thus had a plain, workmanlike, natural appearance. The same would be true of metal fittings like door handles, lamps and window-catches. Colour, whether in textiles, wallpaper or painted decoration, was frequently flat and toneless – the very antithesis of the complex and 'realistic' floral designs of the fifties.

It was not easy to convert an existing house to the Arts and Crafts style, and it was only with new buildings that architects and designers could pursue their ideas to fulfilment. In Britain one among many that can be visited is Blackwell, a house set on a hill above Lake Windermere in Cumbria. It was built between 1898 and 1900 by the architect M. H. Baillie Scott

(1865–1945) as a summer residence for Sir Edward Holt, an industrialist and philanthropist who was twice Lord Mayor of Manchester. Scott wished to use local materials, such as Westmoreland slate for the roofs, and he was fortunate; Ruskin's presence in the area had awakened local interest in artistic craftsmanship, and there were firms nearby that could provide both carving and textiles appropriate to the architect's vision.

Outside, the house is simple and not ornate, lacking the multitude of decorative touches – tiles, coloured bricks, terra-cotta panels – that were still in general vogue at the time. The walls are white roughcast, the windows have no hoods or deep sills, and are of small, leaded-glass panes rather than the plate glass of a previous generation. The chimney-stacks are round, in reference to the traditional style of the region, and the overall effect is vaguely that of a Tudor farmhouse. Inside, the windows have been positioned to make maximum use of sunlight (the drawing-room is oriented to catch the sun in late afternoon). There is a comparative emptiness that is a deliberate reaction against the busy and crowded interiors of the time. Walls in rooms and corridors are covered in a warm, honey-coloured oak panelling that glows in the light. The equally rich wooden floors are uncarpeted, though there would have been rugs in the rooms. There are light-shades of copper. The entrance and the main hall are half-timbered, providing another powerful Tudor echo, as does the use of stained glass, and rooms are focused – as was commonly the case with Arts and Crafts architecture – on large ingle-nook fireplaces. The drawing-room panelling is painted white – the most emphatic contrast to the darkness of earlier Victorian interiors – and the fireplace has a shelf that runs right around the walls; the shelf at 'frieze height' for the display of artefacts was as important as ever.

The chief glory of Blackwell is its décor. There is a riot of carving, depicting roses and rowans. There are friezes in hessian, wallpaper and plaster depicting local plants and birds, and – perhaps most distinctive of all – there are stylized plaster trees. The overall impression is of space and light and a quirkiness of detail that is enchanting.

The Arts and Crafts style, having originated in Britain, spread to America, Europe and Scandinavia. In return, Britain absorbed from Europe in the final years of the reign the style known as New Art. This had much in common with the work of architects like Baillie Scott, for it represented yet another revolt against Victorian 'stuffiness'. It was a new and exciting – even decadent and daring – style in the nineties, and though its presence in the United Kingdom was short-lived, it produced in Scotland an architect and designer of international stature. This was Charles Rennie Mackintosh (1868–1928), who left a number of both exterior and interior masterpieces. His greatest achievement was Glasgow School of Art (1896–1910) and, though he himself described his buildings, with their liquid lines, as looking like 'melting butter', they bear witness to the fact that Britain could, on occasion, match the artistic achievements of Paris and Vienna, a notion that would not have been taken seriously when Victoria was crowned.

5

GETTING ABOUT

Transport Revolution

'When she came to the throne coaches still ran', as Soames Forsyte observed while watching Victoria's funeral procession. He might have added that, by the time of her death, motor cars had begun to run. The age of the automobile had not yet fully arrived, and understandably not everyone could see that horse-drawn transport would soon be extinct, or that powered flight was only a few years away. Nevertheless, people can have been in no doubt that further wonders were on the way, and that the fictional creations of Jules Verne or H. G. Wells might have become fact by the time their children were grown up. Perhaps nothing suggests the extent of the change in British life during her reign more tellingly than this revolution in transport. Its impact on the Victorian experience cannot be overestimated, for it affected virtually every one of the Queen's subjects,

enabling the mass of the population for the first time in history
to travel swiftly beyond the distance they could walk.

In 1897 Walter Besant once again summed up the advances
of the previous six decades for the *Illustrated London News*:

> Steam and electricity have conquered time and space to a
> greater extent during the last sixty years than all the preceding
> six hundred years witnessed. Think of the ocean greyhounds of
> today, capable of crossing the Atlantic in less than five and a
> half days. The broad Atlantic has, indeed, become a mere pond.
>
> The very streets bear evidence to the presence of the god of
> Speed. What would Dr Johnson think if he strolled down Fleet
> Street to-day, with its network of telephone and telegraph wires
> above, that make it the very cradle of the world; with its endless
> stream of hansoms and 'buses and bicycles; with its future
> procession of motor cars? Is there anything more insistent on
> the progress of the reign than that?[1]

These changes altered for ever the familiar patterns of settlement and movement, making it possible to see other places, to
attend events in far-off towns or districts, to work at some
distance from home, meet people from other areas – perhaps
even court someone whose home was scores of miles away. It
was not, of course, only land travel that became easier and
cheaper. The increased speed and relative safety of journeying
by sea made it possible for millions to cross the oceans, as
emigrants or tourists or business travellers. It was in this era
that 'package tourism' was born. Efficient railway travel made
it possible for armies of middle-class Britons to see the vistas
and monuments that had previously been accessible only to the
wealthy or intrepid. Rome, which in the days of the Grand
Tour had taken months to reach by carriage over mountains
and bad roads, was by the 1870s accessible in about sixty

hours from London. Thomas Cook, whose travel agency pioneered the concept of mass tourism, brought so many British visitors to Egypt that the Nile was flippantly dubbed 'Cook's Canal'. In this we can see a striking parallel between the world of the later Victorians and our own, for this democratization of travel was very similar to the budget airlines and other cut-price arrangements that are familiar today. As with the changes in our time, the public was quick to make use of these new conveniences and – within a remarkably short time – to take them for granted.

The End of the Coaching Age

It is true, though somewhat misleading, to say that stagecoaches still ran at the time of Victoria's accession, for the age of steam had by then arrived and they had been supplanted by the railway on some routes. They were, in 1837, already therefore a symbol not of the present but of the past. The railway age had begun as long ago as the reign of George III.

The mail coach did not have a long pedigree. This system for carrying passengers and mail had been organized only in 1784. It had, however, very quickly become the most efficiently run transport network in Europe, and was something of a marvel to foreign visitors. Mail coaches ran from the General Post Office close to St Paul's cathedral in London, departing every evening for destinations all over the British Isles. The service began to decline as the railways provided increasingly efficient competition, and with the massive surge in railway building during the 1840s and 50s, the coach was effectively doomed as a major form of transport.

Mail coaches were extremely elegant. They were painted in a maroon and black livery and sported the royal coat of arms on their sides. Their wheels were scarlet, and their numerous brass and leather accoutrements were always polished and gleaming before they set off. They often had names that suggested either the sleekness of a racehorse, the glories of British arms or the cities that they served – Flyer, Meteor, Wellington, Waterloo, Bristol, Manchester. They could carry only a few passengers – six inside and up to a further six or eight on the roof, next to the driver and guard. The interior contained two horsehair seats that faced each other, and straw would be put on the floor to warm the passengers' feet, for the vehicles were unheated. Those travelling outside, who had to be sufficiently agile to reach the roof by a series of iron rungs, naturally fared badly. They had no protection from the elements except whatever rugs, hats or umbrellas they brought with them. Luggage was carried in a 'boot', or stowed on the roof next to the passengers, who might therefore share their journey with baskets of live animals (before the advent of refrigeration, food had to travel fresh, which meant live). There was little privacy. Cooped up inside, or squeezed together outside, for long hours or even days at a time, passengers would know each other very well by the time they reached their destination.

Coach travel reached a peak of speed and efficiency in the early nineteenth century thanks to the improvement in roads. Road-building techniques had vastly improved through the efforts of two men – Thomas Telford, who devised the right combination of layered gravel and stones to create a permanent stable roadbed, and John Macadam, who invented a process for coating the surface to protect it from pot-holes and mud. A series of toll-houses at which travellers had to stop and pay provided funds for the upkeep of these highways, which were equivalent to – and as innovatory as – the motorway-building of the mid-twentieth century. The principal beneficiaries were the coaches, which could travel faster and therefore run more reliably to a timetable. By the twenties, the journey from London to Holyhead, to take one example, had been reduced from twenty-four and a half hours to sixteen and a quarter hours. Long-distance travel became less of an ordeal and, with more coaches operating, it also became cheaper. In the 1820s fares were fixed at £2 for an outside journey and £4 to travel inside. To contemporaries it seemed as if a transport revolution were already taking place, and that 'distance had been annihilated' – a phrase that would be reused with the advent of railway, steamship, automobile and air travel. Within two decades those who had admired the speed of road transport would find opportunities for travel that would make these attainments seem unremarkable indeed.

En Route

Though the coaches were seen as the epitome of speed, they could travel no faster than fifteen or sixteen miles an hour, which before the railway age was thought to be the most that the human frame could stand. A journey of more than a few score miles would therefore involve overnight stops, and to cater for passengers there was a network of coaching inns, some of which had been accommodating travellers since the days of medieval pilgrimages. In a city such as York, which dealt with a vast amount of coach traffic, these would be very substantial establishments, with several floors of bedrooms, large communal dining- and coffee-rooms, and the necessary stabling, hay stores and carriage houses. They were a prominent part of the community, an important provider of local employment and a source – because of the traffic that passed through them – of news from the outside world. The mere sight of an approaching mail coach would suggest the glamour of speed, the excitement of far-off places and the prospect of interesting tidings, for they brought the newspapers. It is worth emphasizing, however, that although anyone could look at a mail coach, the majority of people could not afford to ride in one. The cost of transport in these vehicles was such that many, in the course of a lifetime, never used them. Others might take a coach only in exceptional circumstances, such as for an annual visit to a large city.

It was during the forties that the competition between train and coach became most acute, for the 'railway mania' in the middle years of that decade began to cover the landscape, and major cities, market towns and even villages increasingly became linked by the 'permanent way'.

The Train Arrives

One aspect of the railway age that became apparent within a matter of years was the decline of the coaching inn. In towns that were not on an important line, or where the local authorities resisted the blandishments of the railway builders, coaching inns ceased to be hubs of news and traffic and became mere local taverns. This could also be seen in London, where a number of famous establishments had hosted travellers before their journeys to all parts of the kingdom. South of the Thames, in Borough High Street and its surroundings, important coaching inns had included the Tabard, from which Chaucer's pilgrims had set off for Canterbury, and the White Hart, scene of Mr Pickwick's meeting with Sam Weller. London's first railway, arriving at the end of the thirties, ran through precisely this area. By the mid-century the inns were either gone altogether or were surviving only as public houses. A later, sentimental desire to preserve some of these obsolete premises for posterity came in time to save only one of them – the George. Much photographed today, its surviving galleries are a reminder of the Pickwickian travellers who, for a few years after the start of Victoria's reign, were roused at dawn to gulp down coffee and cold meat breakfasts while their luggage was loaded and the horses put in the shafts for a long and uncomfortable journey.

By the end of the reign, this simpler world had attracted a good deal of nostalgia. Prints and paintings depicted the sad ruins of once-proud vehicles, forgotten in barns, covered with straw or used as hen houses. In fact, however, coaches did not become extinct. They continued to run in areas where there was no railway access, and within towns provided a service from hotels and coaching inns to the stations – carrying out the same work that was by this time being done by buses. Even at the end of the century, the coach did not quite disappear, for, when it was realized that these noble vehicles were really on their way to oblivion, they began to enjoy a revival in popularity. Sentimental attachment was combined with pleasure in racing or driving them, and coaching clubs became a noticeable feature of upper-class Victorian leisure. It is difficult to identify the precise moment that coaches ceased to be a form of public transport and became a private hobby, for the two functions overlapped. The clubs held runs across country, often departing from the same inns from which in earlier generations the mails and passengers had been carried, and thus momentarily reviving past glories. They might set out to break records over a set distance – or simply to have a pleasant day in the country. Since their roofs were ideal places on which to lunch or watch sporting events, they became extremely popular at race meetings, and continued to appear at the Eton and Harrow cricket match until the mid-1980s. The stagecoach, in other words, was quickly superseded by the railway, but never went away.

On Rails

The steam locomotive had first been publicly demonstrated in London by a Cornishman, Richard Trevithick, in 1808 – though five years earlier he had already used a steam engine to pull colliery wagons along a tracked route in Wales. His machine, called the 'Catch Me Who Can', had been driven round a circular set of tracks. While this may have been an entertaining novelty for those who saw it, there was no immediate progress in the development of passenger rail travel, though an increasing number of steam locomotives were in use in the north (one estimate is that more than ninety were in service by the mid-twenties). A railway was established between Stockton and Darlington in 1825, and four years later a trial was held, at Rainhill in Liverpool, to establish the fastest and most efficient between several types of engine, the winner being George Stephenson's *Rocket*. In 1830 a railway was opened between Liverpool and Manchester, and in 1837 between London and Birmingham, with the capital's first terminus opening at Euston. A few years previously the Great Western Railway, essentially the personal creation of its brilliant chief engineer, Isambard Kingdom Brunel, had been established in the West Country. It was to be the largest of what would ultimately be hundreds of railway companies that began to sprout throughout the country (by the time the railways were consolidated into four major companies in 1921, there were more than two hundred and forty).

Most locomotives ran – following Stephenson's example – on rails that were a standard width apart: 4 feet $8^{1}/_{2}$ inches. This was more or less exactly the width that horse-drawn wagons had been since the time of the Romans. Only Brunel's Great Western differed from this. GWR trains ran on a broad-gauge track whose width was 7 feet $^{1}/_{4}$ inch, and they continued to do so until compelled by parliamentary legislation to convert to standard gauge in 1892, at which time armies of workmen descended on the tracks, lifted the rails and carried out the entire operaton in a single weekend.

Railways made an immense difference to the landscape. They cut across obstacles of whatever kind – ploughing through hills and woods, hurdling rivers, cutting swathes through towns and cities. There was frequently opposition from landowners, though this was rarely effectual. In many cases compulsory purchase was possible, in other instances persuasion was sufficient (townspeople could see the benefits to local trade, estate owners with coal or cattle to sell knew they could move commodities more easily). In some cases it was necessary to divert the line to avoid trespassing on sacred ground. At Cambridge the railway station is a brisk quarter of an hour's walk from the town centre, and when a line was built from Slough to Windsor, it had to make a wide loop to avoid crossing 'the playing fields of Eton'. Sometimes powerful local interests could do the opposite – summoning a railway link rather than keeping it at a distance: at Alnwick, a branch line and a station were built for the convenience of the Duke of Northumberland, whose castle was in the town. Every year there were more miles of track: 97 in 1830, 969 in 1839, 1,775 in 1841, 9,446 in 1861. By the first years of the twentieth century there would be more than 19,000.

As routes opened up, and it was realized that travel by train was not injurious to health, the railways began to do an unprecedented amount of business in transporting people. To begin with it was a thrill to be able to travel at thirty miles an hour – twice the speed, after all, of a coach. As they became widespread, the railways became cheap. In 1844 a Railway Act, as well as laying down obligatory minimum standards of safety and service, established third-class fares at a penny a mile, and sixteen years later workmen's fares were introduced. By the time the novelty had worn off, the convenience of rail travel had won over the public. In the year 1851, 19 million passengers travelled by train.

As the network spread, the railways became an increasingly popular investment. It seemed as if every town in Britain wanted to be on at least a branch line. Railway companies, and shares, proliferated, and a particular peak of hysteria was reached in the mid-forties. To the public, it seemed that investment in these was a sure-fire way to make money, for this new form of transport clearly represented the future. The network could surely only continue to grow, the companies to multiply. The newspapers whipped up a storm of public interest with saturation coverage and advertisements. Interest rates at this time were low, and people were encouraged to invest at once – to catch the moment – while there were shares to be had. It was a rush of enthusiasm something like the buy-to-let property boom of a later generation, and it similarly encouraged those who were not habitual speculators and who had little capital. It was characterized by the number of small shareholders, and many middle-class families committed the whole of their meagre resources.

The result could have been predicted, except that mercifully there was no swift crash. Many schemes had been fraudulent, while other companies had simply been thwarted in their efforts to build. Interest rates went up again, and thousands of shareholders lost their investments; those of most modest means were, as always, the hardest hit. The Railway Age was not without birth pangs.

The creation of Britain's railway system was described by contemporaries as the greatest building project since the Egyptian pyramids. There had certainly never been anything like it in British history. Between 200,000 and 250,000 labourers, many of them from Ireland, worked to create the multitude of lines that ultimately reached to the far north of Scotland. At the height of the railway-building boom, between 1844 and 1847, over nine and a half thousand miles of track were laid and, while the lines stretched out toward remote regions, the suburbs of cities were enmeshed in systems that carried local traffic. Because there were innumerable companies of varying size and ambition, there were hundreds of building projects in progress at once – many of them duplicating services and thus giving towns more than one station – and no unified plan. For passengers on long journeys, the need to book a ticket that involved travelling with several different railway companies created such inconvenience that in 1842 the Railway Clearing House, a centralized booking office, was set up. The railway network that covered the country grew haphazardly, though much of it eventually resolved into a logical pattern that linked together the major cities. The man most responsible for this was George Hudson, nicknamed 'the railway king'. The personification of the get-rich-quick railway decade, he was a Yorkshire businessman who bullied his way to control of several railway companies and then embezzled hundreds of thousands of pounds. His motives were, of course, selfish, and after a few years he was discovered and disgraced. Together with his greed, however, he had had a genuine flair for organization, and had consolidated his various railway holdings into a viable, nascent network, an achievement on which others could build.

Building the Line

The builders – and Brunel in particular – made valiant efforts to blend their work with the landscape. Cuttings hid the line, embankments were sown with grass and planted with trees.

Bridges and viaducts were designed to be graceful, and built with costly materials. The architecture of the railway bridge in the shadow of Conwy Castle in Wales pays tribute to its illustrious neighbour, and the entrance to Box Tunnel, near Bath, is decorated with italianate balustrades and keystoned arches to resemble something from the Renaissance. In the towns, where the coming of the railways had caused the most havoc (for entire districts had been truncated or demolished to allow the tracks through), equal care was taken to make this new intrusion appear dignified and appropriate. Temple Meads station in Bristol looks like a castle but has hints of an Oxford college. There were others that resembled Greek temples or Jacobean country houses. Small rural stations often looked like cottages or farmhouses. Not only the lines and stations were built by the railway 'navvies', but the engineering marvels that carried trains over rivers and through hills and mountains. Their most striking monument is surely the Forth Bridge, completed in 1890.

In London, on which all the main lines converged, there were a number of great termini. Every one of them was built during Victoria's reign, and, because no two looked alike, they usefully reflect the change of taste and the competing styles that characterized the era. The first was at Euston Square, completed in 1838. It was followed by London Bridge, Fenchurch Street, King's Cross, Paddington, Bishopsgate, Victoria, Charing Cross, Waterloo, Cannon Street, St Pancras and Marylebone, which, opened in 1899, was the smallest as well as the last. Euston, with its Doric-pillared arch, was severely Classical. King's Cross was prim and understated, as functional as an engine-shed, while its neighbour, St Pancras, was a colossal neo-Gothic fantasy that looked more like a city hall in Flanders. It is worth remembering that no secular structure on the scale of these buildings had been seen before (with the exceptions of the contemporary Crystal Palace and Houses of Parliament). Even the smallest were as big as cathedrals. Although their architecture often looked to the past, they were a potent symbol of the Victorian present – massive, expensive, technically bold and accomplished, expressive of a great and unassailable confidence.

Even as the railways were covering their own country, British engineers were taking their skills abroad. Western European countries quickly adopted the new form of transport, and lines began extending eastwards and southwards across the Continent. The railway was even more popular in the vastness of India and Russia and of North and South America, where it was not simply a convenience – as it was in Britain – but a crucial link that made life viable in remote settlements. Britain manufactured the locomotives (often tailored to local terrain or conditions), rails and rolling-stock, and sent the engineers, builders, coal, drivers and maintenance men to set up the systems. In the process, they learned to solve problems and cope with extremes that were far greater than anything found at home – jungles, deserts and mountain ranges like the Andes and Himalayas. The manufacture and export of railways was a major industry that employed thousands and earned millions throughout the century.

In Britain, the consolidation of a swift and increasingly efficient railway system had led to the standardization of timekeeping, a concept unknown and unattainable until then. When travel had been slower, every city, or district, could set its clocks as it pleased. With the advent of timetables – and of the electric telegraph through which the railways communicated – it became necessary for far-distant towns to synchronize. 'Railway time' became uniform, and was the standard to which all municipalities, organizations and institutions came to adhere. The result – a single, agreed reckoning of time, based on Greenwich – appears obvious to us. To the Victorians it seemed a miracle.

If the railway stations with their soaring glass-and-iron vaults were engineering marvels, the locomotives that arrived and departed within them were no less impressive. Within twenty years of the Rainhill trial, the engines of the *Rocket* generation looked as anachronistic as a propeller-driven aircraft does to us. Engines were bigger, sleeker and, above all, faster. They had acquired longer boilers, lower funnels, larger tenders to carry more coal and more, and bigger, wheels, driven by pistons (by 1870 the famously elegant Stirling locomotive with its eight-foot driving wheel was in service on the line from London to Scotland). Drivers and footplates were given protection within semi-enclosed cabs, water and coal were made strategically accessible at track-sides so that trains could refuel without lengthy delays. Speed and efficiency were constantly, relentlessly being increased, though there were constant accidents, numerous deaths, frequent official enquiries and several Acts of Parliament aimed at making the service safer.

Passengers were divided, according to their means, into three classes – as they were in society itself. First Class carried the nobility and gentry and the upper middle class. Second was appropriate for the clerk, shopkeeper and suburbanite. Third was for the lower middle class and for workmen. In First Class there were horsehair-stuffed seats. In Second, the seats were wooden. In Third – at least until the 1844 Act – there were no seats, or indeed roofs. The carriages, known as 'standipedes', were simply open wagons in which the travellers huddled, and only gradually did this section of the public gain any basic comforts. The standard of accommodation in all classes improved rapidly, however, once competition for passengers between the companies became more acute.

Though railway travel had ceased to have the excitement of novelty, it came to acquire a different sort of glamour. The longest routes in Britain were those between London and Scotland, and on the east-coast line, to York and Edinburgh, a train left King's Cross at ten o'clock each morning. This, initially called the 'Special Scotch Express', soon took on the more resonant nickname 'The Flying Scotsman', and became one of the world's most famous train journeys. It was known not only for speed but comfort. Engines and rolling-stock were the best available, carriages were well appointed and there was no Third Class. The companies that ran the –slightly longer – west-coast route from Euston had to compete for passengers in what became bitter rivalry, and the 'railway race to the north' saw both sides increase train speeds and shorten passengers' comfort-stops in an attempt to improve the service. This sense of witnessing, or participating in, a sporting event that might involve breaking records (both sides reduced the time of their run to eight hours), increased public excitement and affection for the 'permanent way'.

Because railway travel was within reach of all but the very poorest, it altered the habits of the population. Public events, such as the weekly Saturday afternoon musical concerts at London's Crystal Palace, were attended by thousands who were able to reach its rather off-the-beaten-track location within minutes from Victoria. It became possible for the first time, from the late thirties, for many people to take holidays. Naturally, many wished to go to the coast – although inland spas like Malvern and Buxton, and places of known beauty like the Lake District were also popular – and an increasing amount of railway traffic was devoted to getting them there. It became possible to reach a town such as Brighton or East-bourne, spend some hours there and return within the same day, and thus the 'day trip' became a staple experience for the

lower middle class. Railways also meant that families with
their luggage – and even servants – could be transported to
seaside resorts relatively easily. It was common for a wife,
children and nanny to be installed in a hotel or boarding house
while Father remained in town to work, joining them at
weekends. Traffic to the coast proved so lucrative that railway
companies began promoting resorts themselves, and actually
building piers and other attractions to lure the public. Southend, Seaford, Minehead and Weston-super-Mare were all
created, or improved, by railway companies to generate holiday traffic. With the growth of rail systems on the Continent, it
also became possible for tourists to venture further afield by
catching boat-trains that delivered them to Channel steamers,
and – in another example of a 'shrinking world' – it was
possible to book tickets at the London termini to destinations
all over Europe and Asia. Captain Fred Burnaby, the traveller
who wrote the epic and bestselling narrative *A Ride to Khiva*
about a trek through Turkestan, began his journey, somewhat
prosaically, by boarding the Folkestone train at Charing
Cross.

At Sea

The steam engine could be used, with equal success, to drive
vessels on water. In the United States, Robert Fulton had
patented a steam boat driven by paddles, and tested it on
the Hudson River with a four-day journey from New York to
Albany and back. It represented an important victory over
nature, for it was the first time in history that the propulsion of
a vessel through water did not depend on the power of wind or
muscle.

Steam boats ran on coal, and moved with the aid of paddle
wheels. With one of these at each side, it was possible to turn

the vessel by using one or other of them, though a version with a single, wide wheel at the back was also developed. These boats quickly proved their worth on rivers and in coastal work, and within ten or fifteen years had become commonplace, but they could not easily be used for long sea voyages because they needed constant supplies of coal. When, in 1818, an American steam vessel, the *Savanna*, succeeded in crossing the Atlantic, she did so only with the help of sails.

What caused the revolution in steam navigation was the invention of the screw propeller. Two men developed the idea at more or less the same time. In 1834 a Hampshire clergyman, the Reverend Edward Berthon, conceived the idea that a boat could be driven by a type of finned screw in the vessel's stern below the waterline. He proved it by building a model which performed well in a pond in his garden. Almost simultaneously, Francis Pettit Smith came to the same conclusion, and he too experimented. Both men patented their idea in the same year – 1837 – though Smith was the first actually to build a full-sized boat and sail in it. The Admiralty was persuaded to test the notion, and a larger screw-driven vessel, the *Archimedes*, was built. Her top speed of ten knots meant that she outperformed the *Vulcan*, which was among the Navy's most powerful paddle-steamers. A trial of strength was subsequently arranged between two other boats, this time involving a tug of war. They were of similar size and design, and had the same engines. The *Rattler* was propeller-driven and her rival, the *Alecto*, had port and starboard paddles. A tow-rope was fixed between their sterns, and on a signal they steamed in opposite directions. Watched by an interested crowd, *Alecto* suffered the indignity of being dragged backwards by her opponent. It was a victory for progress. Throughout the twenties and thirties, steam navigation companies came into existence, and steamers began to carry mail for considerable distances – from London to Alexandria, for instance.

In the meantime Isambard Brunel, already heavily involved in building the Great Western Railway, was considering the possibilities of extending its reach all the way to the New World. He wanted to create a shipping service that would enable train passengers from London to disembark at Bristol and directly board a boat to America so that, as he put it, it would be possible to book a ticket 'from Paddington to New York'. He managed to persuade the company's directors to back him. Because Brunel was an engineer and not an administrator, he was less interested in the logistics of the scheme than in the design of the vessels that would make it possible, and he wanted a steamship that could carry enough coal to make the 2,500-mile voyage without recourse to sails. He planned, and built, such a ship, and named it after the railway. The *Great Western* was a paddle steamer, though she had masts and carried sail. At 212 feet long, she was the world's largest vessel, and though built of oak her hull was reinforced with iron. She was launched in the year that Victoria became Queen.

In 1838 she made her first voyage to New York. By the time she departed, she had attracted a rival in the shape of the *Sirius*, another sail-and-paddle hybrid that was attempting to make her way across on behalf of the British & American Steam Navigation Company. They did not set off together – *Sirius* had a head start – but their time across the ocean was measured. *Sirius* arrived first, though only by a few hours, after a voyage of eighteen days. It was a pyrrhic victory. She had run out of coal and been forced to burn all her cabin furniture, and even her doors. When the *Great Western* reached port, having taken fifteen days to make the crossing, she was found to have more than 12,000 tons of coal left.

This achievement was not built upon, and the Great Western Railway failed to create its own fleet. Brunel's ideas, however, moved on. His next ship was even more ambitious. The *Great Britain*, launched at Bristol in 1843, was 108 feet longer than *Great Western* and at 3,500 tons she boasted two important innovations: her hull was completely built from iron, and she had a propeller.

It was this latter feature that made the difference. The screw propeller finally came of age in the 1840s, and shipping experienced something of a renaissance (Samuel Cunard, to cite one example, founded his fleet in 1840). The British shipbuilding industry expanded to meet demand, producing 131,000 tons during the forties – a figure that increased to 314,000 tons for the sixties. This was not simply the result of growing interest in global commerce. The repeal, in 1849, of the Navigation Act meant that all restrictions were removed on the carriage of British goods by foreign vessels. British ships were no longer protected against fierce competition, and it was necessary to fight back. Also significant, however, was the increase in passengers with the immense flood in emigrants from Ireland and the discovery of gold in California and Australia. In addition, during the sixties, British yards built vessels for the Confederate Navy. The slipways were kept busy, and by the fifties it was largely iron ships they were turning out.

Brunel had planned yet another leviathan. In the autumn of 1857 three years' work on the *Great Eastern* was completed at Millwall. Once again this was the largest ship ever built (a record she was to keep until 1906), and this time undoubtedly dwarfed all that had gone before. She was 692 feet in length and 18,915 tons. She had a 24-foot propeller and side paddle-wheels which, at 58 feet, were as high as a three-storey house, though she also had masts and sails. The ship was so vast that she could not be launched bow-first, and she had to be lowered, somewhat gingerly, sideways into the Thames, watched by a crowd that exceeded 3 million.

Unfortunately she stuck, and it required a further three months of careful nudging before she reached the river. Once at sea, her performance was disappointing, for her colossal engines could not coordinate the work of the wheels and propeller, and the ship never reached the speeds expected. Brunel died before she made her maiden voyage, and when she crossed the Atlantic in the summer of 1860, she was welcomed in New York but attracted few passengers. A year later she was badly damaged in a storm while on a return voyage, losing both wheels and what little prestige she had left. In 1864 she was sold to become a cable-laying vessel, and, made redundant from this, in 1886 she became a funfair in Liverpool harbour. Two years later she was broken up.

Great Eastern had symbolized the power of British technology, and her failure was unable to dent the confidence of the engineers and mechanics who continued to design. In the same decade that Brunel's great ship was lying idle, British yards were building more ships than the rest of the world put together. A greater achievement – for it was to power the fleets of the twentieth century – was the steam turbine. This was invented in the eighties by Charles Parsons, who took a further ten years to develop one that could be used aboard a vessel. It was a steam engine that did not use a piston, whose basic principle was the shooting of very hot steam at a revolving set of fan-blades. This simple idea, which was extremely difficult to fulfil in practice, was used for the first time in a small vessel Parsons built called the *Turbinia*, which was able to travel at a speed of thirty-four knots, almost twice the rate of one of the sail-driven tea-clippers, the 'greyhounds of the ocean'. The future had arrived.

While steam navigation represented progress, the sailing ship continued to claim a hefty share of the oceans until the end of the century – in 1865 only a sixth of British shipping was steam-driven – and did not tamely give up its glamour. The clippers that brought China tea and Australian wool to England were the fastest merchant vessels ever powered by wind. The races to the Thames from Shanghai or Melbourne were not only epics of seamanship but major sporting events that attracted wagers and enthralled the public.

'Clippers' were light and fast sailing ships of a type that were first built for the coastal trade in the eastern United States. Only when they began carrying tea cargoes to Britain was the native shipbuilding industry galvanized into competing with them, and soon developed an expertise of its own. Although they carried many types of cargo, the task for which they were celebrated was the bringing of the annual tea crop, in May, to London from ports on the China coast. Because China tea lost freshness if it took too long to reach the consumer – and did not improve at sea – it was a matter of urgency to transport it as swiftly as possible. The first ship to arrive home could command the highest prices, and the crew would receive a substantial bonus. The result was a race across the world – a distance of 14,000 miles – at breakneck speed, by streamlined ships with highly experienced and professional captains and crews. Thanks to the electric telegraph, the progress of these ships could be followed as they dashed across the South China Sea, rounded the Cape and sailed up the Atlantic to the Channel and the Pool of London. Public interest was intense, and mounted steadily as they neared home. The most dramatic of these contests was that of 1866, which was dominated by two ships – *Ariel* and *Taeping* – in a field of sixteen. Though the members of this pack jockeyed for the lead in the opening stages, three vessels pulled ahead and raced for home, crossing the Equator at the same time and exchanging the lead as one or other caught the wind or fell behind. *Ariel* and *Taiping* appeared in the Channel together, and were neck and neck as they rounded the Kent coast into the Thames. *Ariel* arrived first, but *Taiping* was the first to dock, and won by twenty minutes. The third vessel, *Serica*, had joined them within less than an hour. All three had made the journey in ninety-nine days.

When Australian wool was brought from Sydney or Melbourne to London there was a similar interest in the speed of the ships. This voyage involved making for the Channel by the most direct route, around the notoriously rough Cape Horn, and the most famous clipper of all, *Cutty Sark*, gained considerable glory for breaking speed records. Built in 1869 and sold in 1895 – a fate that befell many 'ocean greyhounds' when it became obvious that they could not compete with steamers – her great days were in the eighties when, among other achievements, she made the voyage home from Australia in only seventy-seven days – as opposed to the customary hundred.

The clipper of the *Cutty Sark*'s generation represented the highest attainment of the shipbuilding art as it related to sailing vessels. Technology had already bypassed her when her keel was laid, and her reign was short, for within thirty years her elegance appeared quaint as she lay in harbour alongside the funnels of a new race of ships. Nevertheless she and the other clippers had their place in the epic of nineteenth-century sea transport, and they epitomized something about the Victorians. In their combination of sentimentality and thrusting, materialistic confidence, they were a potent symbol of the era.

On the Streets

At the start of the nineteenth century city streets were filled with people on foot. It was an age of pedestrians, for unless you owned or rented a carriage, and unless you could afford to hire a cabriolet or a chaise or a Hackney – all of which were too expensive for the greater part of the population – you walked. Clerical workers travelled in to their offices and counting houses on foot, great streams of them following the roads in from the suburbs, and plodding home in the opposite direction at the close of business. Though these journeys might take an hour and more, they were seen as an inescapable fact of life. 'Public transport' did not exist.

Although it was the Victorians – during whose epoch the populations of many cities doubled – who solved the problems of moving millions efficiently in and out of great conurbations, the situation had already begun to be addressed before Victoria came to the throne. One answer was the 'omnibus', a vehicle first seen on London's streets in 1829.

The transporting of people in and out of London was, of course, no novelty. As early as 1772 there had been a 'new contrived coach' running between Charing Cross and the Royal Exchange for a fare of sixpence. Like all coaches, this had seating for half a dozen passengers inside and a few more on the roof. Stage-coaches developed runs along short routes in the suburbs, stopping at inns, though they did not follow main thoroughfares into the city centre.

The Omnibus

This situation changed with the opening, in July 1829, of a service between Paddington, at the time outside London, and the Bank, the traditional hub of the business and financial world. It was established by George Shillibeer, a carriage-maker who had worked in Paris and copied the idea direct from the French. Shillibeer designed a vehicle (in fact, he made two of them) that was long, flat-roofed and box-shaped, high off the ground – passengers had to mount three steps to enter it – and drawn by three horses walking abreast. There was a single door at the back, and inside there was room for about eighteen passengers, who sat facing each other on two long benches. The driver's seat was on the roof, directly above the horses. A conductor, who sold the tickets, helped passengers on and off, and called out the stops, stood on the steps at the rear.

Shillibeer's service departed from a Paddington public house, the Yorkshire Stingo, and travelled into the City along Euston and Marylebone Roads. It cost a shilling, at a time when a clerk's wages were between seven and ten shillings a week, so it was not intended to be a democratic form of transport. It offered privacy, and comfort, to the comfortably off. Shillibeer had once been a naval midshipman, and the first two conductors he employed were the sons of naval officers. They were dressed in nautical blue jackets that brought a certain flair to the enterprise, for clearly bus-conducting was initially seen as a career for gentlemen – a notion that did not long survive. The vehicles were painted dark green and each had painted on its side the word 'Omnibus', which Shillibeer had also appropriated from Paris.

His service was an immediate success, prompting him to build more conveyances – within a year he had twelve in operation – and plan more routes, though his vehicles proved too heavy. Later versions were smaller, and pulled by only two horses. Others began almost at once to imitate him, and in less than a decade, when the Victorian era began, there were some four hundred omnibuses operating in London. As the idea spread from the capital to other cities, it spawned local variations: in 1852 a Manchester operator developed an immense vehicle pulled by three horses, which seated no fewer than forty-two. A contemporary newspaper explained why omnibuses were so popular in comparison with the coach: 'In an omnibus there is no delay in taking up and setting down; no calling at booking offices; no twenty minutes waiting at "the Cellar"' (*Morning Herald*, 10 October 1829). In other words, making a short journey to work by suburban coach was as troublesome and time-consuming as going on a long-distance expedition with all its booking and hanging about waiting to board. The omnibus brought a convenience that was refreshing.

This convenience was only relative, for other aspects of travel by omnibus would not become standard practice until the latter part of Victoria's reign. The suburban coaches had had stopping-places, the omnibus did not. It could be hailed, like a taxi, by anyone at the kerbside, and might therefore be constantly stopping – or crossing the road – to pick up fares. As with other vehicles of the time it did not keep to the left, but simply forced its way through the traffic wherever there was a gap. Passengers were picked up or put down in the middle of busy streets and left to fend for themselves. There were no destination boards, therefore the driver and conductor had to tout for custom as they went along, calling out the names of places they were going, and enticing pedestrians to get aboard. As more operating companies came into existence and competition for passengers became keener, rival conductors might even come to blows over whose vehicle a hapless individual was to board. It was not until 1855 that an attempt was made to consolidate the various lines and rationalize the service. When this did happen, the impetus came from an unusual quarter, for the resulting body was called the Compagnie

Générale des Omnibus de Londres, and had its headquarters in Paris. The notion of amalgamating had been conceived by a French businessman, Joseph Osri, and his organization became, with six hundred vehicles, the world's largest public transport provider. It was only after four years that its offices actually moved to London.

The omnibus, its title soon shortened to the more familiar 'bus', remained a single-decker vehicle until the 1840s, and its further development was very gradual. One or two seats were made available next to the driver, and a few more installed behind him, but when in 1847 buses were fitted with roofs that had a clerestory in the middle (to allow headroom in the aisle inside), travellers began to sit on the roofs, leaning against these. By the time of the Great Exhibition, when business vastly increased, some companies had installed plank seats and created the 'knife-board' omnibus, on which passengers sat in two back-to-back rows, entirely exposed to the weather. Their only way on or off was via rungs or a precarious ladder. Nevertheless, many preferred to perch at this height. The inside of a bus rapidly became overheated and claustrophobic, and the stuffed seats, as well as the straw that was put on the floor, were thought to spread infection. The knife-board gradually became less precarious and more comfortable. Steps with a handrail made access easier and guard-rails on either side lessened any sense of vertigo. This style of bus remained in use until the end of the eighties, when outward-facing knife-board seating was gradually replaced by forward-facing 'garden seats' – rickety two-seater wooden benches, on either side of an aisle, a design favoured on the Continent. A set of regulations laid down in 1867 had brought a degree of order, for they allowed local authorities to establish routes, and stipulated that buses could only pick up on the near- (left) side of the road. This meant that instead of a ladder there could be a spiral stair. There was also a substantial rear platform, and there were proper walls around the upper deck. These vehicles could seat twelve passengers inside and fourteen outside, and the new arrangements meant that women could comfortably use the top deck for the first time. By the end of the century hundreds of buses were running on a comprehensive network of routes, many still in operation.

The 'Bus on Rails

Like the omnibus, the tram was an invention that predated Victoria's accession but which came into its own during her reign. The street railway was not a British concept, for in London the thoroughfares were well-paved and buses did not require rails on which to run. In the United States, however, city streets were often so muddy and uneven that a journey in a bouncing, lurching and stalling omnibus was likely to be slow and uncomfortable. It occurred to one operator in Baltimore that by laying rails in which a vehicle could run it would be possible to ensure smooth progress, and a street railway of sorts was in use there by 1828. Four years later the idea was tried in New York. The intention was to lay a track along the roadside and create a railway link between Manhattan and Harlem that would then continue north to Albany. The city authorities did not welcome the prospect of locomotives in their streets, and so instead a horse-drawn bus service that ran on rails was introduced. It was called a 'tramway'. The vehicles, drawn by two horses – whose job was made easier in that they did not have to pull over uneven ground – could carry up to sixty passengers. At first, turntables had to be provided at the end of the route so that the vehicle could be turned round, but before long the easier arrangement of having cars with an identical stair at both ends, and seat-backs that could be tipped to face the opposite way, had been introduced.

The concept was introduced to Europe by the French, who had pioneered so many aspects of public transport. In 1855 an 'American railway' was inaugurated in Paris and, after some initial difficulties, proved a success. Proposals for a similar service in London were floated in 1861, but met with little encouragement. The rails – whether they lay above the road surface and caused other traffic to stumble over them, or were flush with the street and caused carriage wheels to get stuck in them – were unpopular with other road-users. It was for the latter reason that Sir Benjamin Hall, the Chief Commissioner of Public Works (after whom Big Ben was named) refused to allow the laying of rails – his own carriage had once been overturned in similar circumstances. Nevertheless, three experimental lines were built during 1861 and of these one survived. Similar lines had meanwhile been introduced at Liverpool docks and at Birkenhead, in the Potteries and at Darlington. Of these, it was Liverpool that put in place the first comprehensive local service, authorized in 1868 by an Act of Parliament.

In the same year the tide of opinion turned in London and new lines were built, in southern and eastern parts of the city. Because tram lines were excluded from the City and were not wanted among the 'carriage folk' of the West End (whose wheels would become stuck in them), the networks congregated in the poorer parts of the capital, and were particularly extensive south of the Thames. They thus gained a reputation as a poor man's transport, and in fact they deliberately cultivated this. They began operations earlier in the morning than buses did, and pitched their fares to capture the custom of labourers. In the country as a whole this does not seem to have been true, and tram systems spread rapidly in other cities, such as Leeds, Glasgow and Plymouth. While horse power was the usual means of moving tram cars, a wide range of other options was introduced. Steam had been used to drive road vehicles in the 1830s, when several services had been operated (such as that between Cheltenham and Gloucester) by what were, in effect, horseless mail coaches with a boiler and a two-cylinder engine attached. The service had never proved popular and had been disregarded, though forty years later 'steam cars' reappeared. They ran both on tracks and on the roadway, and comprised a locomotive pulling a 'trailer' which carried the passengers. Entire steam-powered systems were introduced, notably at Govan in 1877 and at Huddersfield in 1883. There was at least one line driven by compressed air, and others used steam power to haul the cars by cable (the method still in use in San Francisco). Electricity was first used to power trams in Berlin at the beginning of the eighties, and within a few years an American had invented the 'troller', a wire attached to a set of wheels that ran along an overhead cable, drawing power from it. This was successfully used, but much improved upon when a rigid pole was substituted. Blackpool trams, whose survival has made them the most famous in Britain, started in 1885, drawing electricity from a conduit in the ground but later converting to cables. The first system to be entirely powered by electric cables went into operation in Leeds in 1891. This method was now considered reliable enough to see widespread use, and throughout the decade one city after another festooned its streets with ugly masses of overhead wires.

Trams were now everywhere and they made a massively important change to British life. Before the advent of cheap and convenient public transport, people had had to live near their place of work – or at least within walking distance of it. With the coming of railways, the wealthy were able to live

farther out of town and travel some way to their offices, but
artisans had continued to inhabit crowded and often insalu-
brious city centre districts. The introduction of the workmen's
trains and, to a much greater extent, the trams, meant that for
the first time people's homes and workplaces could be entirely
separate. Many large building projects (King's Cross Station,
for example) had in any case meant the clearing of whole
neighbourhoods, and, with the creation of ever bigger office
buildings, a transformation of the appearance of cities took
place, and the notion of people – of any class – actually living
in a 'business district' began rapidly to disappear. Because of
the tramway system, lower-middle-class suburbs sprouted like
mushrooms, and the outskirts of cities grew on a scale that had
previously been unimaginable. Where a tram stop was designated and people would therefore gather, shops appeared (this
is often the origin of the local 'parade' that is such a feature of
British suburban neighbourhoods). The urban landscape in
which we still live – of scattered miniature communities linked
by the lines of a transport system – began at this time and in
this way. The tram was to become extinct, but its legacy has
remained.

'Trains in Drains'

The congestion in London's streets became steadily worse as
the population expanded. Not only were the streets choked
with disorderly wheeled traffic and with thousands of pedestrians, but users of the various railway termini had difficulty
getting to them. The march of rails across the landscape had
stopped at the edges of London, and a consultative body – the
Royal Commission on Metropolitan Railway Termini – had
decided to keep them there. Railways were not to be allowed
within central London, or at least within an area bounded by

Bishopsgate and Park Lane, New (Marylebone) Road and the Borough. There could be no wholesale demolition in the City or in Mayfair.

Yet a link between the termini was an obvious need, and from the 1830s there had been notions of building it both above street level and underground. In the former case Joseph Paxton, builder of the Crystal Palace, proposed a huge circular glassed-in 'girdle railway' that would run around the centre inside a glass arcade. It was not built – although the notion of an elevated railroad was widely adopted in the United States. The possibility of a subterranean railway seemed even more outlandish. It was difficult to envisage how tunnels could be driven through cramped and densely populated areas without unacceptable disruption and huge compensation claims, or how steam trains could run underground without choking the passengers. Investors could not be convinced of its feasibility, or see how they could make a profit.

It would be immensely complicated, but not impossible. By digging the lines beneath roadways the disturbance and expense of demolishing buildings would be minimized, and a method of doing this, known as 'cut and cover' – digging a short section at a time, laying the tracks and then roofing it over before moving on – would make matters yet easier for those above ground. Only at the eastern end, where the track would go through Farringdon, was it necessary for major demolition, and this was of poorer housing that public opinion wished to see swept away in any case.

The moving spirit behind the dream of an underground railway was Charles Pearson (1798–1862), a London solicitor. He had first proposed the idea in 1845, but had met with scepticism and reluctance, even after Parliament approved in 1853 and 1854 two schemes to build a 'Metropolitan Railway' between Edgware and Holborn. The project flagged and might have died altogether through suspicion, inertia and procrastination had Pearson not lobbied tirelessly to keep it going.

Most of the fifties was spent in raising the capital, but work finally began in the spring of 1860. It was an entirely new venture, and involved the complicated diverting of pipes and drains. Nothing was known about the effects that vibrating trains would have on the foundations of buildings, and there must have been concern that the heavy traffic on roadways above might cause roofs to collapse. With no precedent to follow, it was necessary to trust to luck and rely on the skill of the engineers.

That reliance was vindicated. Though the disruption was immense, the work was finished – somewhat late – by the end of 1862, and service began on 10 January 1863. People's curiosity got the better of their fears, for a total of 30,000 passengers travelled that day. Once the novelty had worn off there was no drop in numbers, indeed the daily average of passengers for the whole of the first year was 32,000. Had there been a serious accident during the first weeks and months, the Metropolitan Railway might have lost favour and perished, but it was known that the safety measures were stringent (the signals were especially good) and this won public confidence. Its sheer convenience, in any case, ensured its popularity. More than 11 million people used it during the first year.

As on the surface, there were three classes of carriage, of which all were comfortable and spacious. It was reported that a six-foot-tall man could stand up with his hat on. First and second class had leather seats and all carriages were lit effectively with gas. The trains were frequent – the number rose to 630 a day – and the journeys were swift, as the trains stopped in stations for only fifteen or twenty seconds. It had been stipulated from the beginning that the railway must provide cheap workmen's fares as a means of encouraging them to move out of the city, and this indeed followed. Most users – almost three-quarters – were Third Class passengers, and these especially appreciated the service. Artisans and their families were able to live farther from the city in more healthy locations, and because the men did not have a lengthy walk home after a day's work, they arrived in a better mood and did not row with their wives!

The dankness below ground was not as off-putting as had been imagined, for a great deal of the line was not tunnel at all but cuttings that were open to the sky, and gas lighting on platforms made them 'more like a well-kept street at night than a subterranean passage'.[2] Nevertheless the dampness was a problem, and injured the health of many staff who had to work long hours below ground. To combat the stench of smoke, the engines burned only coke, and special locomotives were used that carried condensing equipment. Within ten years of opening, ventilation shafts were also being dug. Conditions and equipment on the Metropolitan were therefore better than on any surface railway, though the problem of smoke was never adequately solved until the steam locomotive was replaced by electric trains in 1905.

It quickly became apparent that Londoners – and millions of visitors – preferred the underground railway to the slower horse bus for anything but the shortest journeys, and the cynicism of shareholders quickly turned to euphoria as the service flourished, giving a return of £102,000 in the first year. The line was extended, and carried freight as well as people. Before long there was a Metropolitan line running to Moorgate, and the lines began to spread all over the city. Importantly, links were established with both the London, Chatham and Dover and the London & South Western railways. This meant that underground and surface networks were able to work in tandem and that passengers could travel right through the capital by train without having to use other transport. In

1884, after years of difficulties caused by bickering and obstructions, the pivotal piece of the system – the Circle Line – was opened. The network continued to expand throughout the reign and far into the following century, both linking and creating suburbs. The London Underground, as the various components of the system were collectively termed, was to provide the model for similar networks all over the world, though only one other British city – Glasgow in 1896 – built its own underground during this era.

'Cads on Castors'

As a revolution in transport, the bicycle was second only to the railway, and its importance cannot be overstated, for it utterly changed the view that millions of people had of the world. It was far cheaper, and easier to use and maintain, than a horse, and thus affordable for millions whose only alternative was to walk. The skill of riding, once learned, made possible an entirely new sense of personal freedom and mobility. For women it was especially significant, for it meant that for the first time respectable ladies could go out in public without a male escort. Because it became a popular pastime for couples, it also to a large extent killed off the chaperone.

The country roads of Victorian Britain were not suited to this new mode of transport. The triumph of the railways meant that the building and maintenance of roads had been seriously neglected. Ruts and pot-holes, or rough flint or gravel surfaces, made many of these thoroughfares extremely difficult for cyclists to traverse. At the end of the century, once the bicycle had become first fashionable and then essential, pressure began to build for improvements in the network of rural thoroughfares and this – literally – paved the way for the automobile that was so swiftly to follow in its wake.

The vehicle developed from the *celerifere* or 'hobby horse'. This had first been seen in France in 1791. It was a wooden beam shaped like a horse with handlebars set above two equal-sized wheels. The rider sat on it and propelled it along with strides. There was no way of controlling speed or direction, and there were no brakes. It created some interest as a play-thing in Paris parks before going the way of all fads. In 1817 a German, Baron von Drais, improved the design. He added a saddle and a steering mechanism, and called his machine a *velocifere*. It started a new craze in Paris, and this spread to England. It was briefly seen as a rival to the horse, but was not generally popular because it was exhausting to ride and looked ridiculous – as well as being hard to stop. After a brief vogue in 1819–20 it lost popularity, but though forgotten by the public it did not disappear. Over the next thirty years, three- and four-wheeled machines – the latter called quadricycles or velocipedes – were designed that could be propelled by turning handles or by primitive pedals (one was shown at the Great Exhibition). More importantly, a Scottish blacksmith invented in 1839 a two-wheeled machine that was treadle-operated and driven by connecting-rods. The inventor, Kirkpatrick Mac-millan, used it himself but did not market it. His achievement was to create a velocipede that could be propelled without the feet touching the ground.

It was not until 1863 that the breakthrough in design came with the invention of pedals. The notion of fitting the front wheel of a velocipede with a cranked axle 'like the crank handle of a grindstone, so that it could be turned by the feet of the rider'[3] was carried out by Ernest and Pierre Michaux, two Paris coach-repairers. They saw at once the usefulness of this discovery, and began to manufacture pedalled hobby horses. The result was a return of the craze, which again spread across the Channel. One of the first to adopt it was a Cambridge undergraduate called G. Herbert, who acquired a machine and doggedly practised for several weeks before mastering the technique of getting on and off and keeping his balance. Like all who first saw one of these, it seemed to him nothing short of a miracle that it was possible to remain upright without support. Others followed his example, and the fashion spread.

It is sometimes suggested that the modern bicycle was invented in Cambridge rather than demonstrated there, but it may well have been in the city that it acquired its modern name. The word is a combination of Latin 'bi' (two) and Greek 'kuklos' (circles, or wheels). In the 1930s the writer Augustus Muir met an elderly Benedictine monk at a Highland monastery who told him: 'I rode the first bicycle that was made in England. I was up at Cambridge at the time. I knew the man who was making that strange contraption on two wheels, and I said I wanted to ride it. I did so – and had a spill. When he asked me what to call it I said, "Why, of course – a *bicycle*!" When I got back to my rooms I thought, "What a hybrid name I've given it – part Latin, part Greek! But it was too late. The man had told everybody it was a bicycle, and a bicycle it has remained." '[4]

The bicycle was first demonstrated in London at a gymnasium in 1869. By that time the first cycle race had already taken place in France – though it was won by an Englishman. The machines sold well in both countries, and the mania crossed to America, where a generation of young men sought to learn the mysteries of riding (a cycling school there was called a velocinasium). Bicycling was often carried out, like skating, in indoor rinks, but from the beginning its devotees travelled on roads.

It is difficult from a present-day perspective to appreciate the sense of liberation that the bicycle offered. Keeping a horse was highly expensive, and hiring one was relatively so.

Walking over long distances was slow and tiring. The bicycle solved these problems, and suddenly made it possible to travel without great cost or inconvenience. It was not yet available to everyone, and it was still regarded as a hobby, but its potential was quickly coming to be recognized. As increasingly lengthy journeys were made – three men cycled from London to Brighton in sixteen hours in 1869 – newspapers, and the public, began to take it a good deal more seriously.

The Michaux brothers had had the idea of increasing the speed of machines by making the front wheel bigger than the rear. This quickly led to the exaggerated shape known as the high wheeler (the term 'penny farthing' came in only later) in which the driving-wheel was about four feet high. This type was introduced in 1871 and dominated cycling for the whole of that decade.

The saddle and handlebars were on top of the big wheel, and mounting the machine required a good deal of practice. A contemporary manual described how to do this:

> Hold the handle with the left hand and place the other on the seat. Now take a few running steps, and when the right foot is on the ground give a hop with that foot, and at the same time place the left foot on the step, throwing your right leg over on to the seat. Nothing but a good running hop will give you time to adjust your toe on the step as it is moving. It requires a certain amount of strength and agility.[5]

Getting off again similarly required skill:

> First see that the left-hand crank (pedal) is at the bottom, then throw your right leg with a swing backwards and continue until you are off the seat and on the ground. If you attempt it

when going at all quickly, you will have to run by its side when you are off, which is a difficult feat for any but a skilful rider.[6]

Starting too slowly, or indeed not travelling fast enough at any time, meant falling off. There were often brakes on a penny farthing. If not, the machine could be stopped by back-peddling. The saddle was tiny and uncomfortable, and the handlebars were at arm's length immediately in front of the seat. The resulting posture was arguably better than it would be for those bending forward with hunched shoulders on the later 'safety bicycle', but riding a penny farthing was a difficult and dangerous practice until one had got the hang of it. Perched so high above the ground and entirely exposed to the elements, cyclists would have experienced some difficulty with low branches. There could be no question of dawdling on such a machine. If slowed down by traffic it would be necessary to dismount at once to avoid falling sideways to the ground. On the other hand, its big driving-wheel enabled it to travel faster than almost anything else on the road. To the thrill of speed would be added the commanding view and the exhilaration of hard exercise.

On and Off

Riding one of these machines was as difficult as it sounds. Anyone using a high-wheeler needed legs long enough to work the pedals, and enough physical strength to handle such a big machine. It was not suited to older people or to women. Riding *any* sort of bicycle was not something that could easily be picked up simply by finding a quiet stretch of road and pushing off. It was necessary to have a course of lessons to do it well, and all over the country cycling schools appeared, as ubiquitous in late Victorian Britain as the driving school is in our own time. To us, the instructions seem self-evident, but a generation unused to these practices had to be taught them:

1. Always look where you are going. 2. Always sit straight. 3. Pedal evenly and use both legs. 4. Pedal straight. 5. Keep the foot straight. 6. Hold the handles naturally. 7. Don't wobble the shoulders. 8. Hold the body still and sit down. 9. Don't shake the head.

Once equipped with the necessary skills, many people joined clubs, for there was greater pleasure in cross-country trips with organized groups than in solitude. On holidays, flocks of men in the distinctive insignia of cycle clubs became a noticeable feature of rural life from the seventies onwards, rushing along lanes, congregating at crossroads to study maps, lounging outside the country pubs that were usually their meeting-points or destinations. They often attracted a good deal of ridicule, and local urchins would gather in the hope of seeing them fall off – 'take a spill' in cycling parlance – or might even engineer such an accident by leaving obstacles in the road.

Cycling became established as a sport, with contests in speed and of endurance over rough terrain. Though the British were used to seeing themselves as the inventors of sport, and regarded their country as the home of this one, nobody could dispute the greater claims of the French – especially when in 1903 they were to establish the world's premier cycle race. It also became a national institution in Belgium and the Netherlands, where there were even units of bicycling soldiers with cycling bands.

The tricycle had developed at the same time as the two-wheeled variety, and was popular among those of a less athletic bent. These were driven by levers through a double-cranked axle, or might have a small steering-wheel. With more wheels, it was not necessary to keep one's balance, and thus it was possible to rest whenever necessary. The 'quadricycle' never enjoyed the same public favour, for it was something of a brute to handle. The first model was seven feet wide, and its driving wheels tended to skid when taking corners. Ladies, whose dress prevented them from using a high-wheeler, could, however, sit comfortably on one of these other models, and propel it without loss of dignity. They often cycled in the company of a man, for many versions had two seats – either fore-and-aft or side-by-side (the latter was known as a 'sociable'). This was naturally convivial, and not the least of its attractions was that it offered possibilities for courting couples to out-distance a chaperone. The tandem – a two-seater bicycle of the type still seen today – enabled women for the first time to use an upright bicycle. What a contemporary female author called 'the first revolution' came about when women were persuaded to take the front seat on tandems, 'under masculine convoy and protection'. After this, a two-wheeled bicycle for ladies gradually appeared.

Women cyclists were, to begin with, a source of amusement and a target for ridicule – more likely than their male counterparts to have stones thrown at them by urchins or obstacles scattered in their path, for if all cyclists were eccentric, female ones were also unfeminine and unnatural. The clothing they wore, by necessity, was ugly and unflattering.

What to Wear

While women's everyday outfits were not suited to cycling, even men dressed specially for it, in knickerbockers and short jackets. Because a large proportion of cyclists belonged to clubs, they often wore a quasi-uniform of matching coloured suits or caps sporting an emblem. The Cyclists' Touring Club, which was founded in 1883 and became the supervising body for the sport, recommended garments the fabric and design of which were suited to the level of activity necessary. The CTC even designated a colour – grey – for their members. It became a uniform by which one serious bicyclist could recognize another. As women became more involved, they also wore grey. Mrs Harcourt Williamson, aware of the insult and danger that might await a lone woman in remote areas, valued the anonymity it offered. She wrote, somewhat patronizingly, that 'One reason for the protection which ladies undoubtedly find in the C.T.C. grey uniform lies in the fact that . . . it so closely resembles that ordinarily worn by the wife of a parson or doctor, and therefore the bucolic intelligence sets down the passing stranger in his mind as probably a friend or acquaintance of the local lady.'[7]

The Club made minute recommendations regarding what they should wear too. The list included underwear, for it stated that: 'Nothing but wool should be worn next the skin. A good many riders of both sexes prefer those excellent garments known as "combinations".'[8] It went on to suggest 'a bodice or jacket', a plain skirt, or loose knickerbockers, or 'a pair of trousers cut loose to just below the knee', as well as 'a pair of "Tilbury'd" doeskin gloves' and 'a helmet or hat of the Club cloth, with a special and registered ribbon'.[9] It was, it will be noticed, assumed that cyclists could afford tailor-made outfits for participating in their hobby, but there is a far more important point here: it was also taken for granted that wearing knickerbockers or trousers was acceptable – though these were expected to be covered by a full-length skirt! Female dress was slowly and gradually becoming less cumbersome and more practical, a trend that was to spill over from cycling into golf, tennis and hockey, and into society as a whole. The change came in 1893 with the arrival from France of a movement for what was called 'rational dress'. Until then, the great majority of women's cycling accidents had happened because their long skirts caught in the chain or spokes. Rational dress meant that they could wear leggings and baggy knick-erbockers instead, and after brief initial hilarity these became accepted. The word 'revolution' was indeed appropriate.

The ease of riding in these clothes made a fad of cycling all over again, and this time among a much wider section of the population. Mrs Williamson, commenting on this, makes the point that because the wealthy took it up, bicycling, far from being seen as a socially exclusive practice, was imitated by those lower down in society:

> It might have been always confined to the business of the comparatively few instead of being applied to the many if by some happy chance it had not been taken up by the right people and straightway become the craze of the season.[10]

She went on to explain how bicycle use was spreading not only as a hobby but as a means of travelling to work:

> At a comparatively later date, clerks who lived out of London began to appreciate its uses, and after a time women (also engaged on business) were to be seen winding their way from the suburbs to the City. Then the professional men began to use it a little, [though] still the exercise was condemned by the majority as vulgar, [but now] boys in red uniforms, with the name of 'Gavin' on their caps, may be seen waiting on the steps of Mayfair and Belgravia mansions to clean the aristocracy's bicycles.[11]

Not everyone approved. In Germany Kaiser Wilhelm did not like to see women on bicycles, and reprimanded the American

Ambassador for allowing his daughter to ride one in Berlin's principal park, the Tiergarten.

The Modern Bicycle

What had also made the sport so fashionable had been the arrival, by the nineties, of the 'safety bicycle', which set a seal on the popularity of this form of conveyance and marked the completion of the revolution in personal transport. Anyone could now cycle, provided they could master the steering and brakes and the initially difficult feat of balancing on two wheels. Lessons were still necessary and 'spills' still common, for it was easy to take a tumble, but the time and effort required to cycle well was much less. The machine was lower than previously and thus simple to mount and dismount. It had a chain-driven rear wheel and was easy to steer. It had effective brakes, and it had a guard over the chain to prevent clothes from catching. Like all technological innovations, once the teething problems of the bicycle had been addressed the wider public took the invention out of the hands of specialists and enthusiasts and made it their own.

Back on Four Wheels

Following fast in the wheel tracks of the bicycle came another, even more revolutionary vehicle – the automobile. This too had had a long period of development from crude and impractical prototype to viable machine. Like the bicycle, the first model appeared in France, where an engineer called Cugnot developed a 'steam car' in 1769. It was clumsy, noisy and slow-moving, and did not mark the beginning of a new era. The notion of a steam car had, nevertheless, been established, and was next taken up in Britain. Sixty years after Cugnot, in the 1830s, a number of coaches were introduced that were powered by steam boilers. Technically they were successful, and provided regular service in several parts of the country, but their noise, slowness and potential combustability meant that they never challenged the dominance of the horse. In the same decade the railway became the most important form of transport, and interest in road vehicles waned for half a century.

It was in 1873 that the firm of Leon Bollee began construction of vehicles. Five years later these were displayed at the Universal Exhibition in Paris. In 1885 a wealthy enthusiast, the Comte de Dion, produced another steam vehicle. In 1894 the first actual meeting of automobiles took place. It comprised a trip from Paris to Rouen and back. This was intended to be merely a promenade by the vehicles, but interest in their speed – and in which of them was fastest – gave the event the character of a race. The Dion-Bouton, which had travelled at all of twelve miles an hour, won.

Enthusiasm for this new machine was at first moderate in the United Kingdom, though there were, as there were in France, wealthy men who were interested in a new sport that involved speed, mild danger and expensive equipment. The Hon. Evelyn Ellis, who had been driving for several years in France, brought a motor car to England in 1895. In the same year another motorist, Sir David Salomons, put on a display of vehicles in Tunbridge Wells that attracted some 10,000 people, including several Members of Parliament – and a further exhibition was held twelve months later, this time at the Imperial Institute, an important London venue. By this time the United Kingdom rights for the Daimler patented machines had been bought by a London financier. When, on 14 November 1896, motor vehicles were allowed by Parliament to run on British roads – without the necessity of a man preceding them with a red flag – there was widespread public interest.

Some of those who wrote about motoring matters felt that they were on the cusp of a new era in transport, and could see that attitudes might change sooner than people imagined. With what seems from our perspective a certain naivety, one of them stressed the advantages that could be looked for over the horse, and mentions the type of electric-powered vehicle that might once have replaced the petrol engine:

> It is now admitted by most people that the motor-car has passed the limits of mere experiment, and that it has become a practical vehicle. Motoring has already entered, and will in the future enter yet more largely, into our social life, though we may still be far from the time when the horse-drawn vehicle will be a rarity upon country roads and London has begun to save fifty thousand pounds a year now spent in road scavenging.
>
> The utility of the motor is endless. At whatever distance you may live from your station in the country, the motor is bound to shorten the time occupied on the journey to and fro. Whether you consider the motor from the town or country station point of view, the fact that there are no horses to get tired, and that the motor will run, provided it is efficiently handled, for any hour or all hours during the twenty-four, makes it inevitable that every country house, and nearly every private carriage-owner in London, will have a motor car of some sort in coming years.
>
> There is probably nothing safer in the streets of London to-day than a well-driven electric carriage; there are no horses to fall down when the streets are slippery, and there is brake power available far in excess of any that can possibly be exercised by the horse with his four iron-shod feet on a treacherous surface.[12]

Although the motor car thus arrived in the reign of Victoria, the vehicles were seen – just as earlier the bicycle had been – as a plaything for enthusiasts, who might run races or make experimental journeys over long distances. Not only was the motor car unpleasant – it was noisy, difficult to start and prone to break down – it was also highly expensive and initially beyond the reach even of many 'carriage folk'. The very fact that motoring was included among the subjects dealt with in the Badminton Library of sporting volumes indicates that the car was not yet considered a serious means of transport. The motoring age was not to begin with Victoria but with Edward VII. The Queen herself – though she never personally encountered one – intensely disliked this new invention, saying to the Master of the Horse: 'I hope you will never allow one of those horrible machines to be used in my stables. I am told they smell exceedingly nasty, and are shaky and disagreeable conveyances altogether.'[13] It would only be when her son was on the throne that the Royal Family – which still led fashion – employed automobiles and thus helped to popularize them. It would indeed be in the Royal Stables that they were kept, and the Master of the Horse who would initially supervise them.

6

RELIGION

An overwhelming difference between the twenty-first century and the nineteenth is the presence of active Christianity in society. It is difficult from a modern perspective to appreciate the importance of this influence, not only on individual thought and behaviour but on social convention, general attitudes, and on parliamentary legislation. Religion mattered to the Victorians in a way that is incomprehensible to many people today.

Humbug

The era is perceived, according to stereotype, as one of piety. Churchgoing was commonplace and expected. Family prayers were an equally rigid convention. Missionaries from Britain were sent all over the globe to convert the heathen, supported financially by the pennies of spinsters and Sunday School children. Clergymen lived a rarified, Trollopian existence in cathedral closes and country vicarages, preaching soporific sermons and presiding over tea-parties while their curates fluttered the hearts of local young ladies. The Church – principally, of course, the Anglican Church – was an unflinching upholder of the social order and a sort of moral police force for the nation. Church-sponsored charitable organizations were numerous and, pricked in conscience by the poverty surrounding their own comfort, members of middle-class congregations carried out some useful social work, though this is seen as going hand in hand with humbug and hypocrisy.

Like all stereotypes, this one contains some truth. Observance of the Sabbath was often strict, and was enshrined in law. Clergymen, whether bishops or curates, enjoyed a greater prestige in society than they were later to do. Their opinions, utterances, writings and sermons were respected and heeded and debated, for they were seen as important and well-qualified social commentators whose views carried weight. The Church – not only in its Anglican form but on behalf of Nonconformist and Catholic interests – undertook a huge amount of philanthropic activity that was without precedent in its scope and the zeal of its – largely voluntary – workforce, for the Victorians believed that individuals, rather than the state, should look after society's needs. Though guilt may have played some part in motivating them, it does not detract from their achievement. Waves of missionaries went from the United Kingdom – more of them than from any other country – to Africa and China, Canada and the South Seas to win souls, though they also devoted considerable energy to work at home in 'Darkest England'. All the while their efforts were followed with close interest and supported by the prayers of the congregations that sponsored them.

Storm and Stress

Any notion of uninterrupted peace within the precincts of churches and cathedrals, however, is a serious misconception. The nineteenth century was, for the Anglican Church, a time of storm and stress, of bitter dispute and almost continuous attack from several quarters – from other denominations, from those who held radical or humanist views, and from those energetic and committed evangelicals within its own ranks who wished to refashion it into a less stagnant and more effective organization. Created by the Tudors as a compromise between religious extremes, the Anglican Church was found to be inadequate in an industrial, materialistic and less deferential age. It was in considerable need of overhaul, but this process had begun, and reform was well under way during the decades before Victoria's accession. The characteristics of this National Church as they were before the advent of new enthusiasms was summed up by a late Victorian author as:

> Preaching, without passion or excitement, scholarlike, careful, wise . . . Its average was what naturally in England would be the average, in a state of things in which great religious institutions have been for a long time settled and unmolested – kindly, helpful, respectable, sociable persons of good sense and character, workers rather in a fashion of routine which no one thought of breaking; apt to value themselves on their cheerfulness and wit, but often dull and dogmatic and quarrelsome, often insufferably pompous.[1]

However agreeable the less pompous and more kindly members of the Church may have been, their indifferent and ineffectual outlook was seen by a new generation as a serious obstacle to necessary progress.

Passionate Ideals

As well as those who wished the Church to respond more closely to the needs of society, there was a powerful element that wished it to reform. The most glaring abuse was absenteeism – the holding by a single clergyman of one or more parishes that he seldom visited but from which he received tithes. A parson with several livings could have an extremely comfortable existence, while the services in his various churches were conducted for him by impoverished curates. This practice was gradually brought to an end during Victoria's reign, but it was only one among several major issues that reformers wished to address. A further movement within its ranks sought to rediscover the beauties of the Church's early existence, or at least the purity that was perceived as belonging to the 'Age of Faith' – the Middle Ages. What this meant was in effect a repudiation of the Reformation, a return to ornament and statuary, ritual and – most controversially – devotion to the Mother of God. To some this was simple heresy, a denial of all that made the English Church distinctive. To others it offered a new dimension of beauty and spirituality – something that had been lacking precisely because of the Reformation.

The instigators of this tendency were all linked with the University of Oxford. The oldest of them was John Keble (1792–1866), a brilliant Oriel scholar who took orders and published, in 1827, a book of religious verse entitled *The Christian Year*. It was hugely popular, and so impressively written that he was appointed Professor of Poetry. In 1833 he preached a sermon in the university church that expressed his personal view that Anglicanism should embrace the whole Church, including its Catholic element. What he was saying was, in effect, that it was possible to include Catholic practices without betraying one's Anglican convictions. He did not aim at a reintroduction of

Catholicism, rather the model to which he looked was the Laudian English Church of the seventeenth century. Like others whose thoughts had developed in a similar way, he was also alarmed at the spread of secularism in society. Several of his listeners passionately agreed with him, and between them they formed what became known as the Oxford Movement.

Ecclesiastical Revolution

Their outlook attracted another brilliant mind. Edward Pusey (1800–82) was a clergyman and Fellow of Oriel who joined the debate through academic writing and the publishing of tracts in support of Keble's views, though his influence was so great that those who shared his ideas came to be known as Puseyites. When he was suggested as Regius Professor of Divinity, the unsympathetic Prime Minister, Lord Melbourne, ignored his candidacy and appointed a Low Churchman. This was not Pusey's last rebuff, for he was suspended from preaching a few years later – though he continued to write, and remained a guiding spirit in the Oxford Movement.

John Henry Newman (1801–90) was another Fellow of Oriel inspired by Keble's sermon to develop similar views, and he expressed them in an extensive range of tracts. He wrote nineteen of these, and the fact that several other members of the Movement also published pamphlets gave rise to the term 'Tractarian' to describe the Catholic tendency within Anglicanism. Newman, a quiet and deeply intellectual figure, found himself so drawn to this that in 1845 he converted to the Roman Catholic Church. He continued to write prolifically – his *Apologia pro vita sua* of 1864 was regarded as a masterpiece. He founded the Oratory in Birmingham and became the first Rector of the Catholic University of Ireland. He was created a cardinal in 1879 and died in 1890.

Another convert to Catholicism was Henry Manning (1808–92). The son of a Governor of the Bank of England, and a Prime Minister's godson, he found his way by an indirect route into Anglican orders. He, like Newman, came to prefer the Roman Catholic Church, and converted in 1851. Less intellectual and more worldly than the members of the Oxford Movement, he became actively involved in work among the poor, and was an ally of – or at least a joint participant in various endeavours with – the Salvation Army and the temperance movement. He subscribed fully, in other words, to the Victorian notions of improving the lot of the poor. He also acted as a mediator in industrial disputes (most memorably the 1889 dock strike), and was a vigorous champion of access to education. His concern for the poor was so marked that critics thought him tainted with socialism, but his response was 'People call it socialism, I call it Christianity.' He became Archbishop of Westminster (where there was as yet no cathedral) in 1865, and a cardinal ten years later.

These men possessed some of the finest minds that nineteenth-century England produced. That they should devote the resources they possessed so completely to the service of Christianity suggests not only the important role that religion played in their era but the need they perceived for change, redefinition and reform.

Amid the tensions within Anglicanism, the advantage alternated between evangelicals and traditionalists throughout the century. Prime Ministers, who appointed bishops and could thus shape the character of church leadership for decades to come, were often driven by personal beliefs and preferences. Palmerston and Disraeli demonstrated, in their choice among candidates, a distrust of Tractarians that reflected the traditional English suspicion of ceremonious worship. Gladstone, on the other hand, was a Tractarian himself, and showed a corresponding disinclination to appoint evangelicals.

The Tudor gateway into the Cathedral Close at Canterbury might stand as a metaphor for the position of the Church at this time. It is large, elaborate and impressive, decorated with statuary and coats of arms, and it leads through to a place of peace and privilege. There are massive wooden gates, which still show signs of damage from the mob that tried to break them down during the Reform Bill riots in 1832, so completely was the Church identified with the landed gentry and the old, vested interests. The Church might have seemed secure and complacent, but its influence, its privileges and its possessions were under constant threat.

Fasting, Humiliation and Divine Displeasure

A strict Christian outlook that was manifest in Sabbath observance was not a product of the Victorian era. It had developed by the latter part of the eighteenth century (there were Sunday Observance Acts dating from 1677 and 1780). The battle was not definitively won at that time, for the Victorians were left to campaign for the banning of band concerts in parks on Sundays (they won), the restriction of postal deliveries (reduced to one) and the closing of beer shops (they lost). Nevertheless, it is difficult to imagine any era since the Puritan Commonwealth in which the desire to restrict the pleasures of others would have been taken so seriously. Sometimes tragedy might be interpreted as evidence of divine displeasure. Throughout the railway age, trains ran on the Sabbath on many – though not all – lines. When, on the last Sunday of 1879, the Tay Bridge collapsed in a gale, taking seventy-five people to their deaths, the view was widely held that this had been their punishment for using public transport on the Lord's Day.

Though Scotland, where the disaster had taken place, was a more deeply religious country than England, this attitude to divine displeasure was not uncommon on both sides of the border, and can be seen in the notion of National Days of Fasting and Humiliation. The first of these, proposed by a Member of Parliament at the time of Britain's first cholera epidemic in 1831, had been half-heartedly supported, and the idea was not taken seriously. The next one, held in 1854 and again the result of a cholera outbreak, was more successful. The following year there was a similar observance for the Crimean War, and in 1857 there was another day of self-abasement prompted by the most horrific event of the reign – the Indian Mutiny. A proclamation by the Queen stated that 7 October had been set aside: 'For a solemn Fast, Humiliation, and prayer before Almighty God; in order to Obtain Pardon for our Sins, and for Imploring His Blessing and Assistance in our Arms for the Restoration of Tranquillity in India.'[2] The renowned Baptist, Charles Spurgeon, was the preacher, and the chosen venue was not a church or cathedral but the Crystal Palace. This was necessary in view of the numbers expected: in the event, 23,654 persons attended.

The Evangelicals

Although 'Enthusiasm' – an emotional, demonstrative faith – sat uncomfortably with the British character, it nevertheless took root. It found a response among those who had been cast adrift by the Industrial Revolution, with its destruction of traditional societies and values. By virtue of the number of people who embraced this outlook, it was highly influential during the Regency and pre-Victorian years. While 'Enthusiasm' might have been seen as suited only to the industrial working class, it was given respectability, and appeal at a higher social level, through the involvement of the devout and respected MP William Wilberforce. By the forties it was established as an accepted, important shade of opinion. Evangelicals were to be found both in the Nonconformist sects and in Anglican congregations. It should also be remembered that members of the mercantile and manufacturing elite, especially those who came from areas that were Nonconformist in character, often belonged to this tendency (the Quaker Cadburys of York are one instance among several).

A high incidence of religious enthusiasm and church attendance was not, however, a state of affairs that remained static throughout the reign. Religious revivals, like other popular movements, tend to run their course, peaking and then declining rather than being maintained for decades. Respectable Christianity reached something of a high-water mark in the 1850s, and church congregations were greater from that decade until the end of the seventies than they were to be thereafter. The impetus could, it seemed, not be sustained.

Rome and Nonconformity

As we have seen, the Victorian religious world was not a matter of a single Church existing without rivalry, or without serious divisions within its own ranks. Most legal and constitutional constraints on Catholics were removed in 1829, allowing the re-emergence into national life of a vigorous and experienced denomination that had widespread influence within immigrant communities (Irish and Italians). Nonconformity, which had blossomed in the eighteenth century, continued to have a striking level of influence in the nineteenth. Less socially acceptable than Anglicanism, it appealed to the working and lower middle classes, and was often identified with radical politics and trade unionism. To attend 'chapel' rather than 'church' – to be a Baptist or Methodist rather than an Anglican – was a social label as much as a reflection of a person's spiritual conscience.

If we are tempted to regard the Victorian view of religion, with its emphasis on outward respectability, with scepticism or derision, it is worth remembering two things. Firstly, this attitude suited the spirit of the time. It was considered right and appropriate. In the future a number of our own attitudes – our obsession with 'political correctness', for instance – may seem equally incomprehensible to historians. Secondly, the influence of Christianity enabled the Victorians to accomplish a very great deal of good both in their own country and in the world at large. As a historian has pointed out: 'If some people had not taken a pride, even a pharisaical pride, in being better than their half-barbarous fellows or their morally lax forebears, life in Victorian England would have been worse than it was.'[3]

Victorian Christian Values

The tenets of Christianity as developed in Britain by the end of the eighteenth century fitted well, for several generations in the nineteenth, with the virtues that Victorians admired. They provided a moral code that suited the circumstances, and created the middle-class morality that became so much a feature of the age. The ethos of hard work, frugality, unselfishness in serving others – be they the poor, the community or the nation – drew on roots that went back to the Puritans of two hundred years earlier (and, like the Puritans, many Victorians believed that prosperity was a reward from God for their virtue). In the early decades of the reign, when there was widespread economic hardship and resulting social unrest, the wisdom of avoiding a show of wealth and luxury on the part of the rich was obvious, and this notion of modesty in any case fitted with the national preference for understatement. The encouragement of frugality among the poor was likewise suited to the times. The earnest desire for self-improvement,

again a characteristic left over from the Puritans, but one that
the Victorians continued to revere, stressed the need to put
work before pleasure, obligations before self-indulgence.
However much many people failed to match this ethos of
selfless service in their own lives, they admired it in others, for
moral responsibility was perhaps their most respected ideal.
Probably the two greatest popular celebrities of the age were
David Livingstone and General Gordon. Both were, by any
measure, heroic, but that both were so deeply and obviously
pious added immensely to their appeal, as could be seen by the
number of books about either of them that were given as
Sunday School prizes. These notions of responsible, patriotic
altruism gradually went out of fashion after the Victorian era,
not least because they had become associated with it. They are
not easily understood by societies that are based on entitlement
and the belief that personal desires are paramount.

The Dispossessed

While respectability became a cult among the better off, there
were millions beyond its reach. The Anglican Church remained a middle-class body, and as Nonconformists gained
legal recognition they began to lose the radical, political edge
that had earlier characterized them and to join the social
mainstream. This left a vast section at the bottom of society
that belonged to no denomination and whose plight captured
the attention and enthusiasm of a number of evangelists. At
one end of the doctrinal spectrum, the Catholic wing of
Anglicanism sought to address the plight of those in inner-
city slums. They had some success in building congregations
because their services so closely resembled those of the Roman
Catholic Church, with which the large Irish immigrant community was familiar. In at least one area – south-east London –

they also achieved respect as the only denomination whose priests stayed, and died, during a cholera epidemic.

At the other end of the doctrinal scale, the slum missions and the Salvation Army deliberately pursued those who were considered beyond the reach of churches. William Booth established the latter organization in 1865 as a result of deliberately engineered experiences living in this same corner of south-east London. If it were not possible to induce an audience to come inside a meeting hall, he reasoned that the service must be taken outside. The uniforms in which his followers were attired made them conspicuous, as did the band music they provided. In an era when only ballad-singers, barrel organs and itinerant musicians performed in the streets, this form of free entertainment was popular, though the accompanying tracts and sermons and prayers were not always so welcome. Marching Salvationists were often pelted with missiles. The sturdy poke bonnets worn by women members, which are still seen occasionally even today, had already passed out of fashion by the time the organization was founded, but they were necessary for protection.

The Salvation Army, and similar bodies, did not have the field to themselves, for gradually missions were established in slum districts. The Anglican Church was subject to the 'mission fever' of the mid-century, but found it difficult – perhaps even undesirable – to persuade the very poor to enter its doors. The answer was to copy the Nonconformists and resort to street evangelism and worship in mission halls, practices previously disdained. This type of facility was established not only by denominations but by other types of community; the school or university mission, in which young men volunteered their time and money for the betterment of their less fortunate contemporaries, became an established feature of the urban landscape. Oxford, Cambridge, Eton, Rugby and many other illustrious

(*left*) Symbol of an era: The Queen, depicted in early middle age by the doyen of European court painters, Franz Xavier Winterhalter.

(*below*) A stereoscopic view of the Diamond Jubilee procession passing the National Gallery, 22 June 1897. This event was more than an anniversary; it was a huge celebration of the British Empire and a summing-up of the Victorian age.

Her Majesty Greeting her People, Diamond Jubilee Pageant, London, England.
Copyright 1897 by Underwood & Underwood.

(*right*) Putting on a crinoline, 1850s. Though this is a particularly monstrous specimen, it conveys the sheer impracticality of any 'cage skirt'. One of its component hoops can be seen on the right.

(*below*) Though Victorian children, like those of previous eras, were often dressed as miniature adults, short jackets and sailor suits or dresses increasingly gave them a distinctively juvenile appearance. The young man in an Eton collar is C.T. Studd, later a cricketer, evangelist and missionary, seen here (appropriately) as an Eton boy

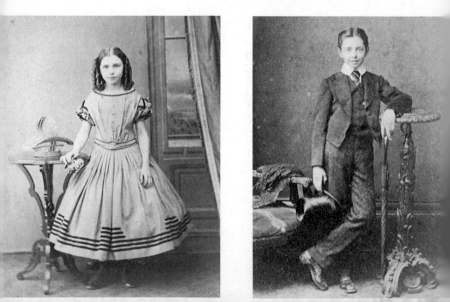

above) A Victorian corner grocer's. One is struck by the large number of staff
for such a small establishment, and by the smartness of the men (for there are no
women). This store is still flourishing at Walmer in Kent.

below) It is often assumed that servants led a dull and cowed existence, yet this
young man – a page or footman in a fashionable quarter of London – is proud
enough of his livery to be photographed in it. The nursemaid pictured on the right
is permitted to wear a stylish straw hat while in the garden with her charges.

Interior. By the time this was taken, in the 1890s, rooms had lost much of their darkness and clutter. Here there are no heavy items of furniture or curtains, thoug there is still the characteristic accumulation of pictures and knick-knacks. The screen was an essential piece of household equipment, for combating draughts.

… and exterior. Albert Place, Kensington, in the 1870s. Many such streets were n accessible to the public, their privacy guarded by gates and uniformed watchmen.

(*above left*) A gentleman of the 1870s still sporting the 'dundreary' whiskers that had been *de rigeur* in the sixties. Though he wears a top hat and sober frock coat, the somewhat shocking loudness of his trousers suggests that men's formal clothes had not yet become the dark uniform of later decades.

(*above right*) William Ewart Gladstone (1809–98), one of several long-serving political giants – others were Palmerston, Disraeli and Salisbury – who shaped events during Victoria's reign. A man of great integrity and undoubted ability, he nevertheless failed to hit it off with the Queen.

The Strand in London on a quiet day in the 1890s. This scene gives little idea of the noise, mess and confusion caused by horse-drawn traffic. Iron-shod wheels, horse dung and falling or shying animals could make travel in such a busy thoroughfare far from pleasant.

(*above*) The Crystal Palace in its new home at Norwood in the 1860s, vastly extended from its Hyde Park original. The towers, designed by Brunel, pumped water for a series of huge fountains in the gardens below. They survived the building's destruction in 1936 but were later demolished.

(*right*) The bill of fare for a private dinner in the 1870s, printed and indented to resemble a plate. Wealthy Victorians showed little interest in healthy eating, preferring to overindulge and then seek medicinal cures such as mineral baths.

87, Eaton Place.

DINER DU 30 MARS, 1878.

Potages
Consommé à la Doria
Crême d'Asperges Faubonne

Poissons
Suprême de Saumon Richelieu
Turbot sauce Crevettes

Entrées
Côtelettes Chasseur aux Pointes
Mousselines à la Princesse

Relevés
Quartier d'Agneau sauce Menthe
Jambon à la Gelée et Mirabelles
Salade assortie

—

Punch au Thé

Rôts
Ramier de Bordeaux
Asperges d'Argenteuil sauce Maltaise

Entremets
St. Honoré aux Pistachio
Abricots à l'Almédorine

—

Corbeilles de Glaces

ockwise from top left)

...each mission at Deal in Kent,
...00, combining relaxation
...h piety. This picture offers
...scinating glimpse of how
...ple dressed, even at the end of
... century, for a seaside holiday.

...erature became a serious industry during Victoria's reign. Not only did the age
...duce British and foreign authors of outstanding ability, a developing popular
...ss and a newly literate public created an almost limitless market for the written
...rd.

...rrow School football XI, an undated image that conveys the structure and
...anization that Victorians brought to traditional games, as well as the self-
...scious prestige of those who played them well.

...oller-skating rink in the 1880s. The Victorians loved novelty and were much
...en to crazes, particularly in the field of amusements.

(*left*) A stoical British 'tommy', as drawn for one of the numerous Victorian boys' magazines. Images like this symbolized, for millions of readers, the qualities that entitled the British to govern the world's largest empire.

(*below*) A gentleman (perhaps a tea planter) and his family, outside their bungalow in Ceylon, 1880s, looking – and dressing – much as if they were in Surrey. The British possessed an extraordinary ability replicate their way of life, and make themselves at home, in all corners of the world.

All illustrations are from the author's own collection.

seats of learning associated themselves with this type of work, and some of their premises were almost overwhelmingly conspicuous: the huge terracotta-fronted Bedford School Mission in Finsbury, built a year or two after Victoria's death, must have dominated the entire street in which it was set.

Christian Charity

While young men might give lectures or teach skills during their spare time at a school mission, it was women who carried the greater part of the burden in terms of church-related charity work, and it is undeniable that Victorian religious work could not have been so wide ranging or successful without them. Women of the middle classes had, during the early and mid-Victorian era, comparatively little else to do. They had no political power, and no prospect of respectable occupation other than the refined end of the teaching profession, while education for them did not begin to be taken seriously until the 1870s. They were often unable, because of the dangers of the streets, even to travel from home without an escort. At the same time rising prosperity meant that in even a moderately wealthy home, the mistress of the house and her daughters would be surrounded by servants who undertook almost all the domestic work and left them prone to boredom. The result was that they channelled their energies into a wealth of 'good works' that filled their empty hands and idle hours. Dickens made gentle fun of this in *Sketches by Boz*:

> In winter, when wet feet are common, and colds not scarce, we have the ladies' soup distribution society, the ladies' coal distribution society and the ladies' blanket distribution society; in summer, when stone fruits flourish and stomach aches prevail, we have the ladies' dispensary, and the ladies' sick visitation committee; and all the year round we have the ladies' child's exam-

ination society, the ladies' bible and prayer-book circulation society, and the ladies' childbed-linen monthly loan society.[4]

He described how swiftly such organizations might spring up:

Mrs Johnson Parker, the mother of several extremely fine girls, reported to several other mammas of several other unmarried families, that five old men, six old women, and children innumerable, in the free seats near her pew, were in the habit of coming to church every Sunday without either bible or prayer-book. Was this to be borne in a civilised country? Could such things be tolerated in a Christian land? Never! A ladies' bible and prayer-book distribution society was instantly formed: president, Mrs Johnson Parker; treasurers, auditors and secretary, the Misses Johnson Parker: subscriptions were entered into, books were bought, and all the free-seat people provided therewith.[5]

If not distributing Bibles, such ladies were often found knitting, sewing or crocheting either for sales of work or for gifts to the deserving – though the suitability of doing even this work on the Sabbath might have been questioned by many. Ernest Shepard – later to win fame as the illustrator of the *Winnie the Pooh* stories – remembered his elderly aunts' habit of filling their Sunday afternoons with work for particular causes:

The Aunts rested or knitted garments for the people of Algoma. Aunt Emily had her own special activity, which was in aid of Deep Sea Fishermen. The garments she knitted, which were of fearful and wonderful proportions, were often tried on Father, who was inclined to make derogatory remarks, while Emily, with puzzled looks, and a knitting-needle in her mouth, would say 'Tut-t-t, very odd. I know I followed the pattern most carefully', and, 'but then, Harry, you must remember they are very *big* men.'[6]

A Revival of Contrasts

Christianity was extremely visible not only in the public recognition given to prominent churchmen and missionaries but in the buildings it created. The Roman Catholic Church was granted freedom to conduct public worship in 1833 and had its hierarchy of cardinals and bishops restored seventeen years later. Emerging from centuries of persecution, censure and disapproval, it began the building of cathedrals and parish churches throughout the British Isles to replace those that had been lost at the Reformation. Much of this naturally went on in Ireland, where the greatest number of Catholics was to be found, but Roman Catholic churches began to share the skylines of towns and cities everywhere. This process culminated in the creation of a cathedral in Westminster – no more than half a mile from the Abbey – when a great Byzantine-revival structure was begun on a site formerly occupied by a penitentiary. Though planned, designed and largely paid for during the Victorian era, this in fact opened the year after the Queen's death, and is still not complete. As well as places of worship, seminaries and Catholic schools became part of the English landscape, and these included those that educated the gentry and even the aristocracy. Downside and Ampleforth, whatever their antecedents, were products of the Victorian era.

At the other end of the spectrum, Nonconformist church building also flourished to keep pace with an expanding population. Baptist and Methodist chapels, particularly common in Wales, the north and East Anglia, were solid and functional, deliberately plain but not without elegance. Typically they were rectangular and designed with a large, square pulpit set above the ground on pillars. This was surrounded on all sides by seating on both the ground floor and in a gallery. Their influence was Classical rather than Gothic, with modest flourishes of ionic column and palmette. Numbers of these buildings are still in use, and such is their functional beauty that many have remained unaltered since they opened.

Within the Church of England itself there was a veritable explosion of church-building. Not only was the populace increasing, but a revival of interest in ritual and the desire to return to the spirituality of the Middle Ages had a considerable effect on the appearance of Anglican ecclesiastical architecture. By the 1840s new churches, influenced by the Ecclesiological Society (founded as the Cambridge Camden Society with the aim of returning church architecture to its medieval splendour), were bristling with statuary and ornament in a way that had not been seen since the sixteenth century. As with the Roman Catholic Church, places of education were founded to provide suitable priests. The most conspicuous, both spiritually and architecturally, was Keble College, Oxford (opened in 1868 and completed in 1876).

Not even the Middle Ages had seen ecclesiastical building on a scale like this. By the mid-1870s the Roman Catholics had erected 738 new churches. The Anglicans built 1,727 and the Nonconformists almost 2,500. These numbers proved somewhat optimistic, and large numbers of pews were never to be filled. Nevertheless the conspicuous presence in towns and cities of these places of worship reminded contemporaries – as the surviving ones continue to remind us – of the confidence, and importance, of organized religion in their society.

The Victorian Sunday

One much-discussed aspect of Victorian religion was the perceived emptiness of the Sabbath. Even in London – let alone smaller cities, towns and villages – shops, places of entertainment and museums were shut on Sundays, and a sense of unspeakable dreariness might prevail. A well-known description of this is given in Dickens' *Little Dorrit*, when Arthur Clennam returns to England after years abroad:

Melancholy streets, in a penitential garb of soot . . . Everything was bolted and barred that could possibly furnish relief to an overworked people. No pictures, no rare plants or flowers, no natural or artificial wonders of the ancient world – all taboo with that enlightened strictness, that the ugly South Sea gods in the British Museum might have supposed themselves at home again. Nothing for the spent toiler to do but compare the monotony of his seventh day with the monotony of his six days, and make the best of it.[7]

In 1851 a Continental visitor, strolling in the City, remarked on this same sense of emptiness:

I walked down Cheapside, which is quite a long street. I would have liked to go into a coffee house for a glass of ale or claret but all the shops were hermetically sealed. Even the front door of my hotel was locked and only if one knew the secret could one turn the right knob and force an entry. I asked for my bill as I have been accustomed to settle my account every day. But the innkeeper politely asked me to wait until Monday.[8]

Even those who had homes to go to were expected to behave differently. William Tayler was a footman in the household of an elderly widow, and kept a diary in the year that the Queen came to the throne. He indicates that a show of respectability was customary even before the Victorian era had properly begun, but that although attendance at a church might be expected and he might set out as if going to one, it was just as likely that he would merely take the air instead: 'This being

Sunday of course I went to church – or rather, I took a little walk elsewhere.'[9] Indeed this was such common practice that, when he *did* actually go to church he made a point of mentioning it in his diary: 'This is Sunday and I have really been to church.'[10]

People attended on Sundays – and in many places would do so at least twice in the course of the day – for several reasons. It might be through genuine conviction, or because it was expected, if not demanded, of them, or because there was simply nothing else to do. In many households the servants would be obliged to go there with their employers – though they would of course sit on benches in the gallery, or in other 'free seats', with fellow members of their class and not in the pews below; church membership, or at least frequent attendance, would have been seen as evidence of good character. For the well-off employers of servants, membership, under the right circumstances, gave an opportunity to flaunt one's respectability, wealth – and dress. The rental of a private pew (obligatory if one wished to impress) would be expensive in a fashionable congregation, and competition for them would be stiff. Since they were prominently situated, other worshippers could not help but see the occupants as they processed down the aisle, or the deference with which the pew-opener – usually an elderly woman – would show them to their seats.

Others were driven by sheer boredom because so little else was open, or by a desire for a warm and dry place to sit on days of inclement weather. Many lodgers were expected to stay out of their homes on Sundays to allow their landlords peace, and this was very commonly the case in cities among the employees of shops and department stores, who lived in barrack-like accommodation on the premises. They were forbidden to stay in their rooms on Sundays, and had little alternative to sitting through services but tramping the streets. In spite of this, church attendance was not as universal a habit as we might imagine. The only census ever taken in Britain of the population's worshipping habits was carried out on Sunday 30 March 1851. Though its findings were not as clear as might be supposed – for no exact and reliable figure was arrived at – it showed that between 47 and 54 per cent of the populace attended a place of worship (the census included all such places, and about half of those worshipping had attended a Nonconformist of Roman Catholic service), though there was no indication whether any of these people were a regular or an occasional worshipper. It was not an encouraging statistic. As one author has said: 'By the standards Victorians set for themselves, it was humiliating.'[11]

The Sunday School – an invention of the previous century – was, until the advent of state education, a place in which children were not only taught about the Gospel but learned to read and write. Even when this task was taken over by local authorities, Sunday Schools remained an important part of national life. All denominations had them, and their popularity with parents was due at least in part to the opportunities it gave for privacy while their children attended. Sunday Schools gave children the exciting feeling of belonging to something worthwhile, for they offered prizes for knowledge and regular attendance, they hosted picnics and outings, and they enabled them to learn about the wider world by saving, or collecting, or making things for missions overseas. Their growth was so dramatic that by the final decades of the century almost three-quarters of British children attended them.

Children not only went to Sunday School but attended adult services too, and could expect to be quizzed on their contents afterwards. In the chapter on 'Our Parish' in *Sketches by Boz*, Dickens describes an elderly widow who, after the service: 'Walks home with the family next door but

one, and talks about the sermon all the way, invariably
opening the conversation by asking the youngest boy where
the text was.'[12]

Sermons

Discoursing on these matters was often a struggle for the
young. Molly Hughes (or Molly Thomas, as she was at the
time), whose family lived in London and attended St Paul's
cathedral rather than some mere parish church, would often
talk with her brothers as they walked back to Canonbury:

> The sermons were usually stiff with learning and far over our
> heads. After one on Solomon's vision, I asked Barnholt on the
> way home whether *he* would have chosen wisdom if he had
> been Solomon. 'Oh no,' said he, 'I've got enough of that. I
> should have asked for a new cricket bat.' The rest of the walk
> home was spent in enlarging on the things we might have got
> from such a golden opportunity.[13]

These addresses were not necessarily given and forgotten. The
notion of the 'popular preacher' is largely unfamiliar today,
because the doings of churchmen no longer excite the same
degree of interest in the public. For Victorians, a visiting
preacher known to be particularly gifted could draw considerable crowds, and members of the congregation would have to
go early to be sure of seats – perhaps arriving an hour or two
before the service began. The same might well be true if the
subject of a sermon were topical – for instance a recent disaster
or a particularly interesting vice – for churchgoers would look
forward to hearing the views of a trained and analytical mind.
Before the arrival of television to provide mass education, the
church sermon could fulfil something of this function, by

providing a concise and reasoned examination of a current question, just as a documentary does today.

If a clergyman were known to be young and handsome, it could be guaranteed that the front pews would be occupied by ladies. Should his sermon prove especially memorable it might well be published, perhaps as part of a collection of his own addresses, or in a volume with those of others. The sermons of a man like Dean Stanley of Westminster sold widely and were not only read at home but even 'recycled' by other preachers. The celebrity achieved by a popular preacher, Anglican or otherwise, is clear in the case of the young and fiery Charles Haddon Spurgeon, the Baptist pastor whose services at his south London church attracted huge crowds. When he married in 1856, the occasion had something of the atmosphere associated in our day with media personalities, as the local newspaper demonstrated:

In point of numbers and enthusiasm it far outstripped any display which the West End is in the habit of witnessing. Shortly after eight o'clock, although the morning was damp, dark and cold, as many as five hundred ladies, in light and gay attire, besieged the doors of the chapel, accompanied by many gentlemen, members of the congregation and personal friends. From that hour, the crowd increased so rapidly that the thoroughfare was blocked up by vehicles and pedestrians and a body of the M Division of the Police had to be sent for to prevent accidents. When the chapel doors were opened, there was a terrific rush, and in less than half an hour the doors were closed upon many eager visitors.[14]

The pastor with personal charisma was likely to attract a host of disciples, almost in the way that a popular musician might today have 'fans'. A book of advice for young women published in 1845 warned against the dangers of taking such an attitude to extremes:

The most objectionable feature which this tendency assumes is an extravagant and enthusiastic attachment to ministers of religion. I am aware that there is in the character and office of a faithful minister, justly calculated to call forth the respectful admiration both of young and old; that there is also much in his pastoral care of the individual members of his flock equally calculated to awaken feelings of deep and strong attachment; and when such feelings are tempered with reverence it is unquestionably right that they should be cherished . . . but there are other young women, chiefly of enthusiastic [evangelical] temperament, who, under the impression that it is right to love and admire to the utmost of their power, give way to a style of expression, when speaking of their favourite ministers, and a mode of behaviour towards them, which is not only peculiarly adapted to expose them, as religious professors, to the ridicule of the world; but which too plainly betrays their want of reverence and right feeling on the subject of religion in general.[15]

A preacher with the eloquence and magnetism of Spurgeon was, of course, the exception rather than the rule, but even with those of lesser ability surviving the sermon need not be the ordeal one might suppose for, especially in illustrious surroundings, the imagination could drift and curiosity might attach to a visiting preacher. Molly Hughes recalled:

Sermons were on the endurance side, but had some alleviations. I had a nice long sit down, and as I was always seated close to the pulpit I enjoyed the colours of the marble pillars, and could weave fancies. If the preacher grew fierce I looked at the statue of Samveli Johnson, whom I vaguely connected with Sam Weller, and if he were gentle I looked at the one of Howard with his keys, a satisfying face and figure. It is curious that during all those years I never inquired who these people were. The sermons were seldom less than three-quarters of an hour. To the preacher it was the chance of a lifetime. He would never again 'address London'. We got to be a bit sorry for him as he went up the steps, conducted by the melancholy-looking verger who certainly must have given him a gloomy foreboding of his reception by 'London'. He did not know how his voice would carry under the dome, and we took joy in seeing whether he would bawl or roar.[16]

Whatever the merits, or otherwise, of the preaching, one might be carried away by other aspects of the experience. Mrs Hughes wondered later:

why we endured those long services. Not from pious or educative motives. It must have been simply for the inspiring music that burst from that organ and that choir. It was worth all the endurance, even of the Litany. No footling sentimental hymns, but Te Deums, Psalms, Creeds, Introits, and Kyries that intoxicated us. During one boy's solo my father was so excited that his fist came thump down on his neighbour's shoulder. We children knew all the chants.[17]

The Scottish Sabbath

North of the Border, the Presbyterian Church was by far the most numerous and influential, but this suffered fragmentation when in 1843 a large segment of it broke off to form the Free Church. In Scotland the Church had an even greater influence on everyday life and attitudes than in England, and the Sabbath was more rigidly kept. Though the strictness of Calvinist influence had softened somewhat since the previous century, a Scottish Sunday – like one in Nonconformist Wales

– was still something that visitors found remarkable for an uncompromising severity enforced by social consensus.

For Nonconformists, or the Presbyterian members of the Church of Scotland, there were few distractions from the strict observance of Sunday. Dr A. K. H. Boyd was minister of the town church in St Andrews, though he had a second career as a bestselling writer whose works sold in the hundreds of thousands. When he took over the parish in 1865 there were three services every Sunday, and a building with seating for two and a half thousand was often well filled during all of them. This was in spite of the fact that here was no organ, or indeed any other accompaniment during the hymns. There was no ritual whatsoever associated with singing and praying, and the intercessions were not recited according to a set formula as in the Anglican Church but extemporized. A sermon was expected to last at least an hour, and an hour and a half would not be thought unusual – something of a burden on the man who had to write them. Boyd was once intrigued to hear his congregation discussing a visiting preacher's style and complaining that he had not moved his hands or body as much during the sermon as they would have liked. That the contents of a sermon would be debated afterwards was natural, but that the accompanying *gestures*, or lack of them, should have been included in the appraisal was a measure of how seriously the matter of a minister's style was taken – or how much it contributed to the entertainment of the populace in a place with few other distractions.

The Rise of Ritual

Boyd did not favour the plainness of these services, and gradually he began to alter them, introducing small innovations that his congregation seemed to accept without demur.

He wrote that: 'The *Saturday Review* was wrong when it spoke of the worship of the Church of Scotland as "the most dismal service ever devised by man." Those who had grown up under it liked it, and found it uplifting.'[18] This is a point worth noting. From a modern perspective, nineteenth-century services may seem unimaginably dull and lengthy, but to those who were accustomed to them and knew nothing else, and whose entire culture had led them to regard these as normal, there was interest and even beauty amid the hard benches and interminable addresses. Changes that we might regard as improvement – such as rehearsed singing by a specialist group within the congregation – could well be seen by traditionalists as a threat to the purity of their beliefs, an attitude shown when a Scottish pastor was taken to a fashionable Edinburgh church: 'An Aberdeen professor went one Sunday to St Stephen's with a worthy Highland parson. The Highland parson listened to the choir in horror, and when the service ended his words were: "If this is to go on, the Church will go down." '[19]

And there were worse offences. The Reverend Boyd received an impassioned letter one day in 1878 following a sermon he had preached at another church. The resulting exchange of letters was subsequently published under the headline: 'DR BOYD OF ST ANDREWS DEFYING THE ALMIGHTY WITH A BOX OF WHISTLES'.

His crime had been to tolerate, and encourage, organ music. His correspondent, a Presbyterian clergyman and the secretary of the Anti-Papal League, thundered that:

In what you did and said about the box of whistles in Brechin Cathedral on the Lord's Day, the 28th ultimo, I charge you with having acted the part of 'the blind leading the blind' because you in reality lifted up your voice against the Almighty while you were pretending to lead worshippers of Him. I charge you in the sight of God with having impiously set at defiance and rebelled against His specification of what praise to Him should be in New Testament times.[20]

Controversy of this sort, the more bitter for the strength and sincerity with which views were held, continued throughout the century. Scottish churchmen, fiercely proud of their national form of Christianity ('Our Zion'), no doubt looked with alarm at the revival of ritual, and were wary of any perceived attempt to spread the infection to their own congregations. In this they largely failed, at least in terms of a number of small gestures that gradually crept in. Boyd described how:

> Dr Robert Lee, of Old Greyfriars Church in Edinburgh, had asked his congregation to kneel at prayer instead of standing, or rather lounging, and to stand at praise instead of sitting. He likewise introduced instrumental music, and began to read his prayers. Now all these things [he was writing in 1892] and more, are found everywhere, it is strange to think how ferociously (no other word will do) they were opposed much less than thirty years since.[21]

His attempts to reform the practices in his own church had begun at about the same time, but he had been surprised at the calm with which his parishioners had reacted:

> It was on July 25th 1869 that I first ventured to suggest to the congregation that it would be decorous and might be helpful if on entering and leaving church they paused for a minute in silent prayer. The Scottish practice was to do neither. And while pronouncing the blessing, one used to see the men smoothing their hats and opening the pew doors, to the end that with the last word a rush might be made as though the building were on fire.[22]

The established Church of Scotland (as opposed to the Free Church, which retained the traditional, purer form of Calvinism and saw itself as a Church of the people rather than the landed gentry) therefore became gradually more liberal as the Victorian era went on, the services in many congregations coming to have more and more in common with Low Church Anglicanism. This was evidenced by the fact that Boyd, during his thirty-four-year tenure as minister, successfully inducted a number of prominent Anglicans, including Dean Stanley and Bishop Wordsworth, to preach or take part in services in his parish.

Sundays at Home

The gloom of a Victorian Sunday has passed into legend, especially through the memories of those who had to endure them as children. Almost everything that gave pleasure seemed to be forbidden, and only improving reading matter was allowed. Ernest Shepard remembered:

> When we got back [from church], Cyril and I were horrified to find our playroom had been tidied up, the toys and games had been put away in a cupboard, and the order had gone forth that we must spend the afternoon in the drawing room. No old *Punch* or *Illustrated London News* volumes to look at: instead, *The Sunday Magazine*, *Leisure Hour*, and *Sunday at Home* . . .
>
> As the afternoon wore on, the only cheerful sound was the ringing of the muffin man's bell as he came round the Square. But, alas! he was allowed to pass unheeded.[23]

Molly Hughes provides a fuller account of what sparse pleasures could be found, especially if one's parents were not too strict themselves in their observance of convention:

The afternoons hung heavy. It seemed to be always three o'clock.
All amusements, as well as work, was forbidden. It was a real
privation not to be allowed to draw and paint. However, an
exception was made in favour of illuminated texts, and we
rivalled the old monks in our zeal for copying Scripture, with
the same kind of worldly decorations that they devised.

Naturally, our main stand-by was reading, but here again
our field was limited by Mother's notions of what was appropriate for Sunday. *Tom Brown*, *Robinson Crusoe*, Hans An-
dersen's *Tales*, and *Pilgrim's Progress* were permitted, but not
the *Arabian Nights*, or Walter Scott, or indeed any novel. We
had to fall back on bound volumes of *Good Words for the
Young*, which were not so bad as the title suggests, and
contained plenty of stories.

Sunday newspapers did exist, but were not respectable. How
horrified my father was on discovering that the servants had
been reading little bits to me out of *Lloyd's Weekly*! My
father's Sunday efforts weakened towards evening, and after
tea he liked to read aloud to us from books that sounded quite
well, but afforded some chance of frivolity. Of course Shakespeare is Shakespeare. *Ingoldsby Legends* were always in
demand, and above all the *Misadventure at Margate*, which
we knew almost by heart. *Pickwick Papers*, by some blessed
workings of Mother's conscience, did not come under the head
of novels. They were 'papers'. She herself led the laughter.
Often my father would read us things that he loved.[24]

Charles Russell, who grew up in Ireland, similarly suggested in
his memories of childhood that not everything about a Sunday
need be dull:

No cooking that might be done on Saturday was allowed. After
dinner each of us had to read a chapter of the Bible aloud, while

mamma and dada listened respectfully. The piano was never heard, except to accompany a hymn; no game of cards was allowed; but all sorts of childish games, such as riddles, conundrums, stories, etc. made our evening cheerful.[25]

William Tayler, the footman, described what must have been for him a fairly typical Sunday in 1837, on which his elderly employer split the difference between respectability and enjoyment, social duty and relaxation:

This Sunday a wet, boisterous day. Been to church of course. Our old lady is got quite well, thinks of little else but playing cards and paying visits all the time. When I went to take lunch up, she was making matches or candlelights. When I took lunch away, she was reading a novel with the Bible laying beside her, ready to take up if any body came in. She had a lady to dine with them. During dinner, the conversation turned on wordly [i.e. worldly] affairs – nothing relating to religion. At tea time, she was talking about china, how much was broke in our house and what it would cost to replace it again. I think these were excellent ideas for an old lady near eighty years of age on a Sunday, but for all this she is not a bad one in the end.[26]

Not Like Other Days

For those who were as concerned with social ritual as with religious duty – or indeed even more so – the Sunday walk was an established routine. During the Season, fashionable families in London walked to the only place it would occur to them to visit – Hyde Park. Even there, it was necessary to be very discriminating about where one went, as the biographer of one young woman recorded:

On Sundays [the highest Society] stayed indoors or were out of town. But the rest, all those who, without being right at the top, were very near it, might be seen sitting on garden chairs or walking up and down a relatively small area of the lawns in the southern and south-eastern part of the Park. The exact spot was determined by fashion, too: 'We went to the grass just beyond the Achilles statue, which is now the thing.'[27]

Clearly, even if there was a broad consensus among society that Sundays should be treated as a day of rest, opinions varied about how strict its observance should be.

It must be remembered that at this time many people worked six days a week. Sunday was not *half* of their weekend but the whole of it. There was not time to cram it with many of the things that for us fill the gap between Friday night and Monday morning. As a result, Sunday was a genuine day of rest whose differences – such as the eating of the week's most elaborate meal and the chance to doze in an armchair after-wards – could be savoured. Where the church was the centre of a family's social life, it provided – as it does to this day – the opportunity to see friends with whom one was not in touch during the week. Because it offered, through its services and social events and choir practices, the company of the opposite sex in surroundings of irreproachable respectability, it fea-tured prominently in the courting of many Victorian couples. Even children, though often imprisoned in starched and un-comfortable Sunday dresses or sailor suits, could enjoy certain pleasures. There was available an extensive variety of maga-zines and journals, with titles like *The Quiver* and *Sunday at Home*, which were intended for family reading on Sunday afternoons and which filled the long afternoon hours with stories, puzzles and games. If the Sabbath must be devoted to worthy thoughts and pursuits, there was at least no shortage of advice available on how to make the most of what was allowed.

Many published memoirs of childhood, like Ernest Shepard's, relate to the last twenty years of Victoria's reign. The older – and often elderly – relatives who dictated their behaviour were therefore products of an earlier mindset rather than typical of current attitudes. By the time the Queen died, the rigidity with which Sunday had been observed in the mid-century seemed more and more of an anachronism. Society, led by the example of the Prince of Wales, had created the 'weekend', for the railways had long since made it possible to travel to country houses far outside London. These gatherings began later – on Saturday afternoon – than would be the case in future generations, and were known as 'Saturday to Mondays'. They gradually popularized the notion that this part of the week could be spent entirely on pleasure. Another factor was that there was simply more to do. New sports and new facilities provided a host of temptations that had not existed, or been so obvious, in the early and middle decades. For those who lived in the burgeoning suburbs there were golf clubs, and for those in town who wished to visit the country there were bicycles. The Sabbath closing of museums was no longer as strictly carried out as in the days of Dickens' Arthur Clennam. The British Museum, if that may be taken as a national litmus test, began opening on Sunday afternoons in 1895.

The Best Tunes

For those who were fond of music – even if they did not, like Molly Hughes, have the resources of a mighty cathedral to entertain them – there was much about a church service to enjoy. Prior to the nineteenth century there had been hymns of beauty that could inspire, but to a large extent the custom had been, in a world of widespread illiteracy in which hymnbooks would have been superfluous, that throughout the service the Bible Clerk would read aloud each line of a hymn or psalm and the congregation would repeat it. This could, of course, be extremely long-winded and uninspiring. The Wesleys and their movement had provided more rousing and memorable hymns, but it was not until religious revival hit its stride in the nineteenth century that there was a flowering of this type of church music, for the Victorians, as it were, mass-produced them. The printing of music became cheaper and easier and this, added to the popularity of sacred subjects, brought a flood of new hymns. One man – H. J. Gauntlett, who wrote the music for *Once in Royal David's City* – allegedly produced 10,000 hymn tunes.

A glance through the Church of England's indispensable *Hymns Ancient and Modern*, itself a Victorian publication (its first edition appeared in 1861), will reveal how many of them – and how many of the great and stirring hymns that are popular even with non-believers – were written at this time. The list includes *Fight the Good Fight, Crown Him with Many Crowns, Alleluia, Sing to Jesus* and *Through the Night of Doubt and Sorrow*, as well as such Christmas favourites as *In the Bleak Midwinter, As with Gladness Men of Old, Shepherds in the Fields Abiding* and *O Little Town of Bethlehem*. Among the mission halls and revival meetings, at which the singing was a good deal less genteel and more hearty, there was similarly a wealth of rousing, inspiring music in the form of 'choruses', many of which are still doing duty in churches today. As William Booth, the founder of the Salvation Army, once put it: 'Why should the Devil have all the best tunes?' The act of worship was rendered much more enjoyable by this outpouring of spiritual creativity.

Why It Mattered

Religious observance was not simply for Sundays. The reading of Scripture or the saying of prayers was a fixture of the daily life of many households, serving several purposes. It was an important part of the Victorian ethos that the servant-keeping class reinforce their authority by setting a good example. For the master of the house to do this by leading worship was seen to add to his dignity and enhance his status. The short service also enabled the household to assemble and begin the day together – no doubt as soon as the devotions were over, the master would use the opportunity to give instructions to the servants, or to speak to any particular one if it were necessary. The mistress could well be inspecting the housemaids' appearance and demanding adjustments if necessary. The cook might be in the habit of staying behind to go over the day's menu. It was, in other words, a small-scale version of a school's morning assembly, and served the same purpose – to provide a formal start to the day by bringing together everyone in the community, and to combine this with an opportunity to sort out the day's administration. In the British Army a daily gathering of a regiment's officers and NCOs to hear the colonel's instructions is still often referred to as 'morning prayers'.

Edith Buxton, the daughter of the missionary C. T. Studd, recalled the formality of this ritual, at which the family was joined – in strict hierarchical order – by the housekeeper, butler, footman and maids:

> The morning began with family prayers. If it was winter a bright fire would be burning in the grate, which reflected in the brass eagles on either side. They held the tongs and poker, and the steel and brass shone to distraction. My Father sat at the table, already spread for breakfast, with the Bible open. There

would be the sound of the fire crackling, and the rustle of Mrs Miles' starched dress and apron as she led the way in, followed by Ryall and Charles, then Jenkins and Roland, the house-maids. There followed the droning of Father's voice, and far away the intermittent sounds of Bayswater Road.[28]

And George Sala, writing of an imaginary household in the fifties, describes the attitudes of those taking part. No one, including the man conducting the service, wants to be there. The servants and the children fidget, their minds on other things. They see this interlude as an unwelcome interruption to the day, something to be got over with:

> The servants come in, not to morning breakfast, but to morn-ing prayers. The housemaid has just concluded her morning flirtation with the baker; the cook has been crying over 'Fatherless Fanny'. The master of the house reads prayers in a harsh, grating voice, and Miss Charlotte, aged thirteen, is sent to her bed-room, with prospects of additional punishment, for eating her curl-papers during matins.[29]

The emergent middle classes, unsure of their status in society and wishing to be punctilious in their observance of conven-tion, aped the perceived behaviour of the aristocracy and gentry. If these occasions were traditional in country houses, then they must be observed in suburban villas too, for a paternalistic interest in the spiritual welfare of one's domestics was clearly a badge of belonging to the 'right sort'. Since servants gossiped a great deal, it might be that the family who employed them did not want news to get out among others of their class that they failed to conduct matters properly.

Missions

Although it is undeniable that many Victorians saw religious observance as a tiresome ritual, we must not underestimate the extent to which a live, sincere and passionate belief influenced people of all classes. The country not only sent missionaries abroad during these years but *received* them, and with results that were often spectacular. The missions conducted by two Americans – Dwight Moody and Ira Sankey – had an effect on Victorians that is hard to underestimate now. Moody was a preacher, his partner wrote and played hymns. They had already had a considerable impact on the faith of their own countrymen when they first came to the United Kingdom in 1875, and they returned in 1884. They brought something of the atmosphere of an American tent mission, and perhaps their approach to conversion was more direct than the British were accustomed to. At any rate, they were highly successful. Moody's preaching was brilliant and inspiring, and the accompanying music in itself was enough to draw many in. They made thousands of converts, and their visits are still remembered as a landmark in British church history. The forceful impact of such an evangelical crusade could result in some unlikely conversions, for it was not only the poor or the dissatisfied who found faith but others who appeared to be content with their lives. One of these was a Mr Vincent, a wealthy retired planter whose passion was for horseracing. Returning from Punchestown races in Ireland one evening, he missed the boat back to England and found himself obliged to stay the night in Dublin. The American evangelists happened to be holding a series of meetings in the city at that time, and by chance he came across them. An author describes how:

> He was at a loose end, and not knowing how to spend the evening, took a stroll. He noticed over a theatre the names

'D.L. Moody and Ira D. Sankey', wondered what Vaudeville Company this was, and went in. He was amazed to find the place crowded out, and on the platform a number of people in ordinary dress and a man singing. He had a wonderful voice, and was singing words such as he had never heard before. He stood absolutely riveted.

The hymn over, he sat down and heard Moody preach, and strange to relate, instead of going home next day, he stayed on day after day. Finally, one evening he followed a great throng of people who rose to go into the Enquiry Room. Moody knelt beside him and simply said, 'Mr Vincent, do you believe Jesus Christ died for you?' 'I do,' he replied. 'Then,' said Moody, 'thank Him.' He did, and he left that room a transformed man.[30]

A short time later, in London, he met an old friend, Edward Studd, who was also a planter and racing enthusiast. He persuaded Studd to accompany him to Drury Lane, to which the Americans had now brought their mission. Studd was in his turn deeply touched by Moody's preaching, and he too returned on subsequent evenings to hear more sermons. Within days he had undergone conversion and his hedonistic, raffish lifestyle had altered beyond recognition:

He withdrew from the Turf, giving a racehorse to each of his elder sons as a hunter, and then sold the remainder. He cleared out the hall of his house at Tedworth and put in chairs and benches; then he rode round the countryside to urge his neighbours to come in on Sunday evenings, and used to get splendid fellows down from London, merchants and business men, to preach the Gospel to the people. They came in their hundreds, filling up the staircase to the first floor, leaning over the balconies to hear. Moody himself came.[31]

Studd's new-found faith was no mere passing fad. He preached relentlessly – and effectively – to all with whom he came in contact. When attending Moody and Sankey's later meetings in London, he took his carriage, and his granddaughter recalled that 'he would come out at half time and send in the coachman and footman, and hold the horses himself.'[32] He also gave financial assistance to the building of the Moody Bible Institute in Chicago, which rapidly became a power-house for the training of evangelists. He died only two years after his conversion, but his family carried on his work, principally in the overseas mission field.

All three of his sons became Christians. They were known throughout the country during the eighties because – as out-standing cricketers – they had all, in succession, been captains of the Cambridge University XI. That one of them, Charles ('C. T.'), became a missionary tells us something significant about the extent to which active Christianity had penetrated the social and intellectual elite. In the late eighteenth and early nineteenth centuries, missionaries had been, almost without exception, poor men from humble walks of life. William Carey, for instance, the Baptist evangelist who made an immense impact in India at that time, was a shoemaker. Missionaries were therefore people who – seen from a worldly point of view – had not given up much in the way of material comfort or future greatness to 'follow the call'. Such was the power of Christian revival that at Cambridge University in 1885 – amid a spate of conversions – Studd and six others volunteered to devote their lives to working for the China Inland Mission. 'The Cambridge Seven', willingly turning their backs on comfortable backgrounds and bright prospects for the work of the Gospel, became national celebrities. Studd's daughter described them. They included:

The stroke of the Cambridge boat, and the stroke of one of the trial eights, a dragoon Guardsman, an officer of the Royal Artillery, and the son and heir of a titled family in Norfolk. In the history of missions no band of volunteers has caught the imagination of the public as much as these seven. Queen Victoria was pleased to receive a booklet giving their testimonies [each one's account of his conversion]. Such was the stir among the universities that their sailing had to be put off so that they could go to Edinburgh and speak at the urgent request of the leading professors. In a hall packed with 2,000 students they were cheered again and again as they rose to speak.[33]

While Studd's father had undergone conversion to the Christianity of the Gospel mission, it is worth remembering that equally sincere tendencies could lead in the opposite direction. John Patrick Crichton-Stuart inherited a vast fortune, together with the title Marquess of Bute, six months after his birth in 1847. His father had belonged to the Church of Scotland and he had been brought up in the Church of England. At Oxford he changed his Anglicanism for an equally devout Catholicism (and was therefore asked to leave); his conversion caused a considerable stir in London society, and was described by Disraeli in his novel *Lothair*. Until his death in 1899, Bute remained a highly influential champion of Catholic interests.

By the end of the century the Church had lost a good deal of its monopoly on charitable work. Secular organizations and political bodies had taken on much the same functions and this meant that religion and charity were no longer seen as synonymous. Science also battered at the gates of Christian orthodoxy. Until Victoria's reign there had been no alternative to belief in divine creation of the world, and it had been established by theologians that this took place in 4004 BC. The science of geology was able to prove that the earth – and even animal life – was very much older than this. The publication of Charles Darwin's *Origin of Species* in 1859 – and the work that followed in 1871, *The Descent of Man* – offered an alternative to the concept that man was created, suggesting that the whole of human life was the result of circumstance. In addition to this, theologians discovered that the translations of the Bible on which Anglican worship had been based for centuries were inaccurate, and therefore that parts of the Scriptures were open to doubt. The unreliability of some of the Bible laid the rest of it open to doubt in many minds. The Christian Church had never in history faced challenges like these to its basic tenets. The apparently flourishing condition of religion at the end of the century, when millions still regularly attended services and religious organizations continued to receive widespread support, is testimony to the strength of faith within all branches of Christianity.

Throughout Victoria's reign, the Christian life of Britain expanded in all directions. The Catholic tendency spread its influence at the same time as the Gospel missions. Religion therefore became much more all-encompassing, and succeeded in offering something to virtually everyone. By the end of the century, no one could possibly accuse the Church of irrelevance, indifference or ineffectuality. It had not solved all the problems that beset it at the beginning of the era, but it had adapted, been revitalized and had managed to give an effective lead in many crucial areas. For all the criticism that it was bound by 'humbug and hypocrisy' it had become more vital, accomplished more, and greatly widened the debate.

ETIQUETTE AND FASHION

Doing the Right Thing

When George IV visited Edinburgh in 1822 it was the first royal visit to the country for over 160 years, and there were no useful precedents to guide the public. Local newspapers received numerous letters from gentlemen asking what was the form of dress to be worn when attending public places such as roadsides to watch the King pass by. There was no such dress, and therefore no satisfactory answer. Nevertheless one member of the public, who seemed to know what he was talking about, wrote that the correct costume consisted of white denim trousers and a navy-blue swallow-tail coat. This was widely accepted, and in the event was worn by many men. Such a situation could have occurred at any time during the nineteenth century, for correct dress was as important as correct behaviour, and those who sought respectability always went in terror of not knowing the right thing to do. An unexplained but categorical sentence in a book on manners that states 'As a matter of course, young ladies do not eat cheese at dinner parties'[1] would have been accepted without demur in thousands of middle-class homes.

This level of respect for conformity is difficult to understand from a modern perspective, but until the 1950s society was run from the top, with modes being created by the aristocracy (the concepts of 'street fashion' and 'street credibility' would have been unthinkable to Victorians other than as a form of fancy dress). This fortunate class, even if it was steadily losing power and influence throughout the reign, still appeared to be a keeper of secrets to which others wished to be privy.

Etiquette was not peculiar to the Victorians, who inherited a good deal of social ritual from the preceding era. In the nineteenth century, as in the eighteenth, there were forms of behaviour that were practised by the 'best people' and imitated to a greater or lesser extent by those farther down the scale. Where there was no established etiquette for a particular situation, it seems to have been necessary to invent it. An authentic-sounding practice might well be thought up on the spur of the moment and become enshrined in custom.

Dos and Don'ts

Victorian society was obsessed with status and social advancement. The era saw the rise of a huge and wealthy middle class whose members – pleased with their attainments but unsure how to behave – looked to the aristocracy for social guidance (the nobility responded with varying degrees of disdain). As a result, what were perceived to be the habits and practices of the traditional ruling class were imitated or adapted in thousands of bourgeois homes. The newly genteel, or the aspiringly genteel, needed a good deal of specific and detailed guidance on how to dress, what to eat, where to be seen and – crucially – how to entertain. Because this class went in fear of committing social *faux pas*, publishers provided them with a battery of books and articles to address these issues. Some were in the form of 'agony aunt' newspaper columns that advised anonymous enquirers about specific difficulties. Others were textbooks of behaviour, some with reader-friendly subject categories that were designed to be kept handy and used for reference. Often they were anonymous, or written under such pseudonyms as 'A Lady' or 'A Member of the Aristocracy', implying that some well-bred personage was willing to pass on, as a public duty, the necessary knowledge. The large number of these produced from the middle of the century is evidence of the extent of society's preoccupation with social niceties.

The Morning Call

Though entirely forgotten today, the complex procedures for giving and receiving social calls occupied the energies of many thousands of women, in towns and cities throughout Britain, until almost within living memory.

'Leaving cards', a handbook on manners informed its readers, 'is the first step towards forming, or enlarging, a circle of acquaintance.'[2] Whether the visiting lady met the owner of the house in person or merely left her card with a servant, this was an important social rite, a way of stating one's own – and one's family's – social credentials (or pretensions) and recognizing those of others. Even at the end of the nineteenth century, when women were increasingly taking advantage of opportunities for education and employment, it was unthinkable for a married woman of the middle class to work. With household staff to relieve them of much of the domestic drudgery, the exchanging of visits and the consequent maintenance of social rituals filled a large part of the lives of many Victorian ladies. The time for making these calls was mid-afternoon, for the morning would be spent planning menus, dealing with household accounts and writing letters. Only at a suitable interval after luncheon would a lady send for her carriage and set out to fulfil her obligations.

Visits were not made before three o'clock in the afternoon, and never after five unless the visitor knew the family extremely well. The convention was that from three to four was the most formal time to visit, suitable for strangers or slight acquaintances; from four to five was a somewhat more relaxed period, fitting for those who may have known the hostess for some time. From five to six was for relations or old friends. In spite of all this, the practice of visiting was referred to as 'morning calls'. Each woman involved knew exactly what was expected of her, either as visitor or hostess. A lady would let it be known among her circle of acquaintance that she was 'at home' to callers on one, or perhaps two, particular days every week. This saved her the trouble of having to remain in her house on the other afternoons. She, and often her female relatives, would then sit in the drawing-room waiting to be visited, while a maid, or in grander houses a butler, would be stationed by the front door. The servants might have prepared some light refreshments, but this was by no means necessary. Calls were brief, and the time was to be spent in conversation. The necessity of feeding a stream of guests – and the guests' need to juggle a teacup and plate while talking – would have made such arrangements difficult, while the fact that callers visited several houses in an afternoon would also have involved the risk of overeating.

The ladies who called would be specially, and very smartly, dressed for visiting, and would change once they got home.

Those that were not 'carriage folk' – unable to afford to keep a vehicle of their own – might have hired one for the occasion, especially if the houses they were visiting were some distance out in the suburbs. Like her hostess, a caller might be accompanied by a sister or daughter. For girls who were not well-connected enough to be presented at Court, taking part in these occasions was their first venture into the adult world and something of a rite of passage. The necessity of sitting without fidgeting in a series of drawing rooms while her mother went repeatedly through the same conversations was probably something of a trial, but there was compensation in the wearing of new dresses or in the feeling that one was now considered an adult.

The girls would be armed with that important symbol of maturity, their own visiting cards. According to established practice and as advised in books on etiquette: 'A lady's visiting card should be printed in a small, clear copper plate type, and free from any kind of embellishment. It should be thin card, and three and a half inches in depth or even smaller. The name of the lady should be printed in the left-hand corner.'[3]

Such young women would long since have been schooled in how to behave when making calls, and they would naturally have learned the corresponding etiquette for receiving visitors – how, for instance, to greet new acquaintances by holding out their right arm with two fingers extended, while family friends and relatives were offered three.

This custom was universal and was in some circumstances also followed by men. Today the use of 'two fingers' has entirely different connotations, and it therefore seems curious to read references to it, as in this account of a visit to Harrow School by Prince Albert: 'The Prince, preceded by the Marquis of Abercorn and two others, advances, bowing low, presents two fingers to [the Headmaster] and is bowed up the steps.'[4]

To us it may seem trivial that anyone should care how many fingers are thrust at them, but to contemporaries it was a small but significant matter, and offence could easily be caused. At the court of the German Emperor – for this practice, like many points of nineteenth-century etiquette, was understood throughout Europe – a visiting Russian princess created outrage in this way. A memoir recalls that: 'she is no favourite with Their Majesties. She gives herself insufferable airs, and only deigns to give the Empress, her hostess, two fingers when they meet, which infuriates both the Emperor and the Empress. It is strange how often princesses forget to behave like ladies!'[5]

Calling was obligatory under some circumstances – to thank those who had shown hospitality, to offer congratulations on a birth or marriage, to commiserate with those who had illness in the family or to offer condolences where illness had proved fatal. Any call paid upon a family had to be returned within a week, or ten days at the most, and failure to do so could cause considerable offence – at least to social equals. A feud that rumbled for many years in one London family apparently began because two daughters had failed to visit their cousins after being invited to a ball. Sometimes, if the caller were extremely fastidious, they might abort a visit for some reason. Ernest Shepard remembered that his maiden aunts used to exchange calls with the clergy of their parish church, but that their violent disapproval of smoking once got the better of their sense of correct form: 'Mr Paget was the rector of St Pancras, and the curates used to make duty calls on the Aunts. It is recorded that on one occasion, while they were returning the call of a newcomer, and were waiting in the sitting room, the Aunts saw on the mantelpiece a TOBACCO PIPE! And that was the end of that call.'[6]

Leaving Cards

By no means all social calls involved actually meeting anyone. It was extremely common to find that the person one was visiting was out – or at least 'not at home'. This meant a further ritual, for a caller would leave a card or, if she were a married woman, three. As ladies were advised in the nineties: 'It is now considered old-fashioned for husbands and wives to have their names printed on the same card: they should have separate cards of their own.'[7] The caller would present one of her own cards and two from her spouse – one for the hostess and one for her husband, who could expect to find a pile of these on a tray in the entrance hall when he returned that evening. It was part of this ceremony that if the mistress of the house had one or more grown-up daughters the visitor would turn down one corner of the cards – by custom the top right-hand one – to show that they had been included in the call. Another aspect of this practice was that a turned-down corner meant the card had been delivered in person by someone who had intended to call, rather than merely handed in by a servant.

If the lady were not at home, her visitor would save time, and could go on to the next address on her list (on an average day, a caller might expect to pay between three and six visits). In the grandest circles, even the simple act of leaving cards could be carried out almost with the pomp of a diplomatic mission. An aristocratic lady would be accompanied on her round of calls by a pair of liveried footmen (always chosen for impressive – and matching – height) who would sit or stand at the back of her carriage. On reaching her destination they would dismount in unison and proceed in step to the front door where, after knocking, they would enquire if the lady of the house was at home. If she were not, they would return to their mistress to receive the necessary number of cards, which they would then march back and deliver to the butler.

Should the hostess be at home, they would fold down the carriage steps and assist their mistress to dismount, then remain outside awaiting her return (and probably spend the time in gossiping with other servants, who were gathered for the same purpose). At the end of the call the departing visitor would leave two of her husband's cards on the hall table, but, the socially unwary were warned: 'Neither put them in the card basket nor leave them on the drawing room table, nor offer them to the hostess, all of which is very incorrect.'[8]

The practice of leaving visiting cards did not date from time immemorial. The use of pasteboard slips bearing one's name and address had developed in France only at the beginning of the nineteenth century, and had attained its level of elaborate complexity in British society by the fifties. However difficult we may find it to understand these formalities, they served a useful purpose. Visiting cards became widespread and popular in Britain for the same reason that the business card continues to be essential today: it was a quick and convenient way of introducing oneself, either to people met in the flesh or to those to whom it had to be sent. It ensured that they had one's details to hand, and perhaps provided some piece of information that would pique curiosity or excite interest.

The present writer's great-grandfather, a tea planter, used a card when in London that simply read: 'Mr George Paterson, Ceylon'. Since tea was the most important business carried out on that island, it gave others a fairly accurate idea of his occupation, and the fact that he had no address in Britain indicated that he was still involved in it. Many such cards, whether used for business or social reasons, would be sent in to someone before their owner was admitted. They were a useful way of assessing a visitor and deciding whether their call was to be received. They thus saved time, trouble and possible embarrassment.

The Hostess

Once inside a house, and after being relieved of outer clothing, the caller would follow the butler or maid to the drawing room. The servant would knock, go in, and announce the name of the visitor before standing aside to let her enter. The hostess was expected to rise and come forward to greet her caller, but under no circumstances to utter such vulgarities as 'take a seat'. Nor was she expected to ask where her guest would *like* to sit. She should simply indicate a chair near her own.

A call would be required to last at least fifteen minutes – the minimum that politeness allowed – but never longer than thirty. By convention nothing but small-talk was permitted. For those who enjoyed serious discussion it would be something of an ordeal, and the more educated and aggressive 'new women' of Victoria's latter years were often impatient with the conversational froth that seemed to satisfy their more traditional counterparts. There was, however, a good reason for this understanding: no subject must be brought up that would either arouse strong feelings or result in lengthy conversation, for both hostess and visitor had to get on.

The filling of the brief interlude would present no difficulty if the hostess were well practised in the social arts, though time might hang heavy in the company of a young and inexperienced wife. It was against the rules to rely on conversational props to sustain a dialogue, as the manuals explained:

A hostess betrays that she is not much accustomed to society when she attempts to amuse her visitors by the production of albums of photographs, books, illustrated newspapers, port-folios of drawings, and artistic efforts of members of the family, and the like. She should rely solely upon her own powers of conversation to make the short quarter of an hour pass pleasantly for the visitor. She should not offer her visitor any refreshments, wine and cake for instance. But if tea is brought in while the visitor is in the drawing room, or if the visitor calls while the hostess is having tea, she should naturally offer her visitor tea.[9]

The Gentlemen

Men were not excluded from these events, but it was taken for granted that they would seldom be present, for it was the duty of women to maintain this institution, and a man might seem as out of place as he would in a milliner's shop. Men would either be earning their living or socializing – at their clubs or on a sports-field – in masculine company. Indeed although wo-men at the end of the Victorian era began to have West End clubs of their own, the afternoon call was in a sense their equivalent. Nevertheless there were, as we have seen, instances where clergymen and others paid social calls on ladies (in an army garrison, newly arrived officers were expected to visit, or leave cards with, the wives of their married colleagues), and the day on which masculine callers – usually young or single – paid their visits was Sunday (confusingly also a day kept for relations and family friends). Should a man arrive, his beha-viour was equally circumscribed:

A gentleman calling should take his hat and stick with him into the drawing room, and hold them until he has seen the mistress of the house and shaken hands with her. He should either place them on a chair or table near at hand, according as to whether he feels at ease or the reverse, until he takes his leave. He should not put on his hat in the presence of his mistress.

To leave his hat on in the hall would be considered a liberty and in very bad taste, only members of the family residing in the same house leave their hats in the hall, or enter the drawing room without their hats in their hands. The fact of hanging up the hat in the hall proves the owner of the hat is at home there.[10]

Should another visitor arrive, it was customary for the first caller to take leave as quickly as politeness allowed, and it is interesting to note that this custom is still often followed in what is perhaps the only remaining situation that resembles a Victorian 'morning call' – the visiting of a patient in hospital, where the length of stay, the possibly stilted small-talk and the sense of obligation to leave once another visitor has arrived are much the same. When a visitor announced her intention to depart, the hostess would shake hands, ring the bell for a servant and see her to the door of the room. The maid, butler or footman would be waiting in the hall to fetch her coat and summon her carriage.

Where, instead of a series of fleeting calls, the hostess actually invited guests to a 'five o'clock tea', the company was more likely to be mixed. Should members of the sterner sex be in attendance, their obligations were explained in a volume called *Manners for Men*:

Their duties are rather onerous if there are but one or two men and the usual crowd of ladies. They have to carry teacups about, hand sugar, cream, and cakes or muffins, and keep up all the time a stream of small-talk, as amusing as they can make it. As regards the viands, a man helps himself, but not till he has seen that all the ladies in his vicinity have everything they can

possibly want. He must rise every time a lady enters or leaves
the room, opening the door for her exit if no one else is nearer
to it and, if the hostess requests him, they must see the lady
downstairs to her carriage or cab.[11]

These social calls were a means by which people of ambition
could attach themselves to a world that they aspired to inhabit,
for if one left a card at somebody's home there was a possibility that it might be acknowledged. People could drop hints
that they wished to be called upon by a particular family,
though this risked a wounding snub. Part of the card-leaving
ritual was the 'cut'. A family that saw itself as above its
neighbours would not acknowledge a card left by them. A
man who was not a suitable companion for a lady's daughter
would not be invited into the house if he sent in his card, and if
someone unacceptable left a card and then saw the recipients
in the street, his greeting would not be returned, thus making it
clear that there should be no further attempts to cultivate their
acquaintance. A cartoon that appeared in *Punch* shows a
matron with her two daughters strolling in Hyde Park. One
of the girls, referring to another woman with similar daughters
whom they have just passed, says: 'There go the Spicer
Wilcoxes, Mamma! I'm told they're dying to know us. Hadn't
we better call?' Her mother replies: 'Certainly not, dear. If
they're dying to know us, they're certainly not worth knowing.
The only people worth our knowing are the people who don't
want to know us!'[12]

While all of this may seem to modern sensibilities both
tiresome and unnecessary, it actually made a good deal of
sense. It offered a means of expanding a circle of acquaintance
while keeping strict control over who was allowed within the
sanctity of one's home. If people would not have made suitable
friends, the system of etiquette made it possible to put them at

a distance while at the same time 'letting them down gently' before a relationship went to lengths that could cause greater embarrassment. Those who think this a dated concept might like to be reminded of two present-day practices that represent precisely the same attitude. If someone receives every year a Christmas card from a person they do not wish to continue acquaintance with, they fail to send a card in return. That is usually enough to make sure that the following year they will not be troubled again. Secondly, a young woman may spend an evening with a man she decides she does not like enough to see again. When he asks for her telephone number, she gives him a false one. Both are ways of 'snipping the thread' of acquaintance without giving serious offence.

Courting

The chaperone is a Victorian stock figure, imagined as a humourless old maid whose fixed purpose was to prevent others from having a type of companionship that she herself had never enjoyed. It is assumed that she was hated by both her female charge and by the young man whose designs she was frustrating. The reality was usually very different. Chaperones – at least the type that appeared at social gatherings – were seldom old maids. No one who did not have a sociable disposition and was not herself at home at a ball or a card-party would be of much use in the role, for part of her task was to introduce her protégé to agreeable companions both young and old. Her duties were defined in a book on manners:

> She must not show fatigue nor look cross, no matter what her feelings may be. It is a part of her duty to be entertaining and agreeable, and thus form an attractive background to her young charge. A brilliant woman who is also an amiable

and unselfish one has great opportunities for helping her young people to 'have a good time'. Young men like to talk to her, and she takes care to introduce them. If she has good spirits, they are contagious to all around her, and her cleverness and ready answers inspire and amuse the young people and put them at their ease. She must not, however, endeavour to shine too brightly, lest she put out the lesser lights which it is her duty to tend and brighten.[13]

A chaperone was very often the young woman's mother. Alternatively she might be a youngish aunt, a family friend or an older sister, married or otherwise. She needed to be someone with experience of Society, for she would have to give advice as well as protection. Her greater experience might have made her conversation interesting and entertaining, so she could be popular in her own right. She had to be not only a guide for the younger woman through the jungle of social behaviour but a mentor, or what would now be called a 'role model', for her behaviour could be studied and her mannerisms copied. One of her duties was to introduce the young lady to her female friends, who could then invite her to their own entertainments. Through her contacts, she could know something of the reputation and character of men who asked her protégé to dance, and would be able to nip in the bud any unsuitable friendships, for chaperones were there to 'guard young girls from bad and designing people, and from penniless young men and rash romantic marriages as well'.[14] She was on the lookout for suitable partners to introduce. When dealing with a gentleman considered worth encouraging, a good chaperone was often adept at disappearing, or becoming distracted, at strategic moments, and many engagements were the result of such tactful momentary withdrawals. A chaperone, after all, would have passed her own rites of passage, perhaps only a few years previously, and could often be relied upon to be sympathetic.

Chaperones were not only to be found at formal evening functions, they went wherever young girls did. They attended the theatre, race meetings, sports matches, picnics. For a debutante to be seen at this type of event without one would have struck others as unusual and improper. One book stated that:

> At country out-of-door gatherings, such as garden-parties, lawn-tennis parties, archery parties and so on, the chaperonage is of comparatively slight nature, but at all other entertainments it is imperative that a young lady be accompanied by a chaperone, whether it be a dinner or a dance, an afternoon tea or an evening assembly, a concert or ball, or theatre etc; and a young lady who attempts to evade this received rule would be considered unconventional and unused to the conveniences prescribed by society. The bias of many young ladies of the present day is to assert as much independence of action as opportunity offers, but any dereliction in this respect is noted to their disadvantage.[15]

Chaperones – and here the girl's mother was most likely to fulfil the function – would also expect to be present when a man called upon her at her home. So long as the mother was present somewhere in the vicinity, it was not necessary for her to be obtrusive – especially if she actually wanted the relationship to develop:

> Mamma does well to sit in the other parlour with her book or work and give the young people a little freedom. Whether she remains in the parlour or not, however, she must never go to bed until all callers have left the house.[16]

It was of course as easy for Victorians as it is for us to become passionate. One important difference was that they knew very little about contraception. Pregnancy in the wrong circumstances would have ruined the prospects of any young gentlewoman (in spite of which it was not uncommon. Ways had to be contrived for the ladies affected to be sent abroad, or into the country, until the child was born and farmed out). It was imperative to keep a daughter's marriage prospects healthy by seeing to it that she had a blameless character – no matter how much this went against her own nature – and to give gossips no ammunition. Such women had to be protected not only against caddish members of their own class but against insolence and embarrassment from those of lower station.

Sound Advice

Books on manners state that it is unthinkable, for instance, that a young lady should arrive at a railway station without having some man to meet her there. If she did not, she would be obliged to secure a porter and a cabbie herself, which could involve her in unpleasant exchanges, or she might get lost, and become vulnerable to comment from undesirables. If a stranger offered to carry her luggage, she would then be put under an obligation to him, which would be awkward. If she were to maintain her good character, she must not be seen with men for whose presence there was not a good explanation. This matter is touched upon by an author in relation to girls enjoying even the company of their own class:

> It seems hardly necessary to say that a young lady must not go to a restaurant with a young man unless a chaperone accompanies them; neither must she go on 'excursions' of any sort. Especially should she avoid the fascinations and uncertainties

of the sailing-boat. If the boat be becalmed, it may be hours before a landing can be affected; indeed, a sailing-party is sometimes obliged to stay out all night. Hence much unfavourable comment arises; and perhaps a single careless act of this sort may be remembered spitefully against a girl for many years. Especially will this be the case if she is pretty and attractive, and if she has frank and cordial manners.[17]

Women in all eras have been subject to both gossip and unwanted attentions. In Victorian times there was no legislation to protect them against 'sexual harassment', and this task had therefore to be undertaken by family and friends. Marriage – the only acceptable domestic arrangement other than spinsterhood – was expected to be entered into responsibly and undertaken only when the man was able to afford it. The passions of young people had to be kept in check until that time. It was also necessary to fend off any unsuitable marriage that might be entered into for romantic reasons. However much a woman's head might be turned by love for someone, divorce was both extremely difficult to obtain and a very considerable disgrace, and would affect not only the couple themselves but their entire families.

Ironically – and this is a sitting target for those who like to dwell on the hypocrisy of the Victorians – it was well known that in the 'faster' sections of Society a young woman, once married, was regarded as having crossed a threshold of sexual availability and that she could have extramarital affairs wherever she wanted. Until then it was accepted that the young and impressionable needed guidance from their elders if they were to avoid rash mistakes that might have consequences for years afterwards. While chaperones busied themselves with arranging the dance-cards of their young women, the girls themselves might be signalling, unobtrusively but directly, to men whom they favoured or wished to avoid.

The Language of the Fan

Until the Victorian era, with its techniques of mass-production, well-made fans had been too expensive for more than a few ladies to use. They were chiefly confined to royal courts, and there was an etiquette regarding their use. They were normally carried closed, and for a woman to manipulate and wave about a fan in the way that the later Victorian code suggests would have been seen as evidence of very low breeding. The Dutch court had, in the eighteenth century, a certain tradition of signalling with fans, though it was not extensive. In the first half of the nineteenth century, the fans carried by ladies in British society came from Paris – as did the etiquette that went with them – but there is little evidence of gestures being used. It was not until the sixties that the great French fan-maker Duvelleroy sent one of his sons to London to open a shop in Regent Street, where it was an immediate success. Its proprietor, however, deliberately fostered the notion of a code of signals – and invented a number of them – as a means of selling his wares. The Victorian language of the fan was therefore to a large extent simply an advertising gimmick.

The fan was an essential part of the social equipment of any female member of polite society. It was necessary not only for keeping cool in overheated ballrooms but for a number of other purposes. Holding it over the face when enduring the conversation of bores meant that one could hide one's expression – and indulge in a surreptitious yawn – without seeming impolite. For those who wished to flirt, or conversely to discourage the advances of others, there was a language of signals that, to those with the necessary understanding, could convey precise reactions or opinions. For instance, touching the right cheek with the fan and leaving it there meant 'yes', doing the same on the left cheek meant 'no'. Fanning oneself slowly gave the information 'I am married'. To fan quickly meant that the young woman was engaged, but to place the fan, in the left hand, in front of the face meant 'I desire to be acquainted with you.' To make this gesture with the right hand was even more unambiguous, for it meant 'follow me'. Opening the fan wide said 'wait for me'. Placing it open over the heart was an admission that a suitor had won the woman's affection, as did the gesture of drawing the fan across the cheek, while presenting the fan closed to someone was a mute way of asking 'do you love me?'. Drawing the fan across the cheek meant that she loved him, and a half-opened fan pressed to the lips invited him to kiss her, though twirling a fan in the right hand informed him that she loved someone else, and drawing it through the hand told him she hated him. An open fan, held clasped in both hands, meant 'forgive me', and drawing it across the eye meant 'I am sorry', while holding it over the left ear signalled that the woman wished to get rid of the man. Dropping the fan altogether meant 'we will be friends'.

Even allowing for the considerable difference in cultures, it is hard to take all this seriously, and one wonders how many young women found themselves half-way to being engaged because of signals they may inadvertently have made while fiddling with fans in mixed company. Though there is often an assumption that Victorian ladies communicated through a widely understood code of such gestures, it is highly unlikely that this was defined and regimented to such an extent – and if it was, everyone in the room would understand the signals, which would ruin any attempt at secrecy!

The Marriage Mart

Regardless of the wiles they employed, many thousands of women stood little chance of marrying. For the Victorian respectable, there were so many restrictions of class and income that a great many women had little hope. There were just not enough men of sufficient wealth and status to go round. William Tayler, the London footman, wrote of a social gathering at his employer's home in 1837, at which he observed women flirting with a touching desperation. There is something deeply sad about the scene he described:

It's amuseing to see the young ladies, how they manover to make the gentlemen take notice of them. They will loose their pocket handkerchiefs or drop their gloves, that the gents may offer to find them, or they will keep a wine glass or cup and sauser in their hand until after the servant is gone out of the room, so that some of the gents mite take it of them. This [gets] them to change a fiew words. The girls are up to hundreds of these little manovers at parties, to induce the men to begin talking to them. Their mothers take care to give them good instruction how to manage before they leave homes. There is very few of them that get husbands after all, except they are very handsome or got large fortunes, as young gentlemen generally place their affections on some poor but pretty girl and takes her into keeping and when tired of her, turns her off and gets another. If a gentleman maries a lady, it's for her money, and in a short time he gets tired of her and takes up with a kept girl again and treats his wife like a dog. Therefore women in high life has not the opertunity of getting married as those in lower stations, as men in lower stations of life cannot afford to keep girls. Therefore they marrey.[18]

Tayler was writing at the start of the reign. Twenty years later, George Sala lamented, in an equally poignant observation, the dreadful dilemma in which society placed many thousands of young people who were expected to remain 'pure' outside marriage, yet who could not marry because they had not the means. This was a particular hardship for women, who had few other options:

> that better part of creation, whose special vocation it is to be marry, but who are oft-times, alas! as hopelessly celibate as the Trappist. One can scarcely go to a wedding without seeing some of these brave knights-errant, these uncloistered nuns. How many women – young, fair and accomplished, pure and good and wise – are doomed irrevocably to solitude and celibacy! Every man knows such premature old maids; sees among a family of blooming girls one who already wears the stigmata of old maidenhood. It chills the blood to see these hopeless cases, to see the women resign themselves to their fate with a sad meek smile. What dullards were those writers in the 'Times' newspaper about marriage and three hundred a year! Did Adam and Eve have three halfpence a year when they married? Has the world grown smaller? Are there no Australias, Americas, Indies? Are there no such things as marrying on a pound a week in a top garret, and ending in a mansion in Belgrave Square? No such things as toil, energy, perseverance? Husband and wife cheering one another on, and in wealth at last pleasantly talking of the old times, the struggles and difficulties? The proper mission of men is to marry, and of women to bear children; and those who are deterred from marriage in their degree (for we ought neither to expect or desire Squire B. to wed Pamela every day) by the hypocritical cant about 'society' and 'keeping up appearances', had much better send society to the dogs and appearances to the devil, and have nothing more to do with such miserable sophistries.[19]

Shawls and Bonnets

As well as the demands of etiquette, women were constrained for much of the era by fussy and impractical clothing, for although fashion changed as completely during three generations as one would expect, it was only at the beginning and end of Victoria's reign that a degree of simplicity or comfort was achieved. Intriguingly, fashion came full circle, for leg-of-mutton sleeves – much in vogue in the thirties – enjoyed a significant revival in the nineties.

During the Regency, women's dress had been influenced by the French Revolution. In their desire to re-create society in keeping with what was to be an entirely new era, the French had searched history for examples of civilizations whose outlook, styles and political structure they could emulate. They sought in their dress to present a complete contrast with the elaborate costume of the *ancien régime,* and for this they chose Ancient Greece. The 'look' they created spread around the world, regardless of the fact that clothing appropriate for the Mediterranean did not suit the cold and damp of other climates. Dresses became simple and flowing, and the figure was deliberately unrestricted by corsets. Sleeves were usually short, necks and shoulders exposed, and the loose drapery was held in place by a sash beneath the bust. The bows and buttons and lace trimmings of the previous century were banished. Shoes were no longer high-heeled. Women and girls wore simple, flat 'pumps', usually slipped on and off but sometimes secured with laces that tied round the ankle. Underwear was minimal. Simplicity dictated a lack of petticoats, and stockings were tied by garters either above or below the knee. Heads were often unadorned (there was a fashion for short, boyish hair). Hats were also relatively simple in comparison with the often huge, elaborate, feathered and ornamented headdress of previous generations. Altogether, the 'profile' of Regency women was simple and unostentatious. This is, essentially, the costume worn by Princess Victoria in portraits, and it continued to be evident in the first years of her reign.

Changes were creeping in as the basic style was modified. Collars and throat-high dresses were seen again, and the waist became the focus of the dressmaker's skill as garments became tight in that area. Ornament – lace collars and buttons – began to return. Balloon sleeves arrived – close-fitting at the shoulder and wrist but baggy in between. This style, worn with hair tied up at the back or sides of the head, is so distinctive of its era that fashion plates can instantly be dated. For girls, whose skirts were well above their ankles, elaborate drawers that came down to the shoes and looked like long, lace trousers became widespread.

The Cage and the Bustle

By the fifties, skirts had continued spreading until it was not possible to support them without the assistance of a framework of hoops and struts underneath. The crinoline, known as a 'hoop skirt' or 'cage skirt', caused more trouble than any other fashion item during the Victorian era. Though it was, arguably, elegant, it took up so much space that ladies could not sit in chairs that had arms (furniture produced at the time had to make allowances for these dresses), nor could they walk easily on crowded pavements or travel comfortably on trains and buses, and they could only sit down *at all* by sinking at the knees. Crinolines were difficult to get into or out of (a contemporary photograph shows a woman assisted by two servants), and could be a fatal fire hazard. A French actress died when her skirt went up in flames – an understandable danger given the gas lighting and limelight in theatres – and a German noblewoman, discovered smoking, tried to conceal the cigarette in her petticoat but set fire to it and was burned to death. Considering its impracticality the hoop skirt had a remarkably long reign – a period of almost twenty years. It was at this mid-point in the century, when fashion had reached heights of impractical absurdity, that a reaction was launched by the American, Mrs Amelia Bloomer. The garment she devized as a sensible alternative was a pair of very loose trousers that were tight at the ankles. They could be worn either on their own or beneath a short skirt. The notion did not catch on, except with a small minority who met with ridicule. Where women did wear them they tended to do so under long dresses, and 'bloomers' simply became an item of underwear.

A small accessory was added to the wardrobe of British women when Alexandra, Princess of Denmark, arrived in 1863 to marry the Prince of Wales. Because she had a mark on her neck, she wore a black velvet ribbon round her throat. This – the Alexandra choker – was quickly imitated everywhere. While it was elegant, and added to the grace of thousands of young women, another fad inadvertently started by the Princess cannot have looked anything but ludicrous. She hurt her leg in an accident, and for a week or more walked with a noticeable limp. In sympathy, modish young women began to do the same and the 'Alexandra limp' briefly became a sign of being in the vanguard of fashion.

The 'bustle', an exaggerated false posterior that was strapped around the hips and jutted out just below the base of the spine, succeeded the crinoline and it too had a twenty-year reign, until the nineties. At the time it was considered daring, indeed erotic and indecent, though this aspect of it is difficult for us to appreciate. The bustle helped to accentuate the slimness of the waist, though the attainment of an exaggerated 'hourglass figure' could lead to frightening extremes. Waists had become so minute – eighteen inches was the measurement to which the slaves to fashion aspired – that some even went so far as to have their lowest pair of ribs removed, and while few followed vanity to such lengths, there were numerous stories of young women fainting from the tightness of their corsets.

Simplicity

By the nineties there was a palpable contempt for the fussiness of past styles, and this decade saw a rationalization of clothing, particularly for women. The blouse and skirt became ubiquitous. The latter, instead of invariably trailing the ground, was often ankle-length, allowing its wearer to walk briskly, cycle and play golf or tennis. Skirts were tight-waisted but less clumsy, and less covered with useless ornaments – such as rows of frills, bows or stitched-in beads – than the dresses of the previous decade had been. Blouses were very high-necked (usually worn with a brooch or tie) and had leg-of-mutton sleeves that were baggy at the shoulder and upper arm but tight from elbow to wrist. Two-piece suits were also cut with these sleeves. Worn with a miniature straw hat tilted forward on the head, the effect was very pleasing. Unlike many Victorian women's fashions, this nineties look can still impress us with its elegance.

Head-gear

Hats were an essential item of dress in a way that we cannot appreciate. No man or woman during the whole of the nineteenth century would have dreamed of going out with their head deliberately uncovered if they could afford not to – indeed to be seen hatless in the street would be considered a sign of eccentricity if not downright madness. Women who would wear a hat when outdoors would often wear a cap when at home. These were of cotton or linen, and might well cover the hair completely, framing the face with an elaborate frilled border. Widows and matrons were expected to wear these all the time, though women and girls of all ages favoured them, and they were often part of the costume of servants. Those too poor to own a cap would wear their shawl over their head, and anyone who had not even this would be subject to derision (in Glasgow the term 'Hairy' – meaning that a woman had no covering at all – was an indication that someone was at the bottom of the social pile).

For the first part of the reign, hats were much the same. The 'poke bonnet' with its coal-scuttle brim was a symbol of the age. This style could be traced back to the previous century – its shape after all derived from tying a wide-brimmed hat under the chin in such a way that the sides were dragged down to cover the face. The bonnets themselves were elegant, made of straw or any of several types of cloth, their wide ribbons tied in a bow that hung decoratively. Wearing one meant that a woman's face could not be seen except from the front, and she herself was effectively blinkered. Nevertheless, these hats had a long run at the height of fashion, combining successfully with the crinoline but fading away in the sixties when the vogue was for small – often tiny – hats that perched on top of the head. Some of these were pillbox-shaped, others were small and shallow imitations of the bowler, and many styles were worn with a veil. Ladies at this time also took to wearing a version of the top hat for riding.

In the bustle era, women's dresses and figures were intended to be admired in profile, and hats – which remained small – tended to be long and narrow. They often trailed veils or ribbons. In the eighties, hats were still extremely small but tended to be high and decorated with vertical ornaments such as sticking-up feathers. By the nineties low hats with brims, worn tilted at an angle over the brow and fixed to the hair with immense pins, had created a style that was to continue throughout much of the Edwardian period.

The Hair

Hair styles altered in keeping with these hats. When the eighteen-year-old Princess Victoria came to the throne in 1837, fashionable ladies styled their hair with curl papers and piled it on the top of the head, often in festoons above each temple. It was also regarded as modish to coil braided hair into a pillbox shape on top or at the back of the head (the Queen wore her hair this way as a girl). The style that lasted from her accession to the end of the sixties, however, was for hair parted in the middle and tied back in a bun. There were variations on the theme. At her coronation, the Queen wore her hair braided in pigtails at the sides and looped back, under her ears, to join her bun. This was either popular at the time or was copied by many of her female subjects, for it appears often in pictures of early Victorian women. Another widely used technique was to tie back centre-parted hair but to leave extensive, shoulder-length bunches at the sides which were then curled. These had the advantage that when worn with a lace cap or a poke bonnet they framed the face very attractively.

With the pillbox hats of the sixties hair continued to be tied back, though it might be bunched more loosely above the shoulders. A perfect image of this style can be seen in the painting *A Girl of the Sixties* (1899) by the Glaswegian artist Bessie MacNicol. With the seventies, hair began to be worn looser, perhaps pinned back but hanging down behind, and in the following decade, with the small, vertical hats of the eighties, hair was teased into tight curls and worn on top of the head. The nineties brought a greater informality in that hair was once more tied back – or 'put up' on top – in a bun, but it was not restrained so tightly, and it was not squashed down by hats. Instead, these perched upon it, held by pins.

The importance of the shawl for women cannot be under-estimated. These were worn by all classes because they were both decorative and extremely practical, and they were produced in all sizes and in every material from silk to tweed. They covered the head and shoulders, acting as both a hat and an overcoat, but they could also be used for carrying children, or shopping or firewood or anything else that could be lifted on to one's back. Though their use was declining as the century went on – by the seventies and eighties elegant women no longer wore them as a matter of course – they continued in use among the poor until well after Victoria's death.

Footwear

Shoes also began to change. The pumps of the Regency, which had been in a multitude of colours and with round or pointed toes, became predominantly black, with toes square or chisel-shaped. Still flat-heeled and flimsy, they were now commonly tied with long laces that criss-crossed over the instep and were wound around the ankle. Worn with white stockings, the effect was extremely attractive.

These had disappeared by the sixties, as had the poke bonnet, and were replaced by elastic-sided boots, which were *de rigueur* for women and girls during the middle decades. Like the male version, they were flat-soled or built up with a slight heel. For ladies they were made in many disparate shades, though black, white and pearl-grey were perhaps the most commonly seen colours. They might be of leather (kid leather was especially popular), silk or satin, and were often given a pretty two-tone effect with toes of patent leather. On an adult woman, the tips of the toes would be the only part of a shoe visible under her dress.

In the seventies high-heeled, slip-on shoes became widespread, as did the lace-up boot. Having spent several decades in flat shoes, Victorian women went almost to the other extreme, for by the nineties such boots had slender lofty heels and sharply-pointed toes. Some versions, especially those seen in pictures of showgirls, came up to the knee. Most were ankle-length or laced up to the shin at the front and were shaped around the calf at the back. These may have been useful for negotiating muddy town streets, but the heels could easily become stuck in tram-lines or fall foul of similar obstacles. Nevertheless they had about them an undeniable elegance that has caused this type of boot to enjoy several revivals. It can still be bought today, which cannot be said for other types of Victorian women's footwear.

Though some Victorian men's styles have survived into the present, female clothing of the era has aroused little envy, or desire for emulation, among women today. Most of it seems absurdly clumsy and uncomfortable, as well as unattractive, to modern eyes. With its emphasis on respectability rather than comfort, and on showy, superficial ornament rather than simplicity – but also because its very elaborateness provoked reactions that took taste in altogether different directions – it is a perfect reflection of its time.

8

THE OFFICE

While a Victorian shopping street might be dominated by the plumage of fashionable women, any business district was the province of men. Even later in the century, when increasing numbers of female 'typewriters' appeared, they were significantly outnumbered in the streets by the dark suits and top hats of their male colleagues.

Dressing the Part

Clothing made up so much of the Victorian human landscape that it is worth examining in detail. Male fashions – as is usually the case – changed much less than those of women during the era, but a man of the nineties would nevertheless have looked very different from his grandfather. In every era but our own, costume was an important indicator of social status, income and circumstances. The Victorians would have marvelled at our abundance of affordable, quality garments, but been appalled by the perverse desire of many well-off people to wear casual or scruffy clothing. Though often impractical and seldom comfortable, the dress of their own clerical and professional classes lent them an undoubted distinction.

Men's clothing was not as sober in the early and mid-Victorian periods as it had become by 1900. The top hat, which dominated the entire nineteenth century, could be grey or white (or even, in summer, of straw!) as well as black. By the end of the reign only the latter was respectable. Waistcoats, an essential garment that no one could think of leaving off even on the hottest day, were of all shades and patterns. Their vivid hues were as much the product of newly available artificial dyes ('chemical colours') as were those on the crinolines of ladies. Loud checks, stripes and designs of fruit or flowers were unremarkable. Gloves were a matter of fashion and not simply for keeping the hands warm in winter. A glimpse of stylish young men at the turn of the sixties is provided by the journalist George Sala, who observed City clerks travelling to work through Ludgate Circus. His description deals with the accessories that indicate their wealth and (questionable) taste. He does not mention that their coats might be of sky-blue and their trousers of pale yellow – a display that would be unthinkable by the time their sons occupied office stools thirty years later:

> These are the dashing young parties who purchase the pea-green, the orange, and the rose-pink gloves; the crimson braces, the kaleidoscopic shirt-studs, the shirts embroidered with dahlias, death's heads, race-horses, sunflowers and ballet-girls; the horseshoe, fox-head, pewter-pot-and-crossed-pipes, willow-pattern-plate, and knife and fork pins. They are the glasses

of City fashion, and the mould of City form, for whom the legions of fourteen, of fifteen, of sixteen, and of seventeen shilling trousers, all unrivalled, patented, and warranted, are made; for these ingenious youths coats with strange names are devised, scarves and shawls of wondrous pattern and texture despatched from distant Manchester and Paisley. For them the shiniest of hats, the knobbiest of sticks, gleam through shop-windows; for them the geniuses of 'all-round collars' invent every week fresh yokes of starched linen, pleasant instruments of torture.[1]

Coats went from the cutaway 'swallow-tail' to the knee-length frock coat. Trousers underwent many changes in the course of the reign. At the beginning, styles were essentially still those of the Regency. Trousers had 'understraps' that buckled underneath the instep and were thus kept taut. There were also 'tights' – skin-tight leggings that buttoned just above the ankle and could be worn with a swallow-tail coat (Dickens' Mr Micawber is described – and usually shown in illustrations – as wearing these). From the late thirties, trousers began to have a single opening at the front – as is universal today – instead of a wide flap that let down. Though 'flies' seem an obvious convenience to us, their introduction caused some outrage among ladies, who felt that this reminder of the male anatomy was indecent. By the 1860s the fashion was for 'peg-top' trousers, and these are particularly evident in pictures of military uniforms, for the shortness of jackets emphasizes their shape. They were tight at the waist and narrow at the ankle, but baggy in between, giving men of that period a somewhat odd outline. In the seventies and eighties trousers became narrower, and might still – following the fashion for 'shepherd's plaid' that dated from the mid-century, be of loud check. It was also not unusual to have the incongruously military touch of a wide black stripe down the leg. The fore-and-aft crease was unknown, but there was at this time a fashion for having perfectly cylindrical trouser legs, and it was possible to buy wooden sets of legs to place in a garment overnight to ensure that they kept this shape. By the end of the reign the cuff or 'turn-up' had come into vogue, though these were not yet a tailored feature of trousers, and men simply turned up the legs themselves – which is why their trousers often look ridiculously short in photographs. George V, whose taste in clothing was formed during the Queen's reign, for the whole of his life wore his trousers with creases at the *sides*.

Sobriety

By the nineties much of the colour noticed by Sala had departed, for sobriety rather than flamboyance had come to be regarded as appropriate for those who handled the nation's funds or ran its government. Black, dark grey and dark blue were the shades favoured by all but the wantonly eccentric. In London's financial quarter:

> every City man [is] strapped into a frock coat one size too small and let into a pair of trousers one size too large. There are collars – four inchers – that lap the whole way round with the neat 4s 6d black silk tie ('all cut from the Spitalfields square') sometimes restrained by black-headed pins. There are top hats that have to be seen to be believed, for each of them is a shining mirror to reflect the virtue beneath and is sent to the hatter's each morning to reflect it. If you buy one, it runs you into one guinea if you want one of the best, although there is an inferior quality at 15s 6d, much affected by office-boy adolescence. For the silk hat means a certain 'five bob a week rise'. It is the insignia of success.[2]

As for coats, the same account states that 'if you are an employer, you wear the frock coat', and that if you are a clerk, you wear a blue lounge suit, 'Navy serge, all indigo-dyed', with a bowler. If you were somewhere in between, you might wear a 'morning coat' – the tail coat still seen at weddings – which was a descendant of the Regency swallow-tail. These too were uniform in colour, though they might vary in style:

> Some morning coats have tails which cling like the wing-cases of a beetle to the waists and nether parts of the wearers, finishing at the bend of the knee. Some, however, the very smart Johnnies, have their tails coming nearly half-way down the calf, and look rather like out of work waiters. But all wear black or grey mixture for the coat, whether frock or morning, and all wear the grey striped or dark mixture of nondescript trousers.[3]

Accessories

The only brief touches of colour might be found in small accoutrements such as ties:

> A few of the ultra-ultras have 'bandana' ties, yellow horrors with red erysipelas spots; they wear their striped cashmere trousers turned up about three inches; and their buttoned boots are varnished, not polished, every morning. Over their arms they carry umbrellas, bamboo-handled with gold or silver studs. And for gloves, they wear lavender or pale yellow kid.[4]

The author concludes by describing the remaining articles in the gentleman's wardrobe. Since he specifies that this is summer costume, we can only wonder how wearers survived the heat of August:

And, of course, what with the impervious vests of thick white linen, the strait waistcoat of a shirt that has a front and cuffs like armour plate (the soft shirt is yet unknown except by 'low workmen'), and the thick woollen undershirt and underpants – every male walks about in a bath of perspiration.[5]

Before the advent of central heating it was necessary, during the cooler seasons, to wear this much clothing to keep warm in an office.

Shoes

Footwear was as prone to change as any other item of clothing. In the thirties men still wore pumps, with buckles or laces, as they had in the Regency, though 'Wellington boots' of the kind worn by military officers were also widespread. By the middle of the reign, boots had gained ascendancy. They were often square-toed and, as readers of *Tom Sawyer* will know, there was a fashion in the forties for having the toes on these curl upwards. Vain young men who wanted to achieve this effect had to force their footwear into the required shape by sitting for long periods with their toes pressed against a wall. The most ubiquitous type of boot, from the fifties to the nineties, was the ankle-length, elastic-sided model. This – revived in the 1960s as the 'Chelsea Boot' – could have either a flat sole or a heel. By the 'nineties, lace-up boots, or boots with buttons up the side of the instep, had become extremely common, and were worn in preference to shoes by millions of men (pictures that show the roadways of Victorian cities, with their heaps of horse dung, will explain why boots were more popular). Buttoned shoes, which were even more commonplace among women and children than men, were very laborious to put on, requiring a 'button hook' for the fiddly task of doing them up.

Nevertheless, they had their devotees. Winston Churchill, another man whose tastes were formed by a Victorian upbringing, continued to wear them until well into the 1930s.

Toppers and Bowlers

Among men, those who were clearly gentlemen wore the top hat. Others, whether gentlemen or not, might wear any one of dozens of type of cap. From the Regency and the Napoleonic Wars had been inherited a number of semi-military forms of headdress – caps with chin straps and peaks and cocked hats of hardened felt. By the middle decades another style had arrived: the round, flat-topped pork-pie hat. A version of this with a small peak that sat flat against the forehead was much more common, and was called a 'cheese-cutter'. These were everywhere during the forties and fifties. They were worn as part of both naval and military officers' uniform, and appear in photographs of Crimean soldiers, though they were even more associated with civilians. They were extremely popular with boys, whether barefoot urchins in city streets or the Queen's children photographed at Osborne. David Livingstone was pictured with one, as was Colin Campbell of Indian Mutiny fame. After Queen Victoria began to spend holidays at Balmoral, her sons were often shown in pictures wearing Highland dress, and this led to another fashion in headgear. Many Sassenach children might not have been willing to put on a kilt, but the Glengarry bonnet with its trailing ribbons became eminently wearable. It was worn, as part of uniform, even for English soldiers. It was popular with men as an informal hat to wear when bicycling, fishing or walking in the country. It was deemed especially suitable for small boys, and became part of childhood for millions of them. It made such an impact that it is still worn by some members of that most Victorian body, the Boys' Brigade, which was founded in 1883.

There were, of course, many other styles. The shovel hat, which was shallow-crowned and broad-brimmed and which was much seen on clergymen, was for some years known as a 'Pickwick' because Dickens' hugely popular character wore one. At the other end of the reign, in the nineties, the 'Trilby' – a brimmed hat with an indented crown – was named after another fictional character, though Trilby was a young woman and the hat got its name through being worn in the 1895 stage production of the novel.

The top hat maintained its dominance throughout the century. It had first been worn in London in 1797, causing such outrage by its strange appearance (no less than four women fainted on seeing it in the street) that its owner, John Hetherington, was charged with breach of the peace and ordered by a magistrate not to appear in it again. Within a very few years it had become universal both in Britain and abroad. The version worn by gentlemen was of beaver pelt – which was prohibitively expensive – but by the start of the Victorian era hatters had discovered the secret of using hardened silk instead. Prince Albert popularized the silk 'topper' which, over a decade or so, effectively killed off the beaver hat.

Toppers varied in style. In the mid-century – the era during which Albert, Brunel and Abraham Lincoln are pictured wearing them – they became higher in the crown (the ones owned by Lincoln were seven inches high, though they looked taller when seen on him) and earned the nickname 'stovepipes' for their resemblance to 'chimney tops with a border'. They had both advantages and drawbacks. Being tall, they blew off very easily, and made it necessary to remember to duck constantly both indoors and out. If sitting taking notes, however, they made an ideal 'desk' when placed on the knees, and they were very useful for storing things in – papers, and even books could be put inside them, and Dickens once encountered a man who kept a large meat pie in his.

In the first half of the century, the top hat in one form or another had been worn even by the poor, and was certainly seen on the heads of policemen, postmen, labourers, street sweepers and young boys. These cheaper models were made from felt or rabbit fur and appeared, when new, acceptably smart. Once rained upon, they quickly looked bedraggled and the fur became shaggy. It was even possible to buy a soft, collapsible and very cheap version that could be stuffed in the pocket. By the time the stovepipe disappeared in the seventies, top hats had become more exclusive, for they had become the symbol of the office clerk and of those above him in society. The notion that those who did not wear a top hat were somehow outside the polite world is one that crops up in Victorian writings. A periodical reviewing a 'decadent' play when it was performed in London sniffed that it was likely to appeal only to 'long haired, soft hatted, villainous or sickly-looking socialists',[6] and when looking back on the Queen's reign at the time of the Diamond Jubilee, the *Illustrated London News* cited as evidence of creeping informality (or, if readers preferred, the country having gone to the dogs) this observation on the House of Commons: 'In the time of Mr Canning, the Minister always came down in silk stockings and pantaloons or knee breeches, and even in the last generation members thought it essential to dress for Parliament at least as well as for a Society call or a garden party. But in recent days unconventionality has been the rule, and low hats and short jackets are quite common.'[7]

By 1897 the top hat had already largely been relegated to formal wear, because another type of headgear had become the customary wear of office clerks. This was the 'bowler', though it was called a Derby in the United States (Americans first encountered it at Epsom) and its inventors, the firm of Lock in St James' Street, called it – as they still do – a Coke. This was a narrow-brimmed hat of pressed felt with a rounded crown. The first of these had been ordered in 1850, from Lock's, by William Coke, the Norfolk estate owner who was later Earl of Leicester. Coke had sought a more hard-wearing hat with which to equip the gamekeepers on his estate, for their top hats were constantly knocked off by low branches. When a prototype was made for him, he visited the shop and tested it by stamping several times on the hat. It withstood his weight, and he ordered more of them. Widely worn in the countryside, the bowler was soon taken up by urban office-workers, and became something of a symbol of the nineties. Sherlock Holmes' assistant, Doctor Watson, was often depicted wearing one.

Whiskers

The hair styles concealed – or set off – by these forms of headgear varied as much as would be expected over a period of sixty-four years. In the thirties beards were almost unheard of and were deeply unfashionable, as they had been all through the eighteenth century. Moustaches were not worn except by foreigners or by somewhat rakish Englishmen (Prince Albert had one, but does not seem to have started a trend). Since before the beginning of the reign, men had had a habit of wearing their hair parted vertically down the back of the head and combed forward at the sides. This style, which can sometimes be seen in old photographs, gave their faces a look that is entirely of the age. Pictures of old men at the end of the century often show them with this hair style, so deeply engrained was the habit that they never broke it. In Dickens' time these side-combed locks, grown long and trained into points thrust forward like horns, were sported by young street-corner men, as can be seen in Cruikshank illustrations.

Whiskers became fashionable at the time of the Crimean War. Partly because the officers in the field were too busy, or too ill-equipped, to shave every day, a certain carelessness in this respect became stylish. The Army had for some time worn moustaches, and in the severe Crimean winter beards were permitted. Dandies in England began to sport facial hair in the hope of being mistaken for returning heroes. Such adornments had, in any case, been out of fashion for so long that it was inevitable they would return. By the sixties no self-respecting 'swell' would be seen about without a pair of 'dundrearies'. These were a combination moustache and side-whiskers, the latter often so long that they hung down to the chest. The name derived from a character – Lord Dundreary – in Tom Taylor's 1855 play *Our American Cousin*. The style, which became as emblematic of the 1860s as the platform shoe was of the 1970s, became particularly associated with foppish, drawling, lady-killing 'mashers' who filled the pages of novels by the then popular author George Whyte-Melville. By the following decade full beards were more common, and these were often worn for the whole of their lives by men of the generation that grew up in the eighties and nineties. By the latter decade small, neat moustaches were considered more suitable, and hair – which in the middle decades had often been grown over the ears (one thinks of John Ruskin) – became neat and short, as it would remain until the 1960s.

Earning a Living

Men commuted to work in several ways. The wealthiest travelled in their own carriages or in hired cabs. Others went by omnibus, though this was initially too expensive a conveyance for the many to use. In the early decades of the reign, when a clerk might make seven shillings a week, the cost of a single journey was a shilling. Only gradually, with the advent of the tram and the Underground, would a majority of London commuters travel on wheels. Prior to that, crowds of them walked to work – a daily journey that might well take an hour or more. One of the sights of the capital was to see them pouring in their thousands through the turnstiles on Waterloo Bridge, paying the toll as they went.

The Counting House

And what of the places of work to which they repaired? The office was an environment that changed between the beginning and end of the reign as completely as it has changed between 1901 and the present. The word 'office', today a catch-all term for any work space that contains a desk, was not applied to commercial premises, where the place for doing paperwork was called the 'counting house'. Readers of Dickens will be familiar with early nineteenth-century clerks – whether Uriah Heep or Newman Noggs – and with the surroundings in which they toiled. Many firms – though they might well be important and successful – were extremely small. Before the monstrous growth of such modern paraphernalia as marketing, human resources and user support departments, a business might, indeed, consist of a single man, who dealt with all the paperwork himself. Equally common would be a proprietor and a single clerk (Bob Cratchit was Scrooge's sole employee), and even this man might be temporary or part-time. A study carried out in Liverpool in the 1870s estimated that the average number of clerks in a firm was four.

A large enterprise, such as a government department, the Bank of England or the East India Company, would have dozens of clerks, and so would a shipping company in any major port. These men often worked in large rooms that allowed even less privacy than the open-plan offices of today. Darkness and cold were familiar problems, for lighting would be provided only by candles or oil lamps, and the stove or fireplace might well be at the far end of a long room. For a clerk to keep his scarf on, as Cratchit did, would not have been unusual. Desks were high and sloping, like that of an old-fashioned schoolteacher, and in a large office could be long enough for half a dozen men to sit side by side, perched on high, backless stools (spinal pain and rounded shoulders were endemic) and perhaps facing a similar row of clerks. Whatever else was to change in the course of the century, offices furnished in this way were to continue in use throughout the reign of Victoria and beyond.

Despite their numbers, the places in which these clerks laboured would have had the stillness of a church, for there was no machinery to create noise. Many counting houses were extremely cramped and unhealthy, for they might be squeezed into back courts in a crowded commercial district like the City of London or, in industrial premises, they might be too close to the noise and fumes of factory machinery. In either case there were no 'health and safety' regulations to ensure access to minimal daylight or fresh air.

Documents were written out in the 'court hand' that the men learned and practised, and a glance at surviving ledgers or letters, in which not a single error can be spotted among the rows of precise lettering, bears witness to their skill. They were required to be equally meticulous in adding columns of figures and entering these in cash books. In an era when the majority of people could not read or write, these abilities represented a valuable asset, and clerks were a small, exclusive fraternity (in 1851 they made up less than 1 per cent of the population). With the coming of compulsory education in the seventies, they were to feel they had lost both professional mystique and status.

They had a life that was relatively secure, but normally without excitement. They were recruited into their positions while in their early or mid-teenage years. A majority came by personal recommendation (a vital element in any Victorian dealings), by family precedent (a great many people of both sexes followed their parents' occupations) or by advertisements in newspapers – a tactic resorted to by both employers and those seeking positions. The notices always asked for the same thing: 'must write a good hand'. The applicant must also, as for any respectable position, furnish testimonials. Once accepted, he might well remain with the same firm for the whole of his working life, for the ethos of the time involved a very high degree of mutual loyalty between employer and employee. Relations within an office might well be highly personal, for companies were family-run to a vastly greater extent than is the case today, and both the proprietors and those who worked for them might bear the same surname for generations. A clerk who served a single family for the whole of his working life was not much different in outlook from a domestic servant who did the same.

A young man in a counting house would serve a five-year apprenticeship, usually under the tutelage of an individual, more senior clerk, before being allowed to see himself as qualified. Clerks were as varied a group as the wide worlds of commerce and administration could produce. Those in banks were considered to be the at the top of the profession, but international commerce was not far behind, for there was always glamour attached to the whiff of exotic places that this brought with it. The men themselves varied between those – the majority – of modest income and ambition and those of comfortable means, who sometimes worked for a few years without pay. These latter were often the sons of merchants, and chose to learn the ropes of their profession before setting up in business on their own. After he had completed his training, a clerk might – if he were in a small firm that had no hierarchy or 'career ladder' – do literally the same work every day until old age or failing eyesight made him unable to continue. In a large organization it might be possible for a valued employee to receive a pension, but this was not something to which most could look forward. In a great many cases, they would hope for a parting gift from their employer, consisting of whatever he was willing to bestow.

Clerks dressed in black, and would have been immediately recognizable in the street from their stooped shoulders, ink-stained hands and general pallor. Their hours of work might be extremely civilized – some government departments began at ten and finished at four, and half-past four or five were typical finishing times – with a break of an hour for lunch. However, clerks had to remain in their offices until the necessary work was finished, and if that took longer than the allotted span of their day, they would simply have to continue. Depending on the nature of their business, there would be busy times of the week or the month or the year, during which they might be expected to work into the night. On Saturdays, when under normal circumstances they could hope to finish at lunchtime and have the afternoon off, they might just as easily have to stay late to complete the week's paperwork. A survey of banks comments that in Manchester in the thirties and forties, before the introduction of Saturday half-days had taken hold, it was 'quite common in the principal banks and warehouses to see every window illuminated up till nine, ten and even eleven p.m., and the longest and sweetest of midsummer evenings often sank in the west before ever a door was locked and a lad set free.'[8] They were not paid overtime, and – like everyone else until the 1930s – had no paid holidays. Though they sat down all day, their work was physically taxing, for until the latter decades of the reign there were no devices to save labour or to lessen the wearisome nature of their tasks.

Dickens, in *Sketches by Boz*, describes an inhabitant of this world, with its:

> dingy little back-office into which he walks every morning, placing his hat on the same peg, and placing his legs beneath the same desk: first, taking off that black coat which lasts the year through, and putting on one which did duty last year, and which he keeps in his desk to save the other. There he sits till five o'clock, working on, all day, as regularly as the dial over the mantel-piece, whose loud ticking is as monotonous as his whole existence: only raising his head when someone enters the counting-house, or when, in the midst of some difficult calculation, he looks up at the ceiling as if there were inspiration in the dusty sky-light with a green knot in the centre of every pane of glass. About five, or half-past, he slowly dismounts from his accustomed stool, and again changing his coat, proceeds to his usual dining-place.[9]

Both clerks themselves and the wider public were well aware they appeared to the world as mindless drudges. B. G. Orchard, in his 1871 report on Liverpool clerks, quoted one man who asked:

> What do we see of real life? What do we know of the world? What do we know of anything? We don't do men's work. We

aren't real men. Think of crossing 't's and dotting 'i's all day long. No wonder bricklayers and omnibus drivers have contempt for us.[10]

As a byword for anonymous nonentity, it was no accident that a clerk – Mister Pooter – was chosen as the hero of George and Weedon Grossmith's satirical novel *The Diary of a Nobody*. As those familiar with this will know, however, the nature of his work does not prevent Pooter from enjoying a relatively varied life – he has his garden, his friends, his hobbies and his visits to the seaside to provide diversion, and he has the luxury of being able to indulge in a sense of self-importance. The life of a Victorian clerk could be more agreeable than a glance at his working conditions might imply.

In the first half of the reign, the only significant piece of office equipment was the pen, though where might also be a need for rulers (in those days cylindrical rather than flat) and the pumice stone that was used for rubbing out mistakes. At the time of Victoria's accession the steel nib had begun to replace the goose quill, but this made very slow inroads. Quills continued in common use for decades afterwards, and were still to be found in many offices at the end of the century. In the absence of photocopiers, all duplicates had to be laboriously written by hand, as did fair copies of letters. The filing cabinet and paper clip, those modern symbols of bureaucracy, did not yet exist. Invoices were stored by being impaled on a spike, in order of arrival, the most recent at the top. Bundles of papers were held together with pins, an inefficient and sometimes painful practice. Many documents were tied together and hung from nails or pegs, and the walls were festooned with calendars, papers and coats and hats. Without telephones, communication was by messenger. If a document was ready to be sent, the ring of a small handbell would summon one. Almost all were small boys or elderly men, who stood about the premises all day awaiting this type of summons, and they knew the geography of a commercial district well enough to speedily deliver letters and packages either within their own building or in the surrounding streets.

The Coming of Machinery

The first manifestation of technology to break in upon the studious hush of offices was the telegraph, invented in 1855, which vastly increased the speed of communications and therefore the volume of business. The telephone arrived a generation later. Invented in the mid-seventies, it began to appear in offices in the following decade. In the nineties the rotary dial was added, creating in effect the instrument we still use today. Though undoubtedly a convenience, the telephone was expensive, and was neither widespread nor popular. Only in the next century did it become more or less universal. Many people – whether clerks or clients – were simply not comfortable using it, and this attitude could still be found as late as the 1920s, when the American President Herbert Hoover objected to speaking on the telephone because he considered it looked undignified.

The typewriter was also to change the nature of office work, and it proved more significant than all the other innovations. It represented a revolution even more important than that which the computer brought in the twentieth century, for it marked the end of the pen and the beginning of noisy mechanization in commercial life. It speeded up the creation and processing of paperwork and, through the development of carbon paper, the copying of documents. The very earliest models appeared in the fifties but it was in the sixties and seventies that the machines began to gain ground. They were large, cumbersome and often difficult to work, but they had come to stay.

Together with the typewriter came the increased use of shorthand. This highly valuable system for speedily recording information was, of course, not new – Samuel Pepys had written his diary in this form, and the young Dickens had used it when working as a legal reporter. It had been popularized at the beginning of the reign by a teacher named Isaac Pitman, whose book on the subject, *Stenographic Sound Hand*, was published in 1837 and enjoyed considerable success. He, and those who followed his lead, taught not only shorthand but other clerical skills such as book-keeping and typewriting. The result was the emergence of the commercial college, in which students of both sexes could be trained for careers in offices. The Dickensian clerk on his own could not possibly have adapted to the expanding needs of administration and commerce, which now needed armies of staff to keep up.

The size of companies, of warehouses, of machinery, increased, as did the numbers that firms employed and the pace of activity. We can see from surviving examples that office buildings from the later part of the century are, for the first time, on a scale approaching that of our own era. Many of them dwarf the counting houses and warehouses of the Georgians.

This revolution took place over thirty or forty years. There was no overnight replacement of Dickensian clerks by 'typewriters' (as the operators of these machines were known). The two worked together in the same offices for many years. The 'Bob Cratchits' largely completed their careers and departed rather than, as would doubtless happen today, facing summary redundancy because they did not understand the new methods. There was still a place – albeit a diminishing one – for their skills until the end of the reign.

Lady Clerks

As if the introduction of so much technology were not change enough, the telephone and typewriter caused large numbers of women, for the first time, to enter the workplace. In 1851, the census showed only nineteen women commercial clerks. Forty years later there were 17, 859. Their numbers would continue to rise until, by the end of the Edwardian era, there would be over 150,000 of them. The change of attitude to some extent resulted from experience in America, where during the Civil War in the 1860s many thousands of women had worked in offices to replace men drafted into the army. In Britain, women in some businesses were initially segregated entirely from men, working in different rooms and even leaving the office at different times to avoid contact. Ironically in view of this, female employees often found no lavatories available to them at their place of work, and were obliged either to use the men's facilities or, if that was impossible, might have to wait until they got home! Their advent in offices and counting houses was inevitably met with some cynicism. A cartoon from the seventies shows an exasperated employer coming into a room to find his female workforce gossiping idly or reading. In reality, employers found that women were actually better suited to working modern machinery than men, whether this was the telephone (the operation of which thus became from the time of their first use a predominantly female occupation) or the typewriter. As a member of the Post Office stated in 1871:

They have in an eminent degree the quickness of eye and ear, and the delicacy of touch. They take more kindly than men and boys do to sedentary employment, and are more patient during long confinement to one place. The wages, which will draw male operators from but an inferior class of the community, will draw female operators from a superior class.[11]

Twenty years later, the great social observer Charles Booth qualified this assessment:

It is said that women are more accurate workers and better copyists than junior male clerks but, for the most part, are inferior to the male clerk over twenty-one years of age. This may be the result of their physical condition and want of experience.[12]

Gradually the sharing of offices became more commonplace. One of the first organizations to try it, in the seventies, reported that the presence of women:

Raises the tone of the male staff by confining them during many hours of the day to a decency of conversation and demeanour which is not always to be found where men alone are employed.[13]

Women represented a saving of money since, regardless of the hours they worked or the duties they performed, they were paid at lower rates than their male colleagues who did the same jobs. As a result, their numbers increased and they rapidly came to form a significant part of the business world. They held no positions of responsibility, and not until almost exactly a century after their arrival would they be paid at the same rate as men. Nevertheless, they had secured for themselves an important bridgehead.

They were described by one writer in the nineties, as they began to contribute to the scenery of London's financial district:

There are very few women in the City crowd. They are so rare that they walk about apologetically and attempt to efface themselves. They try to be businesslike, poor dears, in their linen dresses and blouses, gathered in tightly at neck, waist and wristbands; and their hats are inclined to be pinched and 'perched'. The males scowl at but tolerate them, for they do not know that 'all this rot about women coming into the city is bound to stop. They cant hold their own with us, my boy.'[14]

He revealed something of their appearance – they must have brought a certain colour amid the sobriety of suits – as well as suggesting the difficulty they faced in answering even the most basic needs:

They carry small brown-paper packages tied with white string in a day when 'a lady that is a lady' is not supposed to have a stomach, for in all this big city there is no place where a poor girl may eat and the teashop 'ladies only' department is unknown. When these unfortunate females go into one of the cheap eating-places they are treated as pariahs, and lordly waiters refuse to wait on them. They cannot find a room in which to 'do themselves up' and city employers object tacitly to providing them with the elementary decencies of life in the offices where they hang their diminished heads.[15]

He continues:

However, the typewriter is still frightfully modern and the lordly male does not care too much about working it. It is too like a sewing machine – 'and I'm not a bally nursemaid-office-boy', the comment of a time when women were inferior to men and the men knew it and the women knew it . . .

But they are beginning to be used, all the same, because many of them regard their wages (15s to 30s a week) as 'pin-money' and usually live at home or as they can. But through it all, they are frightfully respectable and apologetic, especially as the night comes on and they have to go home to Finsbury Park or Clapham Junction or Balham or Woodford.[16]

However quaint this sounds to a modern audience, it represented a revolution both in practices and attitudes and a break with custom. From the scribes of the ancient world until the mid-Victorian era, clerical work had been done by men, using the same basic tools. Thereafter, such work was not only done by machine but became so increasingly the province of women that they effectively edged out the male from these regions, and they have continued to dominate them ever since. It was the Victorians who created the world of work that we still inhabit.

9

LEISURE

An Age of Travel

Like our own time, the Victorian era was an age of leisure. Gradually improving working conditions, as well as a rising standard of living, gave people more time and money to spend, while advancing technology increased the opportunities available to them for exploiting these resources. They had more ways of enjoying themselves than any previous generation, just as we – with the technology at our disposal – are perceived to have. The Victorians maintained traditional pleasures such as the theatre (the quality of which had reached commanding heights by the end of the reign, and which was already producing its influential offshoot, the cinema), but developed others beyond the dreams of their predecessors. Most significantly, the advent of cheap travel and organized sports – both of which have undergone equivalent revolutions in our own time – decisively and permanently changed the habits, the outlook and the expectations of the British people.

It was the fruits of the Industrial Revolution that enabled Victorians to travel, conveniently, to the British coasts, as a result of which seaside towns expanded and developed – or in some cases were created more or less from scratch – to feed, accommodate and entertain hordes of seasonal visitors. It was the same technology – the railway and the steamship – that enabled them swiftly to cross seas and oceans and to travel the European Continent and the Middle East, making far-flung regions accessible to the moderately well-off for the first time in history.

It was because of this ease of access to other, and often distant places that the spread of organized games became possible. From this time on it became feasible for teams from other places to play each other. This allowed the creation of sustainable sporting 'leagues' and enabled rules to be standardized. Not only could teams play each other, with the same rules, all over the country but, with the arrival of faster ocean travel, championship matches could be played abroad. The exchange of cricket teams with Australia from the 1860s, and the establishment of the 'Ashes' trophy opened a new era in sporting competition, leading the way to the Olympics – first held at Athens in 1894 – and to the great international events of the following century.

Beside the Sea

Sea bathing was a practice that became established in the latter part of the eighteenth century, as a treatment for ill health rather than a form of exercise or a relaxation. Its popularity was greatly enhanced by the Prince Regent – later George IV – who built a home in Brighton and made what had been an unremarkable fishing-port into an extension of fashionable London. It remained highly select, not least because it was expensive to reach and to live in, but by the end of the Georgian era a fall in the cost of coach travel had begun to nibble at the edges of the town's exclusive character. The coming of the railway, however, was not only to change the resort of Brighton completely (by the end of the reign it was synonymous with cockney day-trippers) but to create a host of imitations. Railways made it possible for large numbers of people to reach the coastal towns with speed and comfort. This led to a seasonal demand for accommodation, for dining facilities and for entertainment. The result was an explosion in building as resorts were created. All over the British Isles, towns that had been largely unknown – or indeed non-existent – became household names: Blackpool and Filey in the north, Llandudno and Colwyn Bay in Wales, Minehead and Weston-super-Mare in the west, Yarmouth and Cromer in the east, Southend and Margate in the Thames estuary, Rothesay in Scotland, Bangor, Howth and Dun Laoghaire in Ireland. Some towns acquired, or maintained, a reputation for smartness and gentility: Scarborough was a cut above any other northern resort. Torquay enjoyed for a time a popularity with the international rich that rivalled the later glamour of the French Riviera. Ramsgate was given distinction by the fact that the Queen had, from girlhood, spent her holidays there. She gave it up only when her summer home was built at Osborne – which led to the reinvention of the Isle of Wight as a summer destination.

In spite of this the seaside as a whole was a classless place. Among the era's well-known images is William Powell Frith's painting *Life at the Seaside*, also known as *Ramsgate Sands*. Bought in 1854 by the Queen, to whom it must have brought back memories, it shows a predominantly upper-middle-class gathering of holidaymakers on a small stretch of beach. It gives what was probably an accurate view of their activities, though the artist has chosen to cram his figures together in a manner that suggests that 'personal space' was not a priority. A modern observer is surprised to see that they are fully dressed. The ladies wear crinolines and shawls, gloves and bonnets, and even a woman who is helping a child to paddle has allowed the hem of her dress to trail in the water rather than hitching it up. The men wear suits and ties – though one of them is in carpet slippers – and there is a sprinkling of top hats. Few people seem very interested in their surroundings, for several read books and papers, women do needlework and some watch an entertainer. There are the usual donkeys and sideshows.

It is noticeable that the attitude of these people to sunburn is the opposite of ours. No one is exposing themselves to the light in order to catch the sun, and the poke bonnets of the ladies, with their wide brims, were specifically designed to keep the faces of their wearers in shadow. For a woman any blush of sunburn would have been seen as unfeminine and unbecoming, which is why the parasol was such an important piece of equipment at this time. Gloves were worn on the beach to prevent hands from discolouring. Only fishwives, or similarly rough local women, would have had complexions that were touched by the elements, and no genteel person of either sex wished to look like that.

No one is swimming. This was not seen as part of the experience until quite late in the century, and those with a taste for salt water tended only to paddle. Sea bathing, since its introduction as a restorative treatment by the Georgians, had been carried out from 'bathing machines' – small wooden huts mounted on high wheels and fitted with shafts, that were towed into the sea by horses. Bathers, segregated by gender, changed into suitable costume before climbing down a set of steps into the water (these steps were sometimes covered by a canopy to protect modesty). The actual bathing consisted simply of immersing oneself a number of times with the help of an attendant. At Brighton and elsewhere, these were typically women, solidly built enough to hang on to, who stood fully clothed in the water. As the notion of actually swimming in then sea gained popularity these attendants became extinct, but the bathing machine (several are visible in Frith's canvas) remained a ubiquitous part of the Victorian seaside until the end of the reign.

In 1897 the cartoonist Phil May drew another picture of Ramsgate Sands. Though there are still rows of bathing machines, there have been a number of changes. The crowd is noticeably more vulgar, even in this select resort, for the seaside has become more associated with the working and lower middle classes, while those higher up the social ladder have by this time taken to holidaying abroad. There are donkeys, ice-cream vendors, pierrots, blacked-up minstrels and several portable photographic studios. The seaside is obviously still a very buttoned-up environment, for though boys have rolled up their trouser legs, their elders are fully dressed. The men are in suits and waistcoats, ties and bowler hats. Women wear corsets, tight skirts and decorated hats. Though not shown in May's drawing, casual dress would have been represented by linen suits, white trousers, striped blazers and straw boaters (Mr Pooter in *The Diary of a Nobody* is proud of a straw sun-helmet he has purchased to wear on holiday). Women might well have had lightweight dresses, but they wore (according to the dictates of fashion) collars and ties and short jackets on the sands, and the young and shapely could not leave their corsets at home without losing the wasp-waisted look that was considered essential. It was in any case part of the Victorian mindset that one dressed up – not down –

to go on holiday. City-dwelling day-trippers would often wear their Sunday best in order to visit the seaside. Those men able to afford it might well wear checked tweed suits and bowler (as opposed to top) hats – the standard costume of relaxation for those on fishing, walking or climbing holidays, but they would never want to look anything but smart.

By the end of the century men and women in appropriate costumes – the latter wearing mob caps to protect their hair, and canvas shoes – would be taking bathing seriously. With the increase in public baths in towns and cities, and the rise of swimming as a sport, growing numbers of people possessed the skills to take to the sea, but given the amount of clothing that would have to be discarded it is not surprising that paddling remained far more popular.

Without a pier, no self-respecting resort could hope to be visited. Originally they had been of stone, and served the simple function of providing a place for vessels to embark or to land goods and passengers. With the technology that had made possible the Crystal Palace, piers began to be made of iron and glass. Sometimes they were built by the very railway companies that brought the visitors and whose stations these structures often resembled. Most piers simply jutted into the sea, though the one at Weston-super-Mare was partly built on an offshore rock. They could accommodate not only sideshows but restaurants, funfairs, theatres and even ballrooms. As the coastal towns attracted a wealth of entertainments – Punch and Judy shows, acrobats, performing animals, 'nigger minstrels' – there developed the notion of marshalling these diversions on the pier. These thus became almost a world in themselves, and often the public was charged admission simply to walk along them. Brighton's two piers were perhaps the best known, though the longest in the country – at Southend in Essex – was over a mile from end to end. It had, and still has, a railway to take visitors along it.

Other traditions gradually accrued. Donkey rides were already customary by the mid-century, but the availability of gimcrack souvenirs increased noticeably from about that time. As well as the ships-in-bottles made by local sailors and hawked around the sands, there were now multitudes of mass-produced (often foreign-made) items of glass, shell or ceramic to clutter the mantelpieces of lower-middle-class households. The advent of the picture postcard in the 1890s added yet another dimension, as it became customary to send greetings, often accompanied by jocular or even scurrilous messages, to those at home. Day-trippers to resorts often sent a postcard as soon as they arrived, knowing that it would have been delivered by the time they returned home that evening.

The boarding house became another staple of the nineteenth-century seaside. Fathers, too busy earning a living to spend weeks on the coast, could send their wives and children – or indeed their offspring in the care of a nanny – to one of these establishments, and join them at weekends. Families developed loyalties to particular resorts, hotels and boarding houses, and made a ritual of the annual holiday.

Field and Stream

Inland there were other types of resort. They were usually chosen for some form of curative facility, and were often within reach of pleasant scenery. Malvern in Worcestershire and Matlock or Buxton in Derbyshire enjoyed a considerable vogue for this reason, all of them having springs of pure water that were beneficial to those who suffered from the heavy, unhealthy Victorian diet. In Scotland, there was a fashion for 'Hydros' – large hotels built for these same purposes of cure and exercise amid beautiful landscapes, such as those at Crieff and Peebles. Several are still in business today.

These were part of a significant increase in internal tourism that gathered momentum as the century progressed. As always, it was the revolutions in transport and communication that made this possible. Trains and boats carried visitors to most parts of the country. Bicycles could take them further into the hinterland. The hotels and other facilities that in turn grew up to cater for these crowds made it easier to visit remote regions. The greater availability of cheap illustrated guidebooks made people more aware of the history and natural wonders of the places they visited, and this in turn increased a desire to protect both landscape and buildings. A new era began, in this sense, with the founding of the National Trust in 1895.

Cultural Tourism

The accessibility of culture made it possible to take holidays that were devoted not only to rest or to exercise but to improving the mind. Great industrial cities such as Manchester, Leeds and Glasgow founded major museums and art galleries to put themselves on the cultural map. These often contained significant treasures that merited a journey. There might also be important temporary spectacles: in 1857 the Manchester Art Treasures Exhibition took place. It was smaller than the Great Exhibition of six years earlier, from which it took its inspiration, and its theme was not technological progress but the glories of art and design. Its 16,000 exhibits were borrowed largely from private collections, and it attracted 1.3 million visitors during the five months that it was open.

While attending such an event is entirely understandable, some aspects of Victorian earnestness can seem distinctly eccentric from a modern perspective. This writer's great-grandmother visited Scotland on her honeymoon in 1887. Staying in Dundee, where the couple view the ruins of the old Tay Bridge (and carry off part of the handrail as a souvenir), she relates in her diary that they 'try to get into a rope manufactory. After a deal of trouble we succeed', but she adds that 'they seemed to be afraid we were spies'. Proceeding to Glasgow, she describes how she and her husband:

> jump on a tram to go out in the direction of the mills, saying to a fellow passenger 'We would like to get into a mill'. He replied 'Come with me' so off we went with him to some large dye works where he had some business, introduced us to the manager & took his departure when we were taken all over the works and shewn every process of dyeing. We said we would like to see another, a weaving mill. So this manager just wrote a note to some man and gave us to take as an introduction. We were admitted at once and after waiting a few minutes were taken over the whole place.[1]

Neither she nor her husband had any connection whatever with the businesses in which they showed such inquisitiveness.

Because it took only hours to reach remote areas, the countryside became increasingly a place of recreation rather than work – a state of affairs that remains true today. Until the middle decades of the century, Britain had depended on its farmers to feed the population. The settlement of huge and far-flung agricultural regions – the prairies of Canada and the United States – and the fact that cheap grain could be shipped, swiftly and safely, from the New World meant that for the first time ever Britain could afford to rely entirely on imports. With the development of refrigeration, meat as well as cereals could be provided from beyond the oceans. Whatever the implications for British agriculture, this increasingly made the countryside a playground for cyclists, walkers and golfers. The advent of the 'weekend' meant that on Saturdays and Sundays, trains disgorged parties of hikers and other enthusiasts to fill the lanes and meadows with noise and movement. For many parts of rural Britain, the peaceful Sunday was becoming a thing of the past, a trend that became even more noticeable with the arrival of the motor car.

On the Water

Not only the roads and fields, but the rivers became a place of entertainment. The Thames, in particular, was regarded by the later Victorian decades as a scene of fashionable resort. Once again it was the railways that brought this change. For the whole of history, the Thames had been a working river, filled with barges that carried, for instance, the stone used to construct many London buildings. When the railway took away this trade, the river was left empty, and it began to be discovered by holidaymakers.

There had already been an element of recreation about the river. Public schools such as Westminster had raced boats on it for some time, and rowing was an established sport at Oxford. The first University Boat Race had been held in 1829, and Henley Regatta – which was soon able to add 'Royal' to its title – began exactly ten years later. While crowds flocked to see these spectacles, there were other attractions: steamers could now bring tourists to view Hampton Court or Windsor. Canoeing and punting – especially popular from the eighties – could make hot summer Sunday afternoons more agreeable. The former was an import from Canada, the latter had developed, earlier in the century, from the flat fishing craft used in shallow water. Because they were easily propelled – by ladies as well as men – punts became a much-used conveyance, giving members of either sex the chance to look graceful and to show off their dexterity. Mishaps were common, however, especially if the pole got stuck in mud, and *Punch* made considerable fun of those who came to grief. The most formidable risk was of being run down by a steam launch. There were so many of these that, in some places, the Thames became as crowded as Ludgate Circus. This was the world so brilliantly captured by Jerome K. Jerome in his novel *Three Men in a Boat* (1889), and he spoke for generations of boating enthusiasts when he wrote that: 'I never see a steam launch but I feel I should like to lure it into a lonely part of the river, and there . . . strangle it.'

The riverside pubs at Bray or Sonning or a score of other places could serve as a rendezvous for trippers, fishermen or rowers. The Thames was a classless thoroughfare, as open to day-tripping East Enders as to aristocrats in their private houseboats. These latter were often as luxurious as country houses, equipped with electricity, pianos, billiard tables and a staff of servants (a number of the vessels that later became Oxford college barges began life as vessels of this sort).

There were also places ashore that took on fashionable importance. Of these, by far the most important was the town of Maidenhead. It owed its status to the arrival there, in 1865, of the Guards Boat Club. It soon attained a prominent role in the Season, and in particular the river there, where it passed through a narrow set of gates called Boulter's Lock, and became the only place to be seen on 'Ascot Sunday' – the day after the races. (Another iconic Victorian painting depicts this occasion. *Boulter's Lock, Sunday Afternoon* was painted by Edward John Gregory between 1885 and 1897. It depicts the lock crowded with craft of all sizes, while both banks are thronging with spectators.) The town itself is some distance from the Thames, but the river front boasted an impressive array of hotels, mansions and private houses, many of which were rented for the very short time during the year that it was fashionable to be there. Maidenhead quickly acquired something of a reputation for raffishness, its hotels and villas favoured by upper class *roués* for rendezvous with mistresses (a row of dwellings opposite the Guards Club was allegedly used entirely for this). Jerome summed it up in *Three Men in a Boat*:

> Maidenhead itself is too snobby to be pleasant. It is the haunt of the river swell and his overdressed female companion. It is the town of showy hotels, patronised chiefly by dudes and ballet girls. It is the witch's kitchen from which go forth those demons of the river – steam launches. The *London Journal* duke always has his 'little place' at Maidenhead; and the heroine of the three-volume novel always dines there when she goes out on the spree with somebody else's husband.[2]

Though a certain notoriety hung about the town until the Second World War, Maidenhead was rapidly to lose its Victorian and Edwardian appeal. Most of the surviving buildings along its riverbanks are in the red-brick, Queen Anne revival style of the latter nineteenth century, attesting to the swift arrival of fashion, and its comparatively swift departure.

Overseas

While the countryside could provide amusement when the weather was pleasant, those in search of more reliable sunshine, or wider horizons, went abroad. The wealthy had always been able to do this, though Europe was also a destination for the genteel poor. Britain was so expensive to live in for those attempting to keep up appearances that numbers of families or individuals gave up the struggle and moved to cities or countries where their means would go further. One such place was Deauville in Normandy, a popular summer destination for English summer visitors but also home to a permanent expatriate community. Similarly Dresden, capital of the German kingdom of Saxony – the 'Florence of the Elbe' – had so many British residents that three English newspapers were at one time published there. Other groups could be found all over Europe and beyond, merging with those fellow countrymen who travelled for health reasons in search of drier climates in which to spend the winter. It was the English who created the French Riviera. Their enthusiasm is thought to have begun with Tobias Smollett, the eighteenth-century novelist whose *Travels through France and Italy* (1766) was a bestseller. By the decades following the Napoleonic Wars, increasing numbers of Britons were settling in the region. One early enthusiast was Lord Brougham, who built a chateau in Cannes in 1836. By that time several resorts – Cannes, Nice, Menton – were being developed with funding from him and from his wealthy compatriots, and Cannes already boasted a *boulevard des Anglais* named in their honour. By 1862 there were almost 500 British families in the area, and by 1900 there were almost 100,000 visitors a year from the United Kingdom. These included even the country's ruler, for Queen Victoria made an annual visit during the last years of her life. (The Riviera was fashionable only during winter, and not until the 1920s would summer visits be popularized by the likes of Ernest Hemingway, who could not afford to live there during the high season.) Two types of people went to this part of France: the wealthy and the sick. The climate was recommended by British doctors to those suffering from tuberculosis. It had not yet been discovered that the Alpine air of Switzerland was more favourable for this (a migration of British invalids in that direction would characterize the later part of the reign), and in the meantime a sizeable community of doctors, invalids and their relatives grew up there.

For those with a bent towards gambling and the necessary social standing, the casino at nearby Monte Carlo was in operation by 1857 and grew into the principal gaming centre of Europe. In less than a quarter of a century it had made such huge profits that the local ruler was able to absolve his subjects from paying any taxes. It at once gained a reputation for high stakes, raffish behaviour (the Prince of Wales was an *habitué*) and suicides among the unsuccessful. As one English observer wrote just after the end of the century: 'When a gambler has become bankrupt at the tables of Monte Carlo, the company that owns these tables will furnish him with a railway ticket that will take him home, or to any distance he likes, the further the better, that he may hang or shoot himself anywhere save in the gardens of the casino.'[3] The resort was widely condemned by the press in Britain, but it nevertheless became an important part of Victorian expatriate life.

For the middle classes, opportunities to travel abroad remained very limited until the spread of the railway. This altered almost overnight the habits and expectations of millions, for within a single generation – from the thirties to the fifties – Continental Europe was brought within reach. It was in the middle of this period that an enterprising Englishman changed the nature of travel for ever.

Thomas Cook was a Baptist and a temperance campaigner. One day in 1841 he organized a train to transport a number of his colleagues from Leicester, where he lived, to a temperance meeting at the nearby town of Loughborough. The excursion was a success, and Cook realized that there was potential in the notion of arranging journeys for others. Not only did passengers have greater pleasure in travelling when someone else had dealt with all the arrangements, the railways were willing to offer more favourable rates when block bookings were made in advance, and they could also schedule trains to suit the passengers.

Within four years, Cook was organizing regular trips with the Midland Railway, providing outings to coastal resorts. A decade later he ran an excursion from Leicester to Paris. His ambitions kept pace with his accomplishments, and the next year – 1856 – he began his 'Grand Circular Tour of the Continent'. He meticulously planned these journeys, reconnoitring in person the routes and the places to be visited, and then accompanying the tourists. Italy, a country that had long fascinated the British, was an extremely popular destination. Cook, as a teetotaller, was often dismayed by his passengers' fondness for local wines, which he assumed – often with justification – would have unfortunate effects on their digestion. In one of the more bizarre quotations to emerge from the Victorian era, he pleaded with them: 'Gentlemen! Do you wish to invest your money in diarrhoea?'

Europe and Beyond

The railway and the steamer opened central Europe to the British in the middle decades of the century. The Rhine was filled with Anglo-Saxon tourists, the castles, cathedrals and hotels on its banks echoing to the sound of their language. Armed with guidebooks from the German firm Baedeker, which have been a ubiquitous symbol of tourism ever since, they were known for their noisy confidence and their perpetual complaints – about the food, the beds, the weather, the cost of things, the rudeness of locals and the lack of cleanliness. They colonized Switzerland in the sixties, and they poured into Italy, familiar to their countrymen since the Grand Tour a century earlier, and now treated as an extension of the Home Counties.

Travellers of this sort were not confined to Europe. By the end of the sixties, the empire of Thomas Cook had reached the Middle East. In 1869 he was a guest at the opening ceremonies for the Suez Canal. He was not alone. A multitude of British tourists were also there, brought by his company. In the same year he hired two paddle-steamers and began running excursions to the pyramids. Egypt became almost his personal fiefdom, for he gained from the Ottoman ruler the exclusive right to run excursion boats on the Nile. With this monopoly went a palpable sense of power. He was nicknamed 'Field Marshal Cook' for the armies of native workers he employed as porters, messengers and guides. He was also referred to as 'the real ruler of Egypt'. He was certainly able to influence events there, for he loaned a number of his vessels to the British Army, which used them to transport troops and supplies up-river in the attempt to relieve Gordon at Khartoum. In 1899 he launched the first of a fleet of luxurious paddle-steamers that opened a new chapter in river-cruising, and the Nile had by this time acquired the nickname 'Cook's Canal'.

The British descended on Egypt, in their thousands, for several reasons. The country's history and culture were of course a source of fascination, and appealed to the Victorian desire to combine leisure with improvement. The warm, dry climate was beneficial for those suffering from consumption at home, and numerous Anglo-Saxons developed the habit of spending winters there. A further inducement was the fact that being abroad gave Victorians a certain licence. Young people of both sexes were able to behave with greater freedom than could be found within the tight strictures that governed them at home. At a hotel in Cairo or Alexandria – as in Interlaken or Biarritz – it was much easier to meet strangers who, at home, might well consider one unsuitable. No matter what the differences in station or in income, one had after all something in common: the experiences of travel. Victorian novels are full of instances of embarrassment caused by holiday friendships that cannot be pursued at home. They are also replete with stories of 'adventures' – flirtations, often passing but some-times serious – that women enjoyed with strangers. For men, a tour in Egypt gave frequent opportunities to help young ladies on and off camels or donkeys, or to assist them up the sides of pyramids. For both men and women, this was not the least among their reasons for wishing to travel.

Britain's dominance in Egypt, begun when Disraeli pur-chased control of the Suez Canal and continuing when the country became a protectorate, was a further encouragement to tourists, who could enjoy the protection of British arms amid exotic surroundings. Because the country remained volatile, however, military adventure was sometimes an in-ducement. The prospect of a naval bombardment and the landing of troops prompted this advertisement in *The Times* on 7 March 1885:

> Advertiser proposes to hire a steam yacht and join her at Alexandria, and proceed thence to Suakin at once, in order to WATCH the OPERATIONS AGAINST OSMAN DIGMA. Would be glad to hear of three others willing to JOIN and share expenses. Time required about six or seven weeks, and total expenses probably £300.[4]

Cook and his employees took much of the uncertainty – and therefore the stress – out of foreign travel. Smartly uniformed company staff escorted tourists to, or met them at, their destinations. They arranged hotels, restaurants, guided tours and – where necessary – medical treatment. This made it possible to spend weeks abroad without needing to speak to a single foreigner, and created the prototype of the modern 'package tour'.

Cook's empire continued to expand. He devoted much of the year 1872 to a trip around the world, scouting new routes and destinations. The company opened offices in Calcutta and Bombay, and with them arrived the whole paraphernalia of agents, native staff and chartered vehicles. Cook's tours then spread to East Asia, and it was soon possible to circumnavigate the world with them.

By the mid-eighties tourists could visit any continent. Each of the huge mail-carrying steamers that plied, with clockwork regularity, between Britain and America, Asia and Australasia could carry hundreds of passengers, and onward travel once they arrived was becoming easier. From 1885 it was possible to make a week-long journey across Canada on the Canadian Pacific Railway, and the Australian outback also became a destination for trippers. The western American frontier was not considered 'closed' (i.e. settled and civilized) until 1890 – in other words, places that were still 'wild', and possibly haunted by bandits and armed natives, were already on popular tourist routes. Just as today, there were complaints that mass travel had made the world smaller, taken much of the adventure out of going overseas and filled the hotels and monuments of the globe with undesirable fellow countrymen.

Playing Fields

At the start of the reign the traditional English 'sports' – hunting, shooting and fishing – went on as they always had. In addition there were 'games', cricket and football, the former well organized. Its rules had been codified in 1788, and it was played by eleven-man sides. Football, on the other hand, was a generic term for numerous forms of scrimmage that might involve scores of players – the male populations of rival villages or entire forms of schoolboys. Such rules as existed usually referred to local circumstances. Few moves were unacceptable; injury was taken for granted and was almost universal. In each of the great schools at which football was played – Winchester, Eton, Harrow, Rugby, Charterhouse, Shrewsbury – a different version had developed, based on local geography and conditions and with its own rules, terminology, scoring and even size or shape of ball. The Rugby game, famously 'invented' in 1823 by William Webb Ellis, a boy who (as a memorial plaque at the school announces) 'first took the ball in his arms and ran with it', was taken up over subsequent decades by so many other schools and clubs that it gained a permanent hold throughout the country and beyond. Even those schools that proudly kept their own version of football came grudgingly to accept the Rugby game and to let it share their playing fields.

England had initially had no monopoly of games. Tennis had come from France, and was played in England, at schools and universities, from the fifteenth century. Cricket may also have originated across the Channel as a game played by peasants using a curved bat and a wicket made from sticks. The Celtic countries had their own bat-and-ball games, shinty and hurley. One of them, golf, had been played in England – as a very minor activity – for centuries (it is thought to have been introduced from Scotland by James I), though it did not become popular in the south until the later nineteenth century.

At schools, whether 'public' or otherwise, pupils amused themselves with the usual playground games and with the rolling of hoops. This was often done competitively – one hoop, or several simultaneously, requiring considerable skill to manoeuvre. As cricket developed in the later eighteenth century, schools that were within reach of each other began to compete in the game. Eton played Westminster in 1786 – the first such inter-school fixture – and began playing Winchester a decade later. These contests were not officially approved, and the teams, supporters, venue and subsequent result had to be hidden by both winners and losers from the authorities. When discovered, those involved were usually thrashed or otherwise punished, a situation that continued until, in the 1820s and 30s, some headmasters gradually accepted the advantages of organized exercise. Despite official disapproval, however, games had steadily increased in popularity, and the school athlete had already become the hero that he has remained.

Character Building

Victorian schools are credited with the invention of team games, partly as a means of channelling aggression and using up surplus energy, and it is true that in the decades before Victoria there were a number of noisy rebellions against authority in public schools, resulting in damage and expulsions. Bored young men tended to create trouble with neighbouring farmers by trespassing, poaching and vandalism, and there were often fights with local roughs. Organized games not only lessened these problems but trained participants in fitness, courage, teamwork, fairness and sacrifice. After the cult of games had become established, one of the most trite misquotations of the era was trotted out to justify it: the Duke of Wellington was reputed to have said that the Battle of Waterloo had been 'won on the playing-fields of Eton', though this was a twisting of his words. Games did indeed help to develop many positive qualities, but they entered the world of the school and university (for old boys took the games to Oxford and Cambridge) gradually and in spite, rather than because, of official endorsement.

Thomas Arnold, the legendary Rugby headmaster whose tenure (1828–42) only just lasted into the Victorian era, has been credited with creating the entire public-school ethos. The school he organized became a model for others, his influence spread by several pupils who themselves became headmasters elsewhere. Games were part of this legacy, though in fact Arnold took almost no interest in them (at least he allowed them to be played openly against other schools, which represented progress!). In fact, the fixation with games had outgrown any opposition by the middle decades of the century.

The consolidation of games had derived, like so much else in Britain during the first half of the century, from improvements in transport. The creation of better roads and the building of railways meant that young men could travel to distant schools more easily. The result was an increase in the number of boarders at the great schools. It also meant that teams could much more easily visit each other's schools – or some other, mutually convenient venue – to play fixtures. The growing wealth of the middle class was meanwhile bringing about the opening of new schools: Marlborough, Radley, Clifton, Wellington, Lancing and Cheltenham, as well as a host of smaller establishments, belong to the middle decades of the century. These quickly developed rivalries both with each other and with their more ancient counterparts. There was suddenly a whole network of opponents, and this helped drive the cult of games that had become a frenzy by the end of the century. The availability of competition also meant an increasing standardization of rules.

Willow

Cricket progressed from a school and village game to a county and national sport, with standards of play becoming increasingly high. Bats lost their curved shape and became straight and flat. Wickets were standardized as three – rather than two – upright sticks with bails on top. Boundaries were introduced, and pitches gradually became smoother, which enabled play to become more sophisticated. One development came not from the deliberations of some committee but from the playing of young people in a garden. The older sister of a boy was bowling at him, but owing to the shape of her wide crinoline skirt she was unable to throw the ball underarm, as was universal practice. She therefore bowled it overarm, with her arm straight. This doubtless seemed absurd at first glance, but it proved a much more effective means of delivering the ball. It gave the bowler much greater speed and enabled the ball to be placed with surprising accuracy. It also meant that a fast-moving ball would bounce on the crease, making it far more difficult, and more challenging, to hit. This method was introduced into matches in 1864, and has been used ever since.

County cricket began with irregular, occasional fixtures, but by the end of the reign there were permanent sides with their own – often hallowed – grounds. National teams toured the country and international competition was also well established by the middle years of the reign, for an English side had first gone to Australia in 1861, and thereafter there were regular exchanges. During one of their return visits, in 1877, the Australian team defeated their opponents so decisively that the British press commented that English cricket was dead and that the Australians had taken its ashes home with them. This jibe gave its name to one of the world's most eccentric sporting trophies – a tiny urn containing the remains of a burnt wooden bail – for which the two countries compete every year. It continues to be one of the great sporting fixtures. The international element in this and other games gave an added glamour and an impetus to public enthusiasm. Crowds at matches became bigger as improved public transport and special trains made it possible for greater numbers to attend, and the facilities – grandstands and permanent clubhouses or pavilions – improved.

As games became more sophisticated, those who played them well became increasingly revered. Though there had been 'sports personalities' in the past (one thinks of Regency prize-fighters such as Daniel Mendoza), the new mass media were able to make household names out of the best of them. The most outstanding – and perhaps the greatest British sportsman of all time, for that matter – was W. G. Grace (1848–1915). A Gloucestershire country doctor, his sturdy build – he was as barrel-chested as a blacksmith – and thick beard became his trademarks. He came from a cricketing family (he and two brothers played in the England side against Australia in 1880). At the age of seventeen, playing for England against Surrey in 1866, he scored 224 runs. Thirty years later he made 257 against Kent. In the course of a lengthy career he scored 54,896 runs as well as taking 2,878 wickets. That he was a kindly and convivial man greatly endeared him to the public, who poured into the grounds to see him play. He was perhaps the first of what has been a numerous breed since his time – the national sporting celebrity.

Leather

The first inter-school football match was played between Charterhouse and Westminster in 1863, but in the same year took place a much more important event – indeed, one of the

most significant moments in British sporting history. The
Football Association was formed by a gathering at the Free-
masons Tavern in London, on 26 October, of old boys from
different public schools, who sought to settle differences in
rules and procedures so that they could play matches against
each other. (The word 'soccer' derived from 'Association'.)
This not only cleared the way for such fixtures but enabled
national sides to play against other countries. The Football
Association (FA) Cup was first competed for in 1871, and the
first international match took place the following year. Two
years after that, Oxford and Cambridge played the first
University Match.

Football had, curiously, taken root at both ends of the social
scale. It continued to be played with enthusiasm by the top-
drawer public schoolboys who had organized it, yet it was
taken up with equal enthusiasm by mill hands, railwaymen
and miners in the north and Midlands. In 1879 Darwin, a team
of mill workers, competed for the FA Cup, and in 1883 a side
of Old Etonians were beaten at the Oval by Blackburn.

The first football club to have a constitution and a set of
rules was established at Sheffield in 1860. Six years later
another club that has represented the city ever since – Sheffield
Wednesday – was started. The oldest 'League club' (for it
was to join the Football League when that was founded) in
England or indeed the world was Notts County, which was
raised in 1866. It was in the same period of roughly a decade
and a half that many of the major teams – the household
names of today – came into being: Glasgow Rangers (1872),
Aston Villa (1874), Hibernian (1875), Everton (1878), Sunderland (1879), Tottenham Hotspur (1882), Manchester
United (1885), Arsenal (1886), Glasgow Celtic (1887), Liverpool (1892) and Newcastle United – an amalgamation of two
earlier clubs – in 1893. Many had origins that were humble but

intriguing: Manchester United was formed by employees of the Lancashire and Yorkshire Railway and was originally called Newton Heath. Sunderland was originally 'the Sunderland and District Teachers' Association Football Club' – something of a mouthful for those cheering its efforts. Everton began life as the team of the St Domingo's Sunday School, while Aston Villa was associated with a local Wesleyan chapel. Stoke City, a club dating from as early as 1863, was founded by old boys of Charterhouse.

Though these sides usually began as a group of enthusiastic amateurs, they quickly developed a more serious outlook, for in the eighties and nineties an increasing number of clubs became fully professional: Everton was entirely so by 1885, Arsenal by 1891 and Tottenham by 1895. It was a notion unheard of before that time, but one with which we are familiar today. The Football League, which allowed for organized competition between teams that could be either amateur or professional or a combination of the two, was formed for the 1888–9 season.

Rugby, like soccer, had for some time attracted devotees among the wider public. Players were amateurs, but this situation began to alter in the nineties, when a number of working-class players – and clubs – in the north-west of England wished to turn professional. They were not allowed to do so within the terms of the game's governing body, the Rugby Union. As a result they set up in 1895 their own equivalent, the Northern Union (later the Rugby League), in which players were initially allowed to receive expenses for participating in matches, and then – three years later – to be paid for their services (in fact it had been common for some time to pay then surreptitiously), provided they had some other paid occupation. Not until the following century would the full-time professional player become part of the sporting world, but the basis of this system was established in the Victorian era. The Rugby League meanwhile drifted farther from its parent sport by developing a number of different rules – most notably the playing of matches between teams of thirteen, rather than fifteen, players. The two forms of the game have remained separate, and separately popular, ever since. Though it cannot be established when professional sportsmen began to appear – for wrestlers and boxers had been paid since time immemorial – this aspect of modern games began with the Victorians, the creators of spectator sport as we understand it.

Oars

The fact that a few schools (Eton and Westminster, most obviously) were situated by rivers meant that rowing gradually became a major sport at public schools, and because the universities too were on rivers it was natural that enthusiasm should spread there. The Oxford and Cambridge Boat Race was first staged in 1829, and inter-collegiate competition also became highly organized. The Regatta held annually from 1839 at Henley became – and long remained – a patrician affair, for there was no aquatic equivalent of Rugby League (it was not until well into the twentieth century that the Thames Tradesmen were permitted to compete) and in any case rowing did not gain any noticeable following outside the confines of muscular Christianity. Henley Regatta was not an entirely British affair, however. Rowing had spread to the older American colleges, which consciously modelled much of their gentlemanly ethos on the English universities. Both Harvard and Yale sent crews to take part in the Regatta. In the Victorian world the great sporting clashes between ancient seats of learning attracted much more widespread interest than they do today, and among the many millions who had no connection with these places there would often be a surprising degree of partisan feeling. The newspapers gave extensive coverage to the Eton–Harrow cricket match, first recorded in 1805, so that by the middle of the reign it seemed like a long-established tradition. It was a two-day contest, and was a recognized part of the Season. It could be assumed that much of the Government and aristocracy, as well as the leadership of the Church, the armed forces and industry, would be at Lord's to see it. The Boat Race was less socially exclusive but attracted greater interest. On the day it took place, the light- and dark-blue ribbons of the rival crews could be seen all over London, even on the hats and coats of workmen and flower-sellers. 'Boat Race night' remained a major event at least until the Second World War, with supporters of both sides creating good-natured mayhem in the streets.

Others

Some games owed nothing to the influence of schools. Golf became popular because it was gentle and unstrenuous but very skilful. This meant that it could be played well by people who lacked the size or the fitness level necessary for other sporting activities. It also required very little equipment, for a set of clubs could often be rented, and it was sociable – even a hard-fought match could have much of the feeling of an agreeable outdoor stroll with one's friends (indeed critics of golf liked to describe it as 'a good walk spoiled'). Despite its relative simplicity, it did not appeal to the British working class, developing instead an image as the epitome of suburban respectability. When women began to take part in games, golf was an obvious choice, for long skirts did not hamper an activity that relied on upper-body strength and hand-and-eye coordination. Women's golf clubs had begun to appear by the end of the reign; the St Rule's Ladies' Golf Club was founded at St Andrews in 1898.

The game was largely confined to Scotland until about the eighties, though the first English club, the Royal North Devon, had been established in 1864. St Andrews, on the east coast of Scotland, had a history of golf dating back to the Middle Ages, and was thus considered the Mecca of the game. It was here in 1857 that the first great modern golf tournament took place. This had, in less than two decades, evolved into the Open Championship (so-called because any player, amateur or professional, could take part) that has been held at different clubs throughout Britain ever since. The first entirely amateur championship was held at Hoylake in Cheshire in 1885. The fact that 'professionals' existed at all in this game says something about the speed with which it had gained popularity. The skills of those who could play well and teach others were considered worthy of respect and remuneration. Of these, the most legendary golfer of all time was the St Andrean Tom Morris (1821–1908), four times winner of the Open Championship.

Golf was not the only gentler game to become characteristic of Victorian Britain. Archery enjoyed a vogue in the early and middle part of the reign. Once again, this was an activity that demanded skill and practice but which involved only the upper body, and was thus suitable exercise for ladies. A more sociable pastime was croquet, a game derived from the old French *pell mell* that had been played in England since at least the time of Charles II. Like golf, this was a sociable, peripatetic activity, but required far less space and, significantly, could be played by men and women together (as a result of which it could become highly flirtatious). 'Lawn croquet' was – as was usual with Victorian sporting passions – thoroughly organized and endowed with a set of rules; the Croquet Association, its governing body, was established in 1896. It also, like so many other games, found a spiritual home, in this case at Hurlingham in London.

Another game had, by the later decades of the century, attained an immense popularity and importance. Tennis was, until the 1870s, still the traditional 'real' game that had been played since the Plantagenets. It had complex and arcane rules, and was played in an indoor space such as can still be seen at Hampton Court. In 1873 an army officer, Major Walter Wingfield, invented a game that he called *sphairistike* which rapidly developed into the more familiar lawn tennis. The game was fast and skilful, required minimal equipment and was suited to a (relatively) confined space. It was equally suited to men, women or a combination of both, with matches between two players or four. The game spread like wildfire throughout Britain, for, the 'weekend' having come into fashion, it was an ideal means of killing time socially at country houses in summer. Crossing oceans, it became equally popular in Europe, in America and throughout the British Empire. Within four years of Major Wingfield's invention, the All England Croquet Club, based at Wimbledon, had added to its title the words 'Lawn Tennis', and held the first world tennis championship, an event it has been hosting ever since. Such was the game's popularity that croquet was swiftly pushed aside.

Billiards was not a British invention, though 'snooker' was a game, and a word, bequeathed to the world by Britons. The term in fact meant a first-year cadet at the Royal Military Academy, Woolwich. Used in the context of an officers' mess to mean an amateur or beginner (one officer is said to have remarked that 'We are all snookers at this game') it enjoyed considerable vogue in the Indian Army. The same was true of polo, a game played in ancient India and Persia but organized with the usual thoroughness by Anglo-Saxons. It perfectly suited the high spirits of young officers stationed in Indian garrisons where there was very little else to do. As readers of Winston Churchill's memoirs will know, several hours every day were devoted to practising and playing, and it was effectively compulsory to have a passion for it. It was taken up by civilians too, and made its way through the English mercantile community to Argentina, where it is still avidly played – yet another British sporting legacy to have put down roots far from home.

A rare example of traffic flowing in the other direction – an unexpected sporting manifestation that was largely confined to the north of England – was baseball. This game, similar to the old English game of rounders, had been organized in the United States in 1839. Sixty years later it was so popular in parts of England that there was a league of professional teams, as well as a number of amateur clubs – indeed the football stadium in which Derby County plays is to this day called the Baseball Ground. It has not been established when or why this sport took root in industrial Britain, nor is it known how or why it declined. A silver trophy in the museum at Stockton-on-Tees bears witness to the prestige it once enjoyed in that area.

Whatever the origins in England of this transatlantic import, native English games continued to proliferate. The public schools had produced the game of fives – a type of contest that involved ricocheting a ball, propelled either by the hand or by various forms of bat, around a court that was either completely enclosed or open at one end. As with other games, each school had its own version that was dictated by local conditions. The most famous of these was, and is, the Eton game, which was played between two of the buttresses of College Chapel. The shape of the 'court' was dictated not only by these but by the jutting, at the left-hand side, into the playing-space of the stone banister from a flight of steps. The game was successful, popular and much imitated. The school itself built rows of fives courts, and the design has been copied internationally. In each instance, the same jutting banister has been included.

From fives developed two games that have outdistanced it in popularity: racquets and squash. Both were developed at Harrow. Racquets was a fast game played with a hard ball in an enclosed court, and required a certain amount of courage. It achieved a slightly wider popularity, during the sports craze of the mid-century, through the efforts of public-school old boys, who had courts built in a few locations in London, but it remained – as it has ever since – confined to these schools and to those who attended them. Squash, on the other hand, is played all over the world. A game for two or four players, it uses a rubber ball and racquets similar to, but smaller than, those used for tennis. It was played – again by the middle of the century – by boys unable to get into the racquets court, who amused themselves by hitting a rubber ball off an outside wall (the ball 'squashed' when impacting on this).

As well as inventing, adapting and playing games, the British copiously wrote about them. *Wisden*, the annual bible of cricket, was begun in 1864 by a cigar merchant of that name, and the *Football Annual*, a similar volume dealing with the other most popular game, began at roughly the same time. The *Badminton Library*, a series of exhaustive reference books on all major and minor sports, was published throughout the later Victorian decades and rapidly gained the reputation of being the 'last word' on questions relating to the subjects. Sets of these were an essential component in the libraries of gentlemen's clubs and country houses. Though subsequent works of reference have been as authoritative, none has been as thorough.

Given British dominance of the world of sport, it might seem surprising that it was a Frenchman – Charles, Baron de Coubertin – who founded the modern Olympic Games. Coubertin, however, a somewhat eccentric character who was a passionate anglophile, was a great admirer of the English public schools and their ethos. He made, in fact, a pilgrimage to Rugby School chapel in 1883 to see the tomb of Thomas Arnold, and fell on his knees beside it in a kind of trance, lost in a sense of deep reverence. His own country had been defeated in war and he believed its future salvation lay in training French youth by the same methods the Doctor had used. Though he failed to make headway with this notion, thirteen years later he presided over the first modern Olympic Games at Athens, and his inspiration was once again the playing fields of Rugby.

Once the machine age had produced greater, and more widespread, leisure it was the British who more or less single-handedly organized the ways in which it could be profitably used. It has proved a more lasting legacy than the nation's military and economic ascendancy.

10

THE PRESS AND LITERATURE

The Papers

During the second half of the nineteenth century two important elements came together to create a revolution in communications. The first was a massive increase in the amount of material published. The second was a massive increase in the number of people able to read. Rapid advances in printing techniques made possible for the first time publishing for a mass market, while the Education Act of 1870 provided, almost overnight, a colossal reading public. In addition to this, following the reforms of 1867 and 1884, this wider public had political power that could be influenced and exploited. The implications of this changed for ever the style and content of journalism and the role of the written word in British life.

From the 1840s onwards, greatly improved machinery enabled newspapers, and other printed materials, to be produced more quickly, more cheaply, in greater quantities and with greater sophistication than ever before. Illustrations could be reproduced with much greater clarity, and by the end of the century it was possible to reproduce photographs and coloured pictures, a fact that was to give rise to a plethora of illustrated weekly papers. The writing and presentation of news also underwent great changes. From the earliest printed periodicals in the seventeenth century until the latter decades of the nineteenth, the format of newspapers had remained essentially the same: though there might be a decorative 'masthead', with bold lettering, a royal coat of arms or even an engraving, the outside of the paper was considered to be of little importance. The front and back pages were used for columns of advertisements because they were regarded as mere wrapping, while the news itself was on the inside pages. Even here, news items were not announced through headlines or bold type, but simply placed in columns according to whether they were domestic or foreign news. The stories were difficult to find amid the bland and uniform layout, and the type was so small that it must have strained the eyes.

A random sample – the *Morning Star* (no relation of its present-day Communist namesake) for 6 July 1857 – may serve as an example. It is four pages long and its name, set between two decorative stars, is in Gothic script. The front page is entirely given over to advertisements for performances at London's theatres, cheap excursions on the Great Western Railway and life insurance. Half a column is given over to advertising coal from different collieries. There is also an intriguing miscellany of other goods and services: 'Water your garden with flexible tube, from 2d per foot'; 'Try Rogers's improved method for Fixing Artificial Teeth'; 'Swimming learnt in an hour'; 'Crimean Tents – A large quantity, available for gardens, lawns &c, to be SOLD'; 'Where shall we dine? –

at the SALUTATION TAVERN, 17, Newgate Street'; 'Washing in Earnest'. Lively though these sometimes are, they are not eye-catching in the way we would expect. Inside, the news is a good deal less interestingly presented: 'Parliamentary Business for the Week'; 'Foreign News' ('The Insurrection in Italy', 'The Ballot in the United States'). Admittedly there is almost a whole page on 'The Glasgow Poisoning' and the trial of Mary Smith, one of the century's most important criminal cases, but it is presented without any attempt to draw the reader's attention or hold his interest. The back page is divided, more or less equally, between theatre reviews and financial news.

Only gradually did this format change, but while daily papers remained conservative in their approach, other periodicals broke new ground. There already existed weekly papers – some of them small enough in format to fit in the pocket – and these had engraved illustrations, on their covers and inside. Such decoration was unheard of in national newspapers, but was popular with the public. A young printer, Herbert Ingram, decided to launch a weekly newspaper that would be heavily illustrated with engravings, and in May 1842 the first issue of the *Illustrated London News* appeared.

Pictorial Papers

It was an instant success. Its masthead featured a beautiful and detailed view of the London skyline, and its sixteen pages – all copiously illustrated – dealt with the campaign in Afghanistan, an exploding steamboat in America, a train crash in France, the candidates for the presidential election in the United States and a costume ball at Buckingham Palace. This first issue, costing sixpence, sold 26,000 copies. It marked the beginning of a new era in journalism, for it enabled the pubic to see the news as well as reading it – an impact similar to that of televised news in a later era. The pictures were usually drawn from descriptions of events, and often owed much to the artist's imagination, but as use of the camera became more widespread, a few subjects – such as machinery at the Great Exhibition – could be engraved from photographs, and the subject could be shown with a good deal of accuracy. The *ILN* quickly spawned imitators, for there were enough national and world events to fill the pages of rivals.

Some of the pictures in the *ILN* were huge. A depiction of a battle, or a royal occasion, could fill the centre-spread, and even more ambitious proportions could be attained by having folding pages. The detail and vividness of these images made them extremely popular, and important events (such as the Duke of Wellington's funeral in 1852) provided scope for special editions that not only showed the public what happened but provided them with a beautiful keepsake. The large illustrations were – as they were intended to be – hung or pinned on the walls of millions of homes, providing a significant influence on the taste of the broad public. A painting from the Crimean War shows a hut in which officers spent the winter outside Sevastopol. Its wooden walls are entirely covered with engravings taken from illustrated papers. Many of these same pictures, expensively coloured, mounted and framed, can be bought today. They have helped define for us an image of Victorians filling their homes with jingoistic visions of imperial glory. Though pride in these achievements will undoubtedly have played its part, it is worth remembering that such pictures represented state-of-the-art news reporting and a triumph of printing technology.

Over the following decades – for it was only towards the end of the century that technical advances made possible the inclusion of photographs in papers – these engraved illustrations became almost an industry in themselves. Imagination continued to guide the artists who drew them (after all, one could not depict a fire or an earthquake in some distant country by any other method) but to a surprising extent they were also based on observation. This was especially the case with military campaigns. Throughout the American Civil War, the Zulu War, the Gordon relief expedition and the Boer War, artists accompanied the armies and sketched the fighting. The 'specials', as these men were known, travelled the world and were as used to the rigours of campaigning as any veteran soldier. They shared all the dangers of the battlefront, and might even join in the fighting, since they often carried a revolver for protection. The extent to which they saw war 'from the sharp end' is witnessed by the case of the most famous of them, Melton Prior. A household name in Victorian Britain, Prior was known to colleagues as 'the screeching billiard ball' because of his high-pitched voice and shining, bald pate. During an attack on British troops in the Sudan, their commanding officer yelled at Prior to keep his head down because its gleam was attracting enemy fire!

The drawings of men like Prior were often made on light-weight paper (for ease of transport) and sent home from the battlefields by whatever means was possible – stuffed in the bags of Army dispatch-riders as far as the nearest town, then brought by railway and steamship back to London. In a matter of days the sketches would be published as engravings. Just as the advent of the telegraph at the time of the Crimean War had made it possible for the British public to read of events over the breakfast table shortly after they happened, so images of great happenings could be examined within a week or ten days. The process by which this was made possible was simple. The artist's drawings would have been glued on to wooden blocks that would then be cut with engraving tools by teams of specialists. The original would be destroyed but the engraved version could be covered in ink and printed. Though a good deal of spontaneity and freshness was lost – the finished product could be lamentably bad in comparison – the result was still impressive and made a powerful impact.

As well as serious news magazines of this sort (*Harper's Weekly* and *Frank Leslie's Illustrated Weekly* are other examples), there were others that dealt entirely with crime. Of these the best-known was the *Illustrated Police News*. This weekly journal, a staple of Victorian barber shops but understandably considered unsuitable for respectable households, was extremely graphic in both its written and drawn depictions of crimes. The issue for 10 June 1882 featured on its cover the 'Horrible Tragedy at Fulham', with sketches of 'Policeman supporting the dying man', 'Body shewing stab-wounds', 'Jury viewing the body' and 'The prisoner, Richard Wells'. In case these details were not enough to tempt purchasers, the cover also showed a young man 'accidentally hanged at Southwark' and – less salaciously – a playground accident that befell a young girl: 'Fatal skipping – Peckham'. With the 'Whitechapel Murders' six years later, sales of this magazine reached a zenith.

By the nineties it was possible to print photographs in magazines. Though this made them somewhat expensive – they sold for shillings rather than pence – it marked the arrival of the modern world in relation to journalism, for photography has dominated the press and periodicals ever since. From the advent of the *ILN* it had been the case that text had to be shortened and fitted around the illustrations, and as a result both the format and the content of periodicals had changed. News had to be told more concisely, and text had to be more eye-catching because it had to compete for attention.

Entertaining Papers

The creation of a vastly expanded reading public through compulsory education also impacted on the presentation of news. The newly literate millions might be able to understand a newspaper, but they did not want to pay to read dry and long-winded articles. They represented a huge market for sales, but to capture it the papers must be made entertaining and readable for those who had a short attention span or limited time. A press like this already existed across the Atlantic, and the same methods began to be copied in Britain. Great issues were presented not in ponderous articles but in short paragraphs designed to be read quickly by people in a hurry. News, instead of mere advertisements, was put on the front page. An important new technique was pioneered in 1884 by the *Pall Mall Gazette* when it published an interview with General Gordon: thereafter, readers could hear the news from those who actually made it. Journalism ceased to be the aloof, semi-academic discipline it had previously been, but the new brash approach could come close to the opposite extreme: 'The news tended to be shorter and often trivial, and lacked the guidance necessary to help its readers understand, or even follow it.'[1] Cheap (halfpenny) newspapers and evening and Sunday papers, as well as the illustrated weekly papers, all became established during this period. This 'New Journalism', consciously modelled on the American press and directed at the lower echelons of the professional class ('written by office boys for office boys'), could control its readers' access to world events and thus direct their thoughts and opinions.

Alfred Harmsworth, the greatest exponent of this New Journalism, launched his *Daily Mail* in 1896 with the state-ment – for he had realized that imperial issues were currently attracting immense public interest – that it stood for 'the power, the supremacy, the greatness of the British Empire'. Harmsworth was a man well suited to the times. Born in 1865, he had been a professional journalist since the age of fifteen, and had become established as a publisher at twenty-two. A man of boundless energy and wide interests, he had quickly developed a firm grasp of 'popular' journalism, and used this to telling effect. In 1894, two years before he established the *Mail*, he acquired the *Evening News*.

This was regarded as the beginning of a new era in Fleet Street. The paper's motto was 'all the news in the shortest space', and its approach to news was gossipy, trivial and concise. Harmsworth paid for some of the best available writers to provide leading articles – prepackaged social and political opinions – that were no more than paragraphs in length. He also studied the interests of the reading public and aligned his publications with their needs. Hobbies, in an age of greatly increased leisure, filled numerous pages: reports of sporting fixtures, discussions of new dance crazes, tips on how to play tennis or ride a bicycle or create a floral paradise in your small back garden. His papers specifically targeted women by featuring pages devoted to fashion, household topics or the sports that they now played. There were crosswords and other types of puzzle to beguile odd moments while one waited for a train, and there were competitions that offered prizes. The technical marvels of the day were described and explained– the motor car, the aeroplane, the cinema. The sheer variety of things to read in a newspaper was bewildering, but this was balanced by a perceived trivializing of important issues and the danger of filling the minds of the half-educated with prejudices. In other words, culture, learning and news were being 'dumbed down' by a mass media – a charge that is often levelled, and with equal justification, in our own time. As in the present day, each successful newspaper or magazine was soon followed by imitators who borrowed the format and filled their pages with similar contents. By the end of the century, station bookstalls groaned beneath the weight of pictorial weeklies (the *Sketch* and the *Sphere* were perhaps the best known), social gossip publications and hobby journals. There were other periodicals devoted simply to providing reading matter. The *Strand* magazine gained immense popularity by publishing the adventures of Sherlock Holmes. For the seriously thoughtful, *Frazer's Magazine* provided quality writing; for the seriously frivolous, *Vanity Fair*, founded by the colourful soldier, traveller and politician Fred Burnaby, provided diversion. This produced a regular series of humorous portraits of political, social and sporting figures, signed with the pen-names 'Spy' and 'Ape' that became hugely popular. Many of them still decorate pubs and restaurants today.

Comic Papers

As well as producing the illustrated magazine, the Victorian age honed the satirical publication to an edge of excellence. For generations prior to the Queen's accession, when the monarchy had been scandal ridden and deeply unpopular, there had been satire in both the written word and the 'public prints' that was disrespectful and vicious. At the lower end of journalism there were cliquish and muck-raking partisan newspapers that defended particular political viewpoints and vigorously attacked others. In the thirties there were several short-lived magazines that took on the function of poking fun at government and Society: *Punchinello*, *Figaro in London*, *Punch in London*, *Charivari*.

In 1841, a group of journalists and authors met at a tavern in Dulwich to establish a more ambitious periodical. *Punch* – its title indicates that it was heavily indebted to its predecessors

– first appeared in July of that year, and was subtitled *The London Charivari* in recognition of the fact that it was inspired by a French publication. It was the brainchild of several gifted men, Douglas Jerrold, Mark Lemon and Henry Mayhew among others, and in its early years was radical and somewhat scurrilous. It also had something of the cheerful amateurishness of a school magazine, for it was put together by a convivial group of friends, and it must have been enormous fun to produce. It attacked social abuses and unpopular governments at home and abroad (it was several times banned in Continental countries), parodied (very cleverly) literature and the stage and filled gaps between articles with often hideous puns. It was illustrated by line drawings, initially to accompany the text, or decorative head- and tail-pieces. Such light-hearted drawings were called 'cuts', but after one of them, depicting an art gallery, was captioned 'Cartoon', this term (which in the art world meant a preliminary sketch) became a catch-all term for humorous illustrations. *Punch*, whose early illustrators included John Leech, the portrayer of Dickens' Mr Pickwick, gradually acquired a reputation as a showcase for drawings that were beautiful and accomplished as well as funny. It outgrew any notion of being copied from French originals and was itself followed by a number of imitators: *Judy*, *Fun* and the curiously named *Ally Sloper's Half-Holiday*. *Punch* artists often worked on these other periodicals, whose style and content were at least superficially similar. Between them, they did much to define our impression of nineteenth-century Britain.

By the end of the sixties, chiefly through the influence of William Makepeace Thackeray, *Punch* had lost its radicalism and positioned itself where it was to remain until its demise in the 1990s – squarely in the upper bourgeoisie. Cartoons were now the major part of its appeal, and this class looked through it to see reflections of themselves and their world. The drawings of George du Maurier captured it during the seventies and eighties, for his images and captions were often drawn from his own family life. As well as merely providing humour, *Punch* produced serious, full-page drawings to commemorate specific events. Many of them depicted Britannia, with helmet, sword and shield, reacting to triumphs and disasters abroad – grim faced while slaughtering Indian Mutineers, or weeping above the caption 'Too Late!' when Gordon was killed at Khartoum. The most famous of these drawing – *Dropping the Pilot* – appeared in 1890 and referred to the dismissal of Bismarck as Chancellor by Kaiser Wilhelm II. Together with Du Maurier's *True Humility*, with the curate saying of his egg: 'Parts of it are excellent', this became the most famous *Punch* cartoon of all time.

The artists who drew these images were at the top of their profession at a time when British pen and ink drawing was at its height. John Tenniel – best known as the illustrator of *Alice's Adventures in Wonderland* – was followed by Linley Sambourne, Bernard Partridge, Harry Furniss, Phil May, Edward Tennyson Reed, F. H. Townsend, Dudley Hardy and many others. Though largely forgotten today, the work of these 'black-and-white men', as they were known, was instantly recognizable to contemporaries, and each had their admirers.

Edifying Papers

Naturally, not all periodicals were trivial. It was entirely in keeping with Victorian earnestness that there should be a wealth of instructive family reading matter, and indeed there were whole publishing houses – the Religious Tract Society, for instance – devoted to this market. Not only was there a demand for light literature that could be read on the Sabbath, there was also a need for wholesome and informative short articles that would fill the minds of the young with useful knowledge, and for innocent games and puzzles that would help to pass the long hours of a rainy afternoon. The publishers' response was a number of titles – *The Quiver*, *Sunday*, *Sunday at Home* – that admirably fulfilled this role. Though the genre was very much a product of its time, and did not survive the Queen by more than a few decades, it was remembered with affection by many of those who read it.

Books

Literature of all kinds was a great deal more widely available to Victorians than it had ever been before, because books had become cheaper and more widespread. A number of technical developments between the twenties and forties had made it possible to typeset, print and bind books more easily, with the result that prices began to fall. Some publishers also issued novels in instalments – *Pickwick Papers* was a notable example of this. It made sense to publish in this way, for interest in the story built up momentum as the weeks went by and sales increased, while for purchasers the cost of the volume was spread in a kind of hire-purchase arrangement – but was greater than it would have been had they bought a complete book. The price of books continued to fall throughout the century. The use of inferior, wood-pulp paper from the seventies and the advent of the paperback at about the same time meant that the craftsmanship involved in making a book might now be minimal, if not non-existent.

This revolution in publishing brought reading, for learning and leisure, within reach of most of the public. One result of this was a great increase in professional writers, as thousands of hacks laboured to satisfy a desire for print that had become insatiable. Whether with established 'classics' or lowbrow fiction, the later years of the reign saw a positive deluge of 'cheap editions', 'pocket editions', 'abridged editions' and, perhaps most significant, 'collected editions'. It became possible to purchase whole collections of poetry, Shakespeare's plays or the entire output of some other writer, in editions with small type and lightweight paper that were cheap enough to give as school prizes and small enough to carry in an overcoat pocket. By this means traditional literature, as well as new works, could be appreciated by anyone in return for a modest outlay, and great poetry and prose could become familiar to millions. This development of accessible, popular literature did not mean, of course, that all books were of a similarly basic standard, as anyone knows who has seen, for example, the presentation volumes of children's books illustrated by Arthur Rackham.

As well as an increase in inexpensive editions, there were more places in which books could be found. The early years of the century had witnessed a spread of libraries – subscription libraries, Mechanics' Institute libraries, public libraries – and the trend continued in Victoria's reign, for her subjects' desire for progress, learning and self-improvement ensured that the momentum was kept up. For aspirational labourers and artisans there were a host of cheap subscription libraries – requiring the payment of an initial fee and then a subscription of a penny a week or so – that offered newspapers, novels and textbooks. There were also reading rooms set up by the temperance movement as an alternative to public houses. The middle classes too had subscription libraries, and these might grow to colossal proportions: Mudie's in new Oxford Street, London, was established in 1842. It lent books all over the country, and indeed the world, becoming a byword for respectable reading matter, for Mudie saw himself as responsible for ensuring that the books he bought, lent out and encouraged the publication of should be beyond reproach. The previous year a rather more studious establishment had already opened: the London Library, begun by Thomas Carlyle, irritated that he could not obtain a book he wanted at the British Library because of heavy demand. It rapidly grew to the proportions of a university library (it too loaned books widely in Britain and abroad) and itself became part of the history of Victorian literature through the numerous writers who became members. Though Mudie's has long gone, the London Library is still in business on its original site in St James' Square. Other cities opened similar facilities, many of which – the Literary and Philosophical Society in Newcastle is an example – continue to flourish.

As with so much else in this era, the spread of literacy owed much to the railway. People making journeys in well-lit carriages had the time and the opportunity to read, and it was not long before it occurred to book-dealers that there was a ready market for their wares at the new stations. The first bookstall opened at Fenchurch Street in 1841, and was quickly followed by one at Euston. Seven years later, William Henry Smith entered this trade. Smith's family was already well established in the business. His father had begun selling newspapers from a shop in the Strand in 1792, and the firm had already cornered the market in supplying these, via stagecoaches, to provincial cities. Where they considered the coaches too slow at bringing news of some great event, they hired their own mounted relays to deliver them. With the building of the railway network, Smith's had been able to speed even further the distribution of newspapers, but they also saw the potential for selling them at stations. Within thirty years of taking over the bookstall at Euston, W. H. Smith was running more than four hundred such stalls throughout the country. Smith was a man of great personal integrity, and, like Mudie, sought to give the public only reading matter that was constructive and edifying. He therefore personally controlled the material on his company's stalls. It was not long before editions of books were being published especially for railway passengers and for the bookstalls that supplied them. Longman's, Routledge and John Murray – all illustrious names in the publishing world – each brought out a series called 'Railway Library' or 'Traveller's Library' and reaped the benefits in sales.

The Victorian era was, by any measure, an age of overwhelming literary achievement. Among novelists it produced Dickens, Trollope, Thackeray and Thomas Hardy, as well as highly popular but less enduring writers such as Bulwer Lytton, Whyte Melville and Benjamin Disraeli. There were outstanding and significant women writers: George Eliot, Elizabeth Barrett Browning and the Brontë sisters. In poetry there were Tennyson, Robert Browning and Rudyard Kipling. There were bestselling travel books such as Edward Whymper's *Scrambles amongst the Alps* (1871) and Frederick Burnaby's *A Ride to Khiva* (1877). The genre of detective fiction, created in the United States by Edgar Allan Poe, was taken to new heights from 1887 onwards by the Scottish author Arthur Conan Doyle with his novels and stories of Sherlock Holmes – achieving a popularity never surpassed by any rival author or character. In children's literature, Charles Lutwidge Dodgson – Lewis Carroll – produced two of the greatest stories of all time in *Alice's Adventures in Wonderland* (1865) and its sequel *Through the Looking-Glass and What Alice Found There* (1871).

Books for Boys

Books for youth became a publishing industry in their own right, appearing in greater numbers than had ever been known. While authors of literature for adults were too diverse and individual to categorize, the work of those who wrote for an audience of schoolboys and adolescents has often been dismissed as a collection of 'ripping yarns' – a genre that has long passed out of favour, except as a curiosity. This is worth examining, however, because it had a profound influence on millions of young men throughout Britain, its Empire and the rest of the world. It reflected a self-image that remained powerful until the Second World War, and which was therefore a significant Victorian legacy.

At the beginning of the reign juvenile literature had been characterized by the scurrilous 'penny dreadfuls' that dealt almost entirely with crime and with the exploits of anti-heroes such as 'Spring-heeled Jack'. Given the climate of increasing respectability that was already taking hold in Britain, it was inevitable that this branch of popular literature would undergo a significant transformation – though this happened somewhat gradually – as attempts were made to provide the young with more edifying reading matter. In 1855 Samuel Beeton (the husband and publisher of Mrs Beeton) produced the *Boy's Own Magazine*. This is not to be confused with the *Boy's Own Paper*, or 'BOP', a later publication that was sold either weekly or as an annual volume, the latter becoming the archetypal Christmas present for Victorian boys. It was to be the forerunner of a type of literature, published in both book and periodical form, that would remain popular for almost a century. Adventure stories enjoyed a huge vogue. Often they were set in far-flung territories of the Empire, which offered – like the American West – a suitably uncluttered environment in which to fight the battles of civilization. The British public already enjoyed a somewhat smug sense of superiority over other nations, and the literature that its younger citizens read reflected this. Because patriotism was a wholesome and worthy subject, stories stressed British virtues such as courage, loyalty and fairness; foreigners were often depicted as lacking these qualities.

The ideals presented to young readers were influenced by two particularly nineteenth-century factors: the revival of interest in chivalry resulting from the novels of Sir Walter Scott – though Scott had died in 1832, his influence continued to reverberate throughout the century – and the cult of 'muscular Christianity' of Dr Arnold's Rugby, which did the same. These spread the qualities and outlook of the archetypal public schoolboy to millions who did not attend such places, and made these attributes characteristic of Victorian Britain.

Alfred Harmsworth's journalistic influence reached into the world of Victorian juvenilia. He was the publisher of several successful boys' magazines – *The Wonder*, *The Marvel*, *Union Jack*, *Boy's Herald* and *Boy's Friend* – whose writers became household names. Much of the sensational, exciting fiction for boys appeared initially in periodicals and was subsequently published in book form (this was the case with one of the century's most famous adventure stories – Robert Louis Stevenson's *Treasure Island*, which came out in 1883). They included R. M. Ballantyne, whose story *The Coral Island* was one of the earliest in the field. W. H. G. Kingston wrote *Peter the Whaler* and *Long Ago and Far Away*. The most prolific, and successful, was G. A. Henty, who produced one hundred and forty-four titles, all of them historical novels set in the distant or recent past and all offering similarly straight-forward stories of youthful courage amid cataclysmic events.

Though they were immensely popular in their time – school libraries often had to limit borrowers to three Hentys at a time – the books became dated and discredited once the Empire that they celebrated had passed from history and had become unfashionable. They have recently enjoyed a revival in the United States, where they are especially popular among conservative parents for the narrative vigour as well as for the moral strength and clean language of their heroes; 'suffused', as one newspaper put it, 'with the high moral expectations of the Victorian era', they have found a new readership. A website has hailed them as 'lessons of honesty, pluck, strength of character and religious tolerance'.[2] Like many aspects of Victorian culture, they may eventually enjoy a renaissance as a wider public rediscovers them.

Whatever form the written word may have taken, the spread of literacy and of the reading habit did much to shape a uniform mass culture (much the way that television would do in the following century), in which literary and fictional references could be recognized by people in all parts of the kingdom.

11

ARMS AND THE WORLD

The Age of Confidence

In 1853 an American author, George Stillman Hilliard, published a description of the English tourists he encountered in the streets and museums of Rome. His comments capture the essence of the Victorian abroad and sum up the Briton's view of his country's place in the world:

They walk over the land as if it were their own. There is something downright uncompromising in their air. They have the natural language of command, and their bearing flows from the proud consciousness of undisputed power. A new sense of the greatness of England is gathered from travelling on the Continent, for, let an Englishman go where he will, the might and majesty of his country seems to be hanging over him like an unseen shield. Let but a hand be laid upon an English subject and the great British lion begins to utter menacing growls. An English man-of-war seems to be always within one day's sail of anywhere. If there be even a roll of English broadcloth or a pound of English tea to be endangered thereby, within forty-eight hours a frigate is pretty sure to drop anchor in the harbour.[1]

This confidence was evident in British travellers up to the time of the First World War and even beyond. It was the product of centuries of conditioning. In Elizabeth's reign the Protestant English had seen themselves as a chosen people and their defeat of the Armada as evidence of divine endorsement. They had become the world's foremost naval power. Over subsequent centuries, numerous victories at sea consolidated a maritime supremacy that came to be taken for granted at home, and which accustomed British subjects to the notion that their government could reach out to the farthest corners of the globe. After the defeat of both France and Spain at Trafalgar in 1805 this confidence increased, for the country's two traditional enemies, and closest rivals, were now removed from the scene. Neither was ever seriously to menace British coasts, or interests, again, and no other power was to threaten British dominance until the end of the century.

While the Royal Navy saw itself as the world's only maritime superpower, the Army was also highly regarded. Entirely composed of volunteers, it was far smaller than the great conscript forces with which Napoleon had fought, and its size was to remain a source of derision for Europeans with mass armies at their disposal (Bismarck once sneered that, if the British Army invaded Germany, he would send the Berlin police to arrest them). Nevertheless, it had centuries of success to its credit. In pursuit of Britain's traditional foreign policy, which was to prevent any one of the European nations becoming powerful enough to dominate the Continent, it had been victorious against the French and Spanish throughout the eighteenth century as well as against Napoleon, and had suffered defeat only from fellow Britons in America.

'Johnny Foreigner'

The attitude of the British to those near neighbours who had been their recent foes was one of smug superiority (the impertinence and disrespect accorded many native-born French masters at English schools throughout the era was typical). It was taken for granted that most other races were lazy and effete, and that they could not compete either in trade or in arms with Anglo-Saxons. As Pip in Dickens' *Great Expectations* had said of the 1820s: 'Britons had at that time particularly settled that it was treasonable to doubt our having and our being the best of everything.'[2] This attitude was equally characteristic of the rest of the century.

Among foreigners, those from northern Europe were the most respected by the British. They were similar in race and religion, and the efficiency of Scandinavians, Dutch and, above all, Germans was admired. These countries were trading nations too, though they were too small, or too little industrialized, to pose any significant threat. Germany had many and obvious links with Britain's Royal Family, and even when in 1871 its disparate states combined to form a powerful nation, Britons saw no cause for alarm. It was only in the last years of Victoria's reign, when the Kaiser's navy began a programme of ambitious expansion, that Germany began to replace France as the most likely opponent in a future war.

Britons viewed Latin nations, whether they were southern Europeans or South Americans, as quaintly amusing. These peoples, their enterprise sapped by hot climates and the overabundance of nature, were seen as lacking the necessary qualities of discipline and determination to deserve prosperity, for great powers must be able to lead by example. Where such countries had colonial empires – as did the Spanish and Portuguese – their colonies were badly run and in decay. When, in 1898, Spain's overseas empire was taken over by the 'Anglo-Saxon' United States, it was assumed that the territories concerned would now flourish.

The colonial peoples themselves rated below even Latins in the pecking order of nations. Despite the fact that British imperial subjects included members of ancient – and undeniably great – civilizations such as China, India and Burma, these peoples were regarded as incapable of self-government. Britain, like France, saw its empire not only as an economic resource to be used for the benefit of the mother country but as the setting for a civilizing mission. Anglo-Saxon efficiency, enlightened religion, British values, sports and education would eventually render indigenous peoples fit to manage their own affairs, but this was not expected to happen soon. The British founded some excellent schools and colleges throughout their Empire – Raffles Institution in Singapore and Mayo College in India are examples – and these created a native elite with the skills and expectations appropriate to an educated class. That there were no opportunities for them to serve in higher administrative, academic or commercial posts created a frustration that was to increase throughout the period of British rule. Uninterested in their colonies until the latter half of the reign, the Queen's subjects discovered an enthusiasm for the Empire only gradually. The title Empress of India, assumed by Victoria in 1877, awakened some pride, and the popularity of Empire increased so much in the following two decades that the Diamond Jubilee was treated more as a celebration of the country's colonial might than of its ruler's sixty-year reign.

The rush to acquire territories by other powers, including the new nations Germany and Italy, spurred Britain to action; the 'Scramble for Africa' in the eighties and nineties was expected to be followed by a Scramble for China, as Europe fought over any land or resources that became available. Though the British Government often did not want to take on the administration of further territories, it might do so to protect commercial interests, to acquire strategic positions or simply to prevent other nations from seizing them. Seeing their country as the heir to Ancient Rome, the British thought themselves better suited to the task of running other parts of the world than any nation. Their attitude was, frankly and unapologetically, that the more of the globe that was run by their countrymen, the better for civilization.

In many respects they were right. However fashionable it has since become to hate 'colonialism', a visit to any former European colony will indicate a legacy of roads, bridges, schools, churches and hospitals that has often served these communities very well. Planting and irrigation schemes have, often, similarly given lasting benefits to the territories concerned (the tea industry in India and Ceylon, for instance). What must be remembered is that, from the seventies onwards, when candidates for colonial administrative posts began to be selected by highly competitive examinations, the young men going out to run overseas territories were of the highest calibre that Britain could produce (the same was broadly true of the other great powers). They must not only have wisdom, common sense and adaptability, but be able to live under the constant gaze of the local and expatriate population, setting an example of incorruptible impartiality as representatives of the Crown. To an overwhelming extent they succeeded, providing one of the finest and fairest administrative bodies the world has seen.

A Worldwide Network

Britain's confidence was built on commercial, even more than military strength. As a seafaring nation and the discoverers of whole continents, the British had learned to make themselves at home all over the world. As a manufacturing nation they had built a vast network of trading links that had given them dominance over entire regions, as in East Asia. The country's commercial network was far greater than its formal empire, covering places, such as Argentina, that were never British territory. No matter where an Englishman went, he would find British products, British traders or agents or representatives. He was always surrounded by familiar goods, accents, uniforms or faces. The knives and forks in a Russian hotel would prove to be from Sheffield. The boat that carried him up a West African river was likely to have been built on the Clyde. The house in which he stayed in Malaya might have been shipped from Birmingham in a crate and then assembled. The railway locomotive that carried him over the Andes might well have been made in Crewe, and the engine driver, the general manager and the engineers would be found to speak in the rich tones of British regions. In any corner of the earth, there was a chance that a Briton would meet some old acquaintance.

As well as the considerable – and expanding – number of territories throughout the world that were governed and garrisoned by Britain, there were informal communities of expatriates to be met with all over the globe. Apart from those who inhabited the French Riviera, or the hills around Florence, there were Welsh settlers in Patagonia who still spoke their native language, and in the Oporto region of Portugal there were English families that had lived for generations among the vineyards whose produce they exported to their homeland. In many instances the trappings of life in Britain – gentlemen's clubs, foxhunts, Anglican churches, cricket teams – were successfully transplanted in foreign soil.

Leading Nation

The country's trade had made Britain the world's richest nation. This position was not to last, but for most of the nineteenth century Britain's financial confidence, and pre-eminence, were unchallenged. Their nation's wealth and financial know-how guaranteed respect for British merchants and, by extension, all of their compatriots. An Englishman abroad would expect the locals to honour his credit notes without demur, and he might well find, in banks or shipping agencies in foreign cities, a young clerk from Yorkshire or Scotland learning the ropes.

The British were not, of course, the only trading nation, but they had an important edge in their reputation for honesty and efficiency. With simple logic, they had long since decided that reliable service and financial probity were the best guarantee of satisfied customers and further orders, and they had succeeded in spreading all over the world this notion of themselves. In parts of South America the expression 'hora Inglese' (English hour) is still used to indicate punctuality. Because of Britain's industrial pre-eminence, the goods they sold were usually as dependable as their timekeeping. The image they projected to others was one that they liked to believe themselves. A book that looked back at the nineties summed up their attitude to the rest of the world, and the way in which commercial and military might were often linked in the minds of others:

> The vision of a Germany in arms had not [yet] come to discomfort. Nor had the sun of these United States. Pugilists and pork-packers and cowboys it might produce. Financiers – never!

Other empires might or might not have gone the way of all flesh. Not so the British Empire. Who was it that had been set over half the world? England. Who was it that knew how to manage the Indian or the African? England. Who had produced General Gordon, with a cane and a prayer instead of a gun and a curse? England. To whom did the Foreigner pay the secret adulation that vice pays to virtue? Victoria – that is, England. And about this there was a magnificent assurance which precluded hypocrisy. The British Business Man of that day may have been many things – he was never a hypocrite, and though an envious world called him that, it respected him and it especially respected his navy.[3]

While British traders and proconsuls presented the world with an façade of unshakeable self-confidence the reality was somewhat different. The country's greatest asset had been the head start given it by the Industrial Revolution. This had enabled British firms to mass produce and export items that in other countries were still made, slowly and laboriously, by hand. It was inevitable, however, that any country that possessed sufficient raw materials and was able to raise, or attract from elsewhere, the requisite funds could have an industrial revolution of its own. This happened in France during the post-Napoleonic decades. It happened with increasing speed in Germany after the country's unification (the German steel industry, in particular, became a serious and growing rival to Britain's). It was most evident in the United States, which had been industrializing since the end of the eighteenth century. By the last years of the nineteenth it was evident that the future belonged to America. Their early advantage had made the British complacent, and they found themselves as the century went on in an increasingly crowded market-place. Foreign goods were often cheaper because labour costs were lower and quality less important. The Paris Exhibition of 1867 showed how quickly France was catching up with British manufactures, and the *Annual Register* of that year lamented that the United Kingdom:

Owes her great influence not to military successes but to her commanding position in the arena of industry and commerce. If she forgets this, she is lost: not perhaps to the extent of being conquered and reduced to a province, but undoubtedly to the extent of giving up the lead, and ceasing to be a first-rate power. The signs, for those who can read, can be plainly seen.[4]

In 1870 James Anthony Froude, the historian and commentator, wrote that:

English opinion is without weight. English power is ridiculed. Our influence in the councils of Europe is a thing of the past. We are told, half officially, that it is time for us to withdraw altogether from the concerns of the Continent: while, on the other side of the Atlantic, Mr Emerson calmly intimates to an approving audience that the time is not far off when the Union must throw its protecting shield over us in our approaching decrepitude.[5]

This was, perhaps, somewhat alarmist. Britain was not a Continental power and did not expect her opinions there – unless she held the balance in wartime – to carry great weight. Disraeli, in any case, was to prove an influential figure at the Congress of Berlin in 1877. In the matter of America, Froude was nearer the mark, for that country's power was increasing so relentlessly that even a long and costly civil war had not arrested its progress. The United States had apparently limitless natural resources, and despite possessing more than enough living space for its large population, by the end of the century it had begun to acquire overseas territories. The famous poem by Rudyard Kipling in which he urged 'Take up the white man's burden' was addressed to America, as a plea for the world's new great power to take on the same role of benevolent responsibility as had the old.

Guardians of Empire

With the defeat of Napoleon, Britain's Empire had been expanded by several strategic new territories, including the Cape of Good Hope and Malta. The Royal Navy, which protected these colonies, was the strongest anywhere. The Army, though small by Continental standards, had seen off the French. Yet once the war was over complacency quickly set in, and the military establishment became the target for cuts. The British did not like standing armies or large peacetime navies and it has always been the practice to disband these forces as soon as possible. A standing army of 150,000 was no longer necessary, and the country in any case was suffering from a recession in the aftermath of the war. The Navy, too, was burdening the taxpayer. One task alone – that of guarding Napoleon in his mid-Atlantic prison at St Helena – was costing £300,000 a year. Retrenchment followed swiftly, with the Navy being reduced by 107,000 men by 1817. The Admiralty also continued to believe in the value of Britain's traditional sailing ships and to resist any suggestion that it convert to steam power.

Throughout the century the Royal Navy was to enjoy immense prestige in the world. The skills of its sailors in manning a ship and in gunnery were unmatched by any rival. It acted as a highly successful international policeman, and no stretch of water in the world was beyond its reach. With no feasible opponent to challenge it, the Navy devoted its efforts for several decades to stamping out the slave trade, not only stopping slaving ships on the high seas but raiding the assembly ports along the West African coast. As a result, more than 150,000 slaves were freed over a period of fifty years. Pirates were another problem. In 1816 British vessels forced the surrender of Algiers, a hornets' nest of piracy for three hundred years. The last battle fought by British sailing ships was at Navarino Bay in October 1827. They, together with French and Russian fleets under overall British command, were assisting the Greeks in their struggle for independence from Ottoman rule, and the Turkish fleet was wiped out. The British public expected its sailors to give equally short shrift to any other international bully.

'Pam'

Between 1830, when he became Foreign Secretary, and 1865, when he died, Britain's foreign policy was dominated by the personality of Lord Palmerston. Twice Prime Minister, he took a view of the world that was common among the upper and middle classes. He epitomized the smug confidence of the world's richest nation and the home of the world's most powerful fleet. He would brook no insult to the British flag anywhere in the world, and had no qualms about exercising his trademark 'gunboat diplomacy' in defence of national interests. This was no mere cliché. A British vessel sent to lie at anchor off a foreign coast was not only a threat of impending violence, but a symbol of the might that could be summoned to reinforce it.

On 30 November 1840, Acre, a Turkish possession in the Middle East, was bombarded with devastating effect, for one projectile hit the gunpowder magazine and blew up the entire port. The local Turkish ruler, Mehmet Ali, withdrew from all his conquests in the region. Infamously, Britain also engaged the Chinese, who were attempting to end the opium trade that was being forced on them by the East India Company. After the seizure of an opium cargo in the Chinese port of Canton by local authorities, Palmerston sent a letter of protest. This was returned. There followed a period of insult and counter-insult, and punitive action by the British then began. The Navy bombarded Canton and several other ports. The island of Hong Kong was seized and the Chinese were forced, by the Treaty of Nangking in 1842, to accept a humiliating peace that opened several ports to British trade and ceded Hong Kong – a valuable entrepôt that would come to dominate trade in the region – to Britain for ever. The result of the opium wars was to confirm British mercantile dominance in the region, a position the United Kingdom would keep until the Second World War.

'Jack'

The Royal Navy was, on the whole, popular with the public. While the Army was used to quell civil disorder (most notoriously in the Peterloo Massacre in Manchester in 1819, when cavalry broke up a demonstration and killed a number of civilians), the Navy did not impinge on the life of those ashore – except in the occasional form of the press gang. This system of compulsory recruiting, the scourge of Britain's coastal towns during the Napoleonic Wars, had often brought misery to those affected, but had benefited the majority by making it unnecessary to introduce conscription. In the decades after 1815 the press gang remained theoretically in existence, but with the reduction in ships it was no longer necessary to fill crews by these methods. However the harsh shipboard discipline of Nelson's era, based largely on floggings, remained, and ensured that the Navy was kept in a state of sullen efficiency. The public loved the sentimental image of the sailor (as opposed to the soldier, whom they usually mocked and disliked). One of the bestselling books of 1841 was a collection of the naval songs of Charles Dibdin, with illustrations by the Dickens illustrator George Cruikshank, of which Queen Victoria bought fifty copies and the Admiralty five hundred.

Flogging, like the press gang, declined in use rather than being abolished (the last flogging in the Royal Navy took place in 1880) as conditions gradually improved. In 1831, small pensions were granted to sailors with twenty-one years' service. Regular long-term engagements for sailors were introduced in 1853, and all who signed on for these were entitled to pensions. Though there was a Naval Hospital at Greenwich for the care of old and wounded sailors this closed in 1867, for the Navy had been involved in so few major actions by that time that there were not enough veterans to make it worthwhile. The pensioners were sent home and paid what was owing to them there. For officers, there was no question of superannuation. They did not retire, for they held commissions for life. They were put on 'half-pay' (in practice often less than half) and sent home, in theory to be called back when circumstances required. Because no officers left the Navy except through death, junior men – whether able or otherwise – could not gain promotion except on the principle of dead men's shoes, and many naval officers remained captains, lieutenants, or even midshipmen, throughout their careers. Those at the top, in the Admiralty, could retain their posts in perpetuity. The result was a moribund and ineffectual body that had no taste for innovation and did not grasp the importance of new technology. Only in 1860 – presumably after the last Napoleonic relic had left the Admiralty –

did the Navy have its first ironclad warship. The conversion to steam was followed through, slowly and late, for the same reason.

'Tommy'

When Victoria came to the throne, the British Army was largely still a relic of the Napoleonic Wars, its recruits drawn, in the Duke of Wellington's much-quoted phrase, from 'the scum of the earth, enlisted for drink'. Fully a quarter of its manpower came from the poorest part of the United Kingdom – Ireland – and one of them described it as: 'the dernier resort of the idle, the depraved and the destitute', adding that 'the larger part . . . make good soldiers, and useful, if not valuable, servants of the state.'[6]

The Queen's reign would see constant warfare, though most of it would be minor. Only in a single year – 1862 – would her soldiers not be involved in conflict somewhere in the world. These actions would accustom British troops to fighting on all continents and in all conditions, and render them the world's most battle-hardened army. There would be a steady evolution in their tactics, weaponry, organization, planning and quality throughout the Victorian era, though the reign would end in military ignominy with the Boer War, and the quality of the British soldier – in terms of initiative rather than bravery or doggedness – would still leave something to be desired. Only two years before the outbreak of the South African conflict, Besant wrote what he may have assumed would be an end-of-term report on Victoria's Army. His choice of battles is interesting, for several of those he mentions were embarrassing debacles, while others are entirely forgotten. One of them, the landing at Tel-el-Kebir, was not even opposed:

If, during this period, our Navy has proved our 'first line of defence', it is equally true that of our Army that it has been employed as our 'first line of offence' in almost every quarter of the globe., and in no era of our history of the same length have our soldiers reaped so many laurels. They have had their reverses, their checks and their disasters; but their colours have also been blazoned with some of the proudest victories in history. Alma, Balaclava, Inkerman, Sevastopol, what heroic memories do these not recall! They have quelled the unruly tribes of the Niger, broken the military power of the brave savages south of the Zambesi, subdued an Egyptian rebellion on the Nile, and inspired with a wholesome dread of the British name the death-despising hordes of the Soudan; and the Queen's troops are prouder of no victories than those of Tel-el-Kebir, El-Teb, Tamai, Abu-Klea, Kirbekan, and Tofrek.[7]

In peacetime the Army was scattered throughout the world, manning garrisons in colonies and protectorates and spheres of influence. The forces involved varied in size from the vast armies (mainly native) in India to the single soldier – a bombardier – garrisoning Tristan da Cunha in 1841. Like other armies in colonial situations, they were not only soldiers but policemen and engineers, creating roads, towns and bridges and surveying territory. Units would be sent around the world as circumstances required, postings perhaps including Ireland, Canada, India, South Africa and Bermuda as well as spells at home in stations like Aldershot, Colchester or Hounslow.

In 1854 the total number of men in the British Army was 140,043, of whom 29,208 were in India and 39,754 in other colonies. From the 1870s onward, local forces in the self-governing colonies took a more prominent role in the defence of their territories, freeing British troops from some of this duty. In 1860 the members of Volunteer units totalled 124,000.

At the beginning of Victoria's reign the Army was reduced to the level at which it had been after the defeat of Napoleon. It was to be built up again only when circumstances made this necessary, at the time of the Crimean War and Indian Mutiny, and when the Boer War broke out. In between, many regiments were reduced to a single battalion.

Conflict

Any notion that British armies took success for granted was disproved almost as soon as Victoria became Queen. The first conflict of her reign took place in Afghanistan between 1839 and 1842. Indian Army troops, on the orders of her Government, invaded the country, seized its capital, Kabul, and installed a pro-British native ruler. They then occupied Afghanistan through a series of garrisons. Two years later, rebellion against their puppet ruler, Shah Shuja, broke out and spread. The country was too dangerous for a small and scattered British force, and their commander negotiated with the rebels the safe withdrawal of his men. They retreated south towards India, through freezing mountain passes, but rebel promises regarding their safety proved worthless and their numbers were reduced by constant attacks (the last stand of the 44th Regiment at Gandamak provided the subject for William Barnes Wollen's heroic painting with that title, done in 1898). Only one man – Dr William Brydon – out of a force of 4,000 succeeded in reaching the safety of British-held territory in January 1842. Losses included almost 12,000 camp followers, though not all were killed. The Afghans took both soldiers and civilians hostage, and these were held throughout most of the year until a punitive force was able to release them. Though Britain won the war, the retreat from Kabul and anxiety over the hostages had been a major humiliation.

Confronting the Bear

The Crimean war broke out in the autumn of 1853, and Britain joined the following spring. While the nation's armies could fight successfully against ill-equipped natives, they were inadequate to take on the forces of the Russian Empire – even though these too were ineptly managed and badly equipped. Once again the difficulty was not with the quality of the soldiery or the leadership of junior officers but with the bureaucracy.

The war was a disaster in terms of organization. The public, accustomed to effortless British supremacy at home and abroad, was horrified by the muddle and incompetence, and filled with resentment at the generals – who, like their naval counterparts, were relics of an older generation, a forgotten war and an antiquated mindset. Men like Lord Lucan, Lord Raglan and the Earl of Cardigan owed their positions to aristocratic influence and the sense of entitlement that the upper classes cherished for higher state positions. Commissions in the Army could be purchased, and most regiments looked with disdain on middle-class applicants. As in other European armies, the cavalry, infantry and guards regiments were aristocratic in tone. Only the artillery and engineers, in which technical ability was necessary, were open to a wider range of background, as were navies for similar reasons. (In the British Army there was no purchase of commissions in the technical branches.)

The emerging middle classes, who were used to running their businesses with punctuality and efficiency, were scandalized by the incompetence with which the War Office carried out its tasks. They hated the Army, too, for its unreformed aristocratic nature – since the 1832 Reform Bill that had restructured a similarly moribund political world had had no effect on military affairs – and for the fact that their own sons were kept out of its smart regiments.

The Crimean War was the only European conflict in which Britain was involved between 1815 and 1914. It was caused by the designs of Nicholas I, the Russian tsar, on the Ottoman Empire. Nicholas claimed the right to protect Christians in Ottoman territories, which included the Holy Land. Though the cause of the outbreak was trivial, the wider issues – who was to dominate the eastern Mediterranean? – were more serious, and both France and Britain decided to come to Turkey's aid. Less than thirty years after fighting the Turks at Navarino, Britain was their ally. Enthusiasm for the war built up in Britain, which saw Russia – a former partner against Napoleon – as a natural enemy and a bully who needed to be faced up to. Britain declared war on 27 March 1854. Queen Victoria – and many of her enthusiastic subjects – saw off the soldiers and the ships as they set out.

The public, expecting swift victory, was disappointed. It took almost ten weeks to get an expeditionary force of 18,000 troops to the Dardanelles, and the men were felled in droves by cholera. The British plan was to cross the Black Sea to attack the Crimea and capture the port of Sevastopol. Having landed the troops, the allies enjoyed some quick successes, expelling the Russians from the heights above the Alma River within six days, and setting off a burst of triumphalism at home. Instead of following this up by attacking Sevastopol, which might well have fallen quickly, the armies proceeded to dig siege positions around the city. There was a notable lack of cooperation between the allies, or even the two British services. The Navy began bombarding the city, and the Army commander asked them to stop.

The most famous event of the war, from a British viewpoint, took place on 25 October 1854 at the small port of Balaclava, where the supplies were landed. A Russian force tried to seize it but were repulsed by Highland troops. A cavalry unit, the Heavy Brigade, counter-attacked but its counterpart – the Light Brigade – misunderstood orders to attack and advanced straight into the fire of enemy artillery. The operation was a disaster – about a third of the 673 men involved were casualties – but the public thought it a magnificent example of British courage, and it was quickly to pass into legend.

Winter came, and the war ground to a halt. The weather was extremely bitter, supplies were inadequate, especially in terms of uniforms, greatcoats and boots, and were not efficiently distributed. Men suffered, and died, in the siege-lines through lack of equipment, blankets or medicines. One of the most famous cartoons to appear in *Punch* – which was an unrelenting critic of the War Office – depicted two ragged, starving and bandaged soldiers in a snow-covered landscape. One says: 'Well, Jack! Here's good news from Home. We're to have a medal.' The other replies: 'That's very kind. Maybe one of these days we'll have a coat to stick it on.'[8]

The commanders came in for a great deal of public ridicule. Lord Raglan, the British commander-in-chief, was a one-armed veteran of Waterloo who had never even commanded a battalion in the field. He wore civilian clothes, and repeatedly referred to the enemy as 'the French', so much was he stuck in the thinking of a previous era. However out of touch with reality he may have been, he was aware of the criticism that was heaped on him by press and public at home, and of the mutterings of his men. Through the bleak winter of 1854, morale plummeted. When, the following July, Raglan died of dysentery at the age of sixty-five, he was replaced by another Napoleonic relic, Lieutenant General James Simpson, three years his junior.

The Navy did not fare much better. It too was run by men in their sixties who had had to wait decades to achieve command rank, and who had come to prominence too late. The Navy played no significant role in the conflict other than transporting men and supplies, and bombarding enemy territory. Their ships were embarrassingly outdated in comparison with those of their French allies, for they had no steam-powered vessels. Government refusal to spend, as well as nostalgia in the Admiralty, had prevented any modernization of the fleet. For the same reasons there was no rifled gunnery and there were no ironclad ships.

The uniforms worn in the Crimea, like those worn everywhere on campaign by the Army, were the same tight-fitting, conspicuous and impractical ones in which they mounted guard at home. Only under the stresses of battlefield conditions and prolonged living in the field did this begin to change. Officers, in particular, improvised warm clothing – the Balaclava helmet and the cardigan – that have seen service among both the military and civilians ever since. After the harsh winter of 1854, Highlanders were at least given permission to abandon the kilt for tartan trousers. Soldiers were, however, still required to wear a tight leather stock that severely restricted movement.

The Crimean was the first war in which the public were given a relatively clear idea of what the fighting was like. In the same way that, in the following century, television brought the Vietnam War into the living-rooms of America, the electric telegraph brought the Crimean conflict to the front parlours of Britain. It was made real for those at home by illustrated newspapers, published photographs and by the forcefully written despatches of William Howard Russell, war correspondent for *The Times*. There had never before been so much written and visual information available. Because the British had embraced the war with such enthusiasm, and had been so appalled by its conduct, they followed its developments attentively. They sympathized with the plight of freezing, ill-clad soldiers, felt outrage at the conditions in which the wounded were left in the hospitals, and applauded the work of Florence Nightingale and Mary Seacole to alleviate their suffering. This feeling of concern for the private soldier would evaporate once the war was over, but it marked something of a new departure for public opinion.

Mrs Seacole, a West Indian hotelier, travelled to the war at her own expense. She pioneered the concept of 'comforts for the troops' by providing them with refreshments and leisure facilities at the battlefront. She also took her considerable nursing skills into the trenches and treated the wounded within sight of the enemy. 'Mother Seacole' became so loved by the troops that she was cheered wherever she went.

Miss Nightingale became a national heroine. The condition of the wounded was the greatest scandal of the war, and she managed to rectify the situation almost single-handed. Though she was assisted by a band of nurses, it was she who organized their transport, brought the funds and equipment that created clean and pleasant wards, and dealt tactfully with the senior Army administration, while undertaking in person an exhaustive amount of nursing and cleaning. Because this work received a great deal of attention she gained, in the process, recognition for nursing as an honourable profession, and established principles of hygiene and patient care that were adopted thereafter. These women represented yet another Victorian revolution, the only useful legacy of a pointless and harrowing war.

The public was aware of the hardships faced by the troops, but they were, through the same channels, also aware of the bravery of many individuals. Medals were not yet commonplace in the British Army. The first generally available one had been awarded to those who fought at Waterloo. In 1847 a Military General Service Medal was authorized for those who had served in the Napoleonic Wars. A similar award was struck for naval personnel to cover actions up to the bombardment of Acre in 1840. A campaign medal was to be given for the Crimea, but in 1856 a new gallantry award was instituted. Conceived by Prince Albert but named after the Queen, the Victoria Cross was to be given to men of any rank who performed a single act of valour. The creation of this medal had been inspired by a particular deed. On 21 June 1854, HMS *Hecla* was attacking the Bomarsund fortresses in the Baltic. The ship was only 500 yards offshore when a live shell clattered onto the deck, its fuse hissing. Charles Davis Lucas, a twenty-year-old Irishman, picked up the red-hot projectile and threw it overboard seconds before it exploded. He received the first of the new medals almost exactly three years later, though he did not lack other rewards, for he had been promoted immediately from mate to lieutenant. He was ultimately to become a rear-admiral.

As the Queen stated, the medal was not an order like those that were in her gift. It brought with it no title and had no classes (unlike its French equivalent, the Legion of Honour). It could not be gained through position or privilege, and this was significant, given the aristocratic nature of the Army leadership. Not even the sovereign herself was entitled to it, and no member of the Royal Family has ever held it. Victoria Crosses were bestowed by the Queen in public ceremonies, in Hyde Park or at Horse Guards, and the actions for which they were given were extensively detailed in the press, a process which strengthened the bond between the armed forces and society.

The siege of Sebastopol was the largest event of the war. It lasted a year, from September 1854 to September 1855, before the Russians withdrew from the city. The whole enterprise had been pointless, wasting vast quantities of ammunition and causing needless death and misery among the troops encamped around its defences. It was somehow characteristic of this hopelessly muddled war that, though the fighting was over, it was a further six months before peace was signed.

Though the soldiery might still have merited Wellington's dismissive comment, they did not compare badly with their counterparts in the mass armies of Europe, the French and Prussians. They were of noticeably higher quality than many of their opponents, as one Russian officer – the writer Leo Tolstoy – observed when he encountered wounded British and French prisoners while serving in the artillery at Sebastopol:

> Every soldier among them is proud of his position and has a sense of his value, he feels he is a positive asset to his army. He has good weapons and he knows how to use them, he is young, he has ideas about politics and art and this gives him a feeling of dignity. On our side; senseless training, useless weapons, ill treatment, delay everywhere, ignorance and shocking hygiene and food stifle the last spark of pride.[9]

They also showed the combination of aggressiveness and endurance that had typified them for generations. As so often before and since, it was Highland soldiers that made the greatest impression on the enemy. The sight of kilted soldiers, advancing to the slow and menacing tunes of bagpipes, with their tall feather bonnets and short 'skirts' was so outlandish that it caused panic among the Russians. (When 'kilties' again saw action in the Indian Mutiny their opponents, watching them advance in the distance, believed that the British had run out of men and were sending women. This impression will not have lasted long, for Highlanders were as fierce as they looked.)

Though it has been commonplace since the end of the Crimean War to see it as a scarcely mitigated disaster, modern scholarship has offered a more positive view. So much was weighted against the British – the distance from home, the bad communications, the hostile terrain – that any success (they and their allies won, after all!) seemed an outstanding achievement. There were unquestionable, and serious, shortcomings in supply and medical care, but these were largely solved, for lessons were quickly learned. Though the British were not as successful in the war as the French, their army was brought to a state of – relative – efficiency and even excellence by its end. War, as always, is the quickest and most effective teacher of armies.

It was increasingly clear that efficiency was hampered by the purchase system through which commissions were obtained, for they were seen as creating an officer corps that was untested, aloof, arrogant and uneducated. Prices varied according to the social 'smartness' of the unit, but at the time of the Crimean War a captaincy cost about £3,500. A majority was in the region of £5,000 and the rank of lieutenant colonel might cost up to £9,000 if it were in the Guards. When the scale of Crimean ineptitude became apparent, there was talk of abolishing the sale of commissions, but it took an entire generation – until 1871 – before this was done. It must be said that purchase of rank by no means inevitably led to incompetence. Many members of old military families had imbibed enough from their backgrounds to make adequate officers. For those who did not enter a regiment directly by recommendation there was training provided at military schools – Woolwich and Sandhurst. The former, if not the latter, was adequate.

Mutiny

The Crimean conflict was followed by an even more distressing event farther from home. The sub-continent of India – like all other British territories in the East – was governed by the Honourable East India Company, a commercial enterprise that had first traded with, and then administered, these countries. Based in London, the Company had such power that it minted its own coinage, protected its merchant fleet with its own warships, and garrisoned its provinces with its own army. The soldiery – a private soldier was called a sepoy – was recruited from among the native peoples. The officers were British, trained at the Company's military college in Addiscombe. They were despised by officers of the regular British Army ('Royals'), who saw them as social inferiors, for there was no purchase of commissions in the Indian Army, but most were effective officers. Their troops were also largely loyal and efficient, though there were issues that caused discontent among the disparate castes and religions: they resented attempts to convert them to Christianity; they objected to a number of land reforms; they were annoyed by the discontinuation of certain allowances.

The final straw was the introduction of new cartridges that were alleged to be greased with cow or pig fat. One animal was sacred to Hindus, the other unacceptable to Moslems. All cartridges were paper-covered and the end had to be bitten off before use. For adherents of either religion this was unthinkable. The authorities realized this, and sought to ensure that the cartridges were issued only to British troops, but it was too late to change the perception. On 9 May 1857, Indian soldiers in Meerut refused to load their rifles and were jailed. The next day, the sepoys in the garrison mutinied and the first of several hideous massacres began.

The uprising spread from Meerut to Delhi and then Cawn-pore, where two hundred women and children were murdered after British troops had surrendered. At Lucknow, both sol-diers and civilians survived only because they succeeded in barricading themselves inside the Residency, where they sat out a lengthy siege until relieved by British forces. Delhi was recaptured only after bitter street fighting, and it was the summer of 1858 before order was restored.

The Mutiny had not drawn in all Indian troops. Indeed only the sepoys of Bengal were involved. The ferocity of these rebels, however, had persuaded opinion at home that the whole man-agement of India would have to be reconsidered. The East India Company was liquidated, its military element transferred into the British Army and its administration given over to govern-ment civil servants answerable both to a Viceroy and to the India Office in Whitehall. The Queen issued a proclamation that treated the rebels with some clemency – guaranteeing, for instance, freedom of worship and respect for religious customs, and these things became enshrined in the India Act of 1858.

For those who had taken part in the Mutiny, however, there was a rougher kind of justice. Not only was British feeling understandably outraged by their atrocities, but it was thought necessary to stamp out any similar tendencies for the future. Rebels were executed with a savagery that matched their own, though the British pointed out, as evidence of their greater civilization, that they spared women and children while their opponents had not. The Lucknow Residency – ruined and pock-marked by shells but with the Union Flag flying above it – was preserved as a memorial until the British departed in 1947. A monument at Cawnpore, built on the site of a well into which the bodies of women and children had been thrown, also remained until Independence. No Indian was allowed to enter it.

The Indian Army was rebuilt, though many of the old officers, disgruntled at the pay and status they were offered, departed. It had much to do in the northern reaches of the sub-continent. In this mountainous terrain there were constant feuds, skirmishes and minor rebellions that necessitated the sending of punitive expeditions to restore order or simply show the flag (between 1858 and 1897 there were thirty-four of these). Had they not been deadly affairs – for the tribesmen were extremely warlike, as well as crack shots – there would have been something of a sense of fun about these expeditions. They were certainly regarded by ambitious young officers as a means of earning both medals and promotion. The most testing campaigns in the region were those against Afghan tribesmen.

This mountain kingdom was not a British possession, simply a neighbour that had to be kept under control. The country lay between British India and the Russian Empire which, expanding south-eastwards by the 1880s at a rate of twenty-five miles a day, posed a serious threat. Afghanistan was impossible to conquer or to police effectively, and even its borders were not defined. Britain wanted this buffer state between its own and Russian territory, and to ensure friendly relations insisted on sending an envoy to the court of the Amir. When this request was refused, the British sent an expedition to install him. He was murdered a few months later, and another expedition was then sent to invade the country. Commanded by Lieutenant-General Roberts, this force advanced on the capital, Kabul, in December 1879. They defeated an Afghan army and put in place a more sympathetic Amir. Hearing that another British force was besieged in Kandahar, in the south of the country, Roberts' men set off at once on an epic speed-march through rough terrain and fierce extremes of temperature. Arriving exhausted, they nevertheless drove off the attackers and raised the siege. Roberts – who had already won the VC in India – became a hero in Britain, and was made a baronet.

Adventure

It must be remembered that, from the 1870s (by which time memory of the Crimea and the Mutiny had faded) until the rude shock of the Boer conflict, war came to be seen by many Britons as something of a lark. With no 'civilized' enemy to fight, for Russia – the obvious candidate for several reasons – was unwilling to pick a quarrel, the Queen's soldiers devoted their energies to colonial conflicts. For the public at home these were distant, small-scale affairs which they expected their soldiers to win without difficulty. Casualties were light, because the enemy were always at a disadvantage. The British troops, after all, had not only discipline and valour on their side but modern weaponry – which by 1889 included the Maxim machine gun.

Colonial wars provided excitement, cheaply won victories, enhanced prestige and a sense that Britain's mission in the world was being fulfilled. The exploits of generals and young officers were thrillingly told in fiction (*With Kitchener in the Sudan, With Buller in Natal*) and newspaper reports made celebrities of many commanders. Sir Garnet Wolseley, who defeated the armies of the Asanti king in West Africa and whose troops made yet another epic march in abominable conditions, was a textbook example. A dapper little man of distinguished appearance, he became highly popular, and was commemorated in contemporary slang with the expression 'All Sir Garnet!', meaning that all was well.

The public could see that the Army was changing. Not only did weaponry improve, but appearances altered. The Guards might still wear bearskins and scarlet tunics at Buckingham

Palace, but finery of this sort was vanishing from the battle-field. The last occasion on which troops wore scarlet in action was the Egyptian campaign of 1882. The previous year, fighting the Boers in South Africa, colours had been carried in battle for the last time. Uniforms – at least those worn on battlefields – were khaki, a pale-brown shade that had been created in India at the time of the Mutiny, allegedly by dyeing the cloth in tea. It was extremely practical for overseas service, though the public at home did not become fully aware of it until large numbers of troops marched through their streets on the way to the Boer War. Two of Galsworthy's female characters illustrate what may have been a common civilian reaction, when discussing such a spectacle:

> My dear, but they've been so progressive. Think of their having given up their scarlet. They were always so proud of it. And now they all look like convicts. They must feel it very much. Fancy what the Iron Duke would have said![10]

Officers and Gentlemen

Whatever the social qualifications necessary to be an officer, there was no requirement for great intelligence. The British, and especially the upper classes, had a traditional antipathy toward those who thought too much, and their ideal of an officer was that he be – in a famous phrase of Henry James – 'opaque in intellect but indomitable in muscle'. Officers were expected, during the vast amounts of time at their disposal (they were granted five months' leave a year) to indulge passionately in sports. If they were stationed in India it was unheard of that they should not play polo, for the game was something of a secular religion. Otherwise, foxhunting was more or less compulsory in smart regiments, the more so as it was believed to sharpen officers' skills – improving their 'seat' through practice, accustoming them to risk and teaching them to 'read' a landscape through observation. Team games were seen as useful preparation for war.

In no other army was this sporting ethos found. Officers in the Russian or Austrian service, for instance, might cultivate an aristocratic languor even greater than that in British regiments, but they regarded it as beneath their dignity to exert themselves or get dirty. Though they might ride for pleasure, their off-duty hours were spent in drinking, gambling, pursuing affairs, fighting duels and surviving the crushing boredom of small garrison towns. While British officers might be fitter, their brains were not exercised. Within their regiments, much of the training and drilling of the men was done by senior non-commissioned officers. In the Prussian Army – which after defeating France in 1871 became the dominant power in Europe and a potential future adversary – it was the officers themselves who carried out these tasks. As a result they knew their men very well, and had a firm grasp of administration and leadership, while at the same time they were required to study to pass promotion exams. The Prussian officer was often expected to be a professional. His British counterpart preferred to behave like an amateur.

Though the stereotype of the Victorian officer – and the pages of satirical magazines were filled with caricatures of them, stroking their moustaches and speaking in a languid drawl ('fwightfully!') – suggested that the officers' mess was a rarified, patrician world beyond the reach of others, yet it was not impossible to rise to the highest ranks of the Army without an aristocratic background. While Wellington, Roberts and Buller were all Old Etonians, Sir Colin Campbell – later Lord Clyde – was the son of a Scottish carpenter, Sir Garnet Wolseley was the son of a small-town Irish tradesman and

General Hector Macdonald ('Fighting Mac') made an even more spectacular ascent. Beginning life as an Inverness draper's assistant with a passion for military history, he enlisted in 1870 as a private in the Gordons and ended his career as a major general, a Knight of the Bath and an ADC to both Victoria and Edward VII. All three were extremely popular with press and public, in an era that treated victorious generals with the same adoration as film stars now command. A glance through an antique shop will often reveal souvenirs – teapots, plates, badges – commemorating Victorian military heroes, especially those, like Roberts and Baden-Powell, from the Boer War, upon whom the nation's hopes rested.

These men had won promotion through their abilities in the field, and every ambitious soldier, whatever his background, looked for opportunities to follow the same path. Even with a small Army and a constant succession of colonial campaigns, however, it was difficult to see action. Postings in Britain, or in Canada, New Zealand or Bermuda, for instance, might be pleasant enough but meant years of uneventful garrison duty. The same was true of India, where unless a regiment was sent to the North-West Frontier, there would be little for officers to do but play polo. Those without the patience to wait for battle experience often sought to be seconded to other units in order to go with them on campaign. The most glaring example of this type was the young Winston Churchill, whose tireless lobbying and social connections enabled him to take part in actions in both India and the Sudan by joining other regiments. When he entered the Army, in 1895, soldiers were very conscious that there had been no war against a white army since the Crimea. There was a professional curiosity to know how they would perform in a well-matched, major conflict. Churchill also dreaded seeing out his military career without gaining any medals, for his commanding officer had spent a lifetime in the Army without once seeing action. The prospect of war was therefore something to be sought out and valued – a rare opportunity to test one's skills, gain experience and hope for distinction. In his memoir *My Early Life*, he wrote of this attitude:

> In the closing decade of the Victorian era the Empire had enjoyed so long a spell of almost unbroken peace, that medals and all they represented in experience and adventure were becoming extremely scarce in the British Army. The veterans of the Crimea and the Indian Mutiny were gone from the active list. The Afghan and Egyptian warriors of the early eighties had reached the senior ranks. Scarcely a shot had been fired since then, and when I joined the 4th Hussars in January 1895 scarcely a captain, hardly ever a subaltern, could be found throughout Her Majesty's forces who had seen even the smallest kind of war. Rarity in a desirable commodity is usually the cause of enhanced value; and there has never been a time when war service was held in so much esteem by the military authorities or more ardently sought by officers of every rank. How we young officers envied the senior Major for his adventures at Abu Klea! How we admired the Colonel with his long row of decorations! How we longed to have a similar store of memories to unpack and display!
>
> The little titbits of fighting which the Indian frontier and the Soudan were soon to offer, distributed by luck or favour, were fiercely scrambled for throughout the British Army. But the South African War was to attain dimensions which fully satisfied the needs of our small army. And after that the deluge was still to come![11]

The excitement both of young officers looking for action and of a public reading about their exploits at the breakfast table suggests a confident assumption that events would always turn out in Britain's favour. In reality there was a good deal less complacency than this image suggests. For one thing, the British did not always win. In 1879 the expedition of Lord Chelmsford against King Cetawayo suffered 1,329 fatalities when Zulus overran their camp at Isandlwana, and only the valour of defenders at Rourke's Drift on the same day – for which seven Victoria Crosses were awarded – saved Britain from humiliation. Two years later, the Queen's soldiers faced South African Boers after the latter refused to accept British rule over the Transvaal. British columns suffered terrible losses from the superb marksmanship of their opponents, and after securing the summit of the strategic Majuba Hill on 26 February 1881, they embarrassingly lost it the following day, being driven down the slopes in confusion and suffering heavy casualties.

Another factor was that even glory did not make the army popular enough to entice young men to join. It was said in the countryside that 'Jack Frost was the Army's best recruiter', for only failed harvests or harsh winters could bring men into the ranks in numbers. Unlike her Continental neighbours, Britain did not have a standing army, and recruiting was an uphill struggle, even during the depression of the 1870s. In order to make the military profession more attractive, and to eliminate the worst abuses, reforms had been carried through at the beginning of the decade. The purchase of commissions had been abolished, and enlistment, which had been for a period of twenty-one years, had been reduced to twelve, of which only six were spent on active service. The branding of deserters – an especially barbaric practice – was discontinued in 1871, and flogging was abolished a decade later. This notwithstanding, the pay of private soldiers could not compete with the wages of civilian tradesmen or skilled labourers, and the Army re-mained too small to fulfil its worldwide commitments.

Comrades

One solution was increasing reliance on units of local troops under the command of British officers. Throughout the Empire a number of these – often with highly specialist roles – came into existence during the latter half of the century, and caused a good deal of interest when they sent contingents to London for the Queen's Diamond Jubilee: the Gold Coast Hausas, the Singapore Engineers, the Hong Kong Regiment, the Sierra Leone Frontier Force, the British Guiana Constabulary, the Mauritius Royal Artillery, the Malta Submarine Mine Engineers. Numbers of these soldiers could be sent around the Empire to fill gaps where British troops were withdrawn, or simply to support a particular campaign. British punitive expeditions in West Africa relied heavily on black soldiers of the West India Regiment, who proved very able, one of them winning the VC. When in 1882 Wolseley, the hero of West Africa, landed a force at Tel-el-Kebir in Egypt to protect the Suez Canal from anti-European unrest, Indian Army native troops took part. When Egypt itself became a British protectorate shortly afterwards, local units of British-trained men were raised. These in turn helped to defeat the armies of the Khalifa at the Battle of Omdurman in 1898.

Showdown

Egypt was officially part of the Ottoman Empire, but in practice the Sultan's government did not have the power, or the will, to run it effectively. The Sudan, a vast area of desert to the south of it along the Nile, was an Egyptian fiefdom – a colony of a colony, as it were – and here a rebellion against Egyptian rule was fomented in the early 1880s by a self-appointed local leader who called himself the Mahdi, or messiah. His followers, 'dervishes', were Muslim fanatics of a sort once again familiar. They were heavily armed, though with obsolete weaponry, and without mercy to those, whether locals, Egyptians or Europeans, who fell into their power. They were a major, and growing, threat to the whole region.

General Charles Gordon, a distinguished soldier, was sent by Gladstone's government to evacuate civilians from the Sudan. He arrived in the principal city, Khartoum, but after organizing one evacuation he decided to remain and defy the rebels. He had Khartoum turned into a fortress, and by March 1884 it was under siege. Gordon was hugely popular at home, and the public expected a relief expedition to go at once to his aid. Gladstone, who hated such measures and whose trust Gordon had betrayed by abandoning his original mission, procrastinated for several months as British outrage rose to fever pitch. When at length Wolseley led a British force to the Sudan, time had run out. It was necessary to fight the dervishes on the way, and in one action, at Abu Klea, the rebels overran a British defensive square. British gunboats arrived offshore on 28 January 1885 to find that two days earlier the Mahdi's forces had broken through the defences and wiped out those within. Gordon's body was never found. The Mahdi died a few years later but a new leader – the Khalifa – took his place, and the dervish threat remained.

Far from feeling complacent about exotic wars and imperial adventures during the last decades of Victoria's reign, the public was highly anxious. Majuba and Khartoum were international disgraces that cried out to be rectified. The Boers – who had proved the most charming of enemies (they treated the British wounded, and the defeated commanders, with outstanding kindness) – were regarded as backward farmers, while the dervishes were the most rapacious and savage opponents Britain had faced since the Indian Mutiny. Both enemies must be dealt with for the sake of national honour, but long years passed, and it was only after a change of government that opportunities for revenge could be found.

Firstly, the dervishes. General Kitchener, the 'Sirdar' or commander-in-chief of the Egyptian Khedive's forces and another military celebrity, led an expedition to occupy the Sudan in 1896. He slowly and carefully built and equipped an Anglo-Egyptian force that set out off southwards at a leisurely pace. Gunboats sailed up the Nile, while engineers constructed a railway over the desert to move supplies. It was not until September 1898 that his force arrived within sight of Khartoum and, opposite it, the city of Omdurman. The dervish army was not in the city but out in the desert, and the Sirdar had time to organize a formidable defensive position with its back to the Nile. The battle was fought on his terms.

It began the following morning, 2 September. The dervishes – like some other peoples whom the British encountered in colonial wars – believed that they could not be killed by bullets. Their whole army therefore made a frontal attack on the Anglo-Egyptian defences, with a result afterwards described by a war correspondent as 'not a battle but an execution'. The defenders had artillery as well as the gunboats that were firing from offshore. They had well-disciplined, volley-firing infantry and were equipped with Maxim guns. The dervishes were shot down in droves, the number killed being somewhere between ten and eleven thousand (Kitchener's casualties were 80 dead, 472 wounded). Khartoum was captured and the Mahdi's tomb blown up – by Gordon's nephew. Rebellion simmered for a few years afterwards, but Mahdism was a dead letter.

Although Gordon was now avenged, the public was not as euphoric as might be expected. Some elements of opinion felt that the enemy should not have been shot down wholesale, as if it were unfair to use modern technology against medieval weapons. There was also some outrage at the desecration by Kitchener of the Mahdi's tomb. The Sirdar was rumoured to have carried off the head as a trophy – an act which won him a personal rebuke from Queen Victoria. Versions of the story state that he meant to have it made into a drinking vessel, that he returned it for burial or that he donated it to the Royal College of Surgeons. Whatever the truth, this was not in keeping with the sense of moral superiority with which the British had endowed themselves.

South Africa

The Boer conflict resurfaced in 1899, following the discovery of gold in the Transvaal. This brought thousands of British prospectors to the area, where their presence and behaviour put them at odds with the devout and simple Boers. The latter believed – with perfect justification – that there were British plans, though perhaps only unofficial, to annex their republic. If enough of the incomers qualified to vote and opted for union with the neighbouring British territories, the Transvaal was finished as an independent state. To prevent this, the Boers stiffened the qualification for citizenship, enabling the British to see themselves as a persecuted minority whom it was the duty of the mother country to help. Others shared this view, including the vastly influential Cecil Rhodes, and when the Boers asked for negotiations the British sought to ensure that they failed. War broke out in October, but did not result in the quick victory that the public had expected.

The Boers were well equipped, for their country's gold reserves enabled them to buy sophisticated weaponry that was often superior to that of their enemy. They fought in small, mobile units called commandos, but also had artillery, which they used to effect. They possessed an excellent knowledge of the country, an ability to move fast and live off the land, and the same skill in marksmanship that they had displayed at Majuba.

They besieged three towns – Kimberley, Ladysmith and Mafeking – and thus added another epic to the annals of Victorian heroism. In fact these encirclements were carried out with the usual Boer good humour (on Christmas day 1899 they sent plum puddings to those inside Ladysmith) and bore no resemblance to the horrors of Lucknow. The British Army, meanwhile, suffered three defeats within five days, a period christened 'Black Week'. At Stormberg a failed British attack left 600 men prisoners. At Colenso ten artillery pieces were captured – though others were rescued – and Lord Roberts' son won a posthumous VC in trying to save them. Worst of all, at Magersfontein British troops attacking a ridge and expecting to find the enemy at the top found them dug in at the bottom instead, from where their withering fire caused such casualties that the attackers turned and ran. Though not a familiar name in Britain, Magersfontein was considered the country's worst military defeat for a century.

With the customary British talent for turning defeat into epic, the 'Saving of the Guns at Colenso' was presented as an act of heroism that outweighed the embarrassment of losing a number of them. Meanwhile war fever gripped the British public. The soldier, a despised figure in years of peace, suddenly once again became a hero, immortalized – through a reference to a line of Kipling's – in countless gimcrack ornaments as the 'Absent-Minded Beggar' and depicted with bandaged head and bayonet fixed, ready to resist any threat. Kipling brilliantly captured the mood in his lines:

> It's Tommy this, an' Tommy that, an' 'Chuck him out, the
> brute!'
> But it's 'Saviour of 'is country' when the guns begin to shoot.[12]

Britain not only lost battles but a good deal of face. Her Continental neighbours could barely restrain their glee at the sight of the world's greatest power being tied in knots by a small nation of farmers. At the same time considerable hatred was evident in many quarters. Feeling ran so high in France that the Queen was obliged to cancel her annual visit to the Riviera. In the Netherlands, where the Boers were regarded as relatives, anyone who looked or sounded like an Englishman was likely to be abused or mobbed in the streets. In Germany, where Britain was increasingly regarded with envy and dislike, there was open rejoicing. Volunteers from these countries, and from America, Ireland and Russia, went to join the Boers or sent declarations of support. Britain used a phrase at this time to describe her status in the world – 'splendid isolation' – which suggested a power so great that it needed no foreign alliances to keep it in place. In fact it was making a virtue of necessity.

The news continued to be bad. In January 1900 the Boers inflicted another defeat – and over a thousand casualties – at Spion Kop on the Tugela River as Buller's forces attempted to get through to Ladysmith. In the same month Britain's most popular soldier, Lord Roberts ('Bobs'), arrived in South Africa to take charge. Matters began to improve almost at once, for increasing numbers of troops were being sent, not only from Britain but from elsewhere in the Empire. Kimberley was relieved in February, the Tugela Heights were captured, enabling Ladysmith to be freed, and a British victory at Paardeberg resulted in the surrender of Cronje, one of the Boers' most able commanders. Bloemfontein was occupied in March, Mafeking was relieved on 16 May (causing a disproportionate amount of rejoicing in Britain) and in June British forces entered Johannesburg and Pretoria.

The war, however, went on. Roberts had rejected any question of negotiations, insisting that surrender must be unconditional. As in all such cases, this stiffened the enemy's determination to fight, and the Boers continued to wage guerrilla warfare from remote areas while their President, Paul Kruger, eluded the British and escaped to Europe to drum up support. Though fighting still went on, there were no further major battles, and both Roberts and Buller had gone home before the end of the year. When the Queen died the following January, the conflict seemed to a large extent over.

In fact, it had changed from full-scale war to a police action. Kitchener had been left in command, and his task was to mop up remaining resistance. Because the Boers received considerable assistance – in terms of shelter, supplies and information – from their families and from other non-combatants in the countryside, the Army had made a policy of burning farms and scattering livestock that might be used to feed the enemy. Another method was to round up local civilians and accommodate them in 'concentration camps'. These were communities of huts within barbed-wire enclosures. They were basic, but in theory adequate, though it was not long before overcrowding and lack of sanitation, and resulting deaths from disease, made them notorious (it is thought that up to 20,000 died in them – an appalling statistic). Lurid artists' impressions of the camps were shown in illustrated papers all over the world, pushing Anglophobia to unprecedented levels. Their existence also caused outrage among sections of opinion at home. Concentration camps were not a British invention. They had been used by the Spanish authorities in Cuba during the rebellion in the 1890s, but they became a symbol of British oppression. Visited, and condemned, by both British and foreign observers, they were eventually closed down. They had, in any case, proved somewhat counter-productive. By freeing the Boer guerrillas of responsibility for their families, they had made it easier for many of them to pursue the war.

By the summer of 1901 the Orange Free State was entirely under British control, and in the Transvaal resistance was slowly eradicated. Negotiations led to an eventual settlement, signed at Vereeniging on 31 May 1902, that gave the Boers many of the guarantees and concessions they had wanted, and paid for the reconstruction of their country. It occurred to many of those who had fought on the British side that their efforts had therefore been in vain. The Empire had won, eventually, though only after deploying almost 450,000 troops, of whom more than 21,000 had died. Boer combatants suffered about 4,000 fatalities from a strength of 70–80,000. It was victory, but only just. This had been as much of a trauma as the Crimean War fifty years earlier, and it caused a great deal of national soul-searching.

The Old Enemy

Unlike all of her Continental neighbours, Britain did not have military service, and as a result had a domestic army that was pitifully small in comparison to those of the European powers. The country's defence posture was based on the notion that the Royal Navy – by far the largest fleet in the world – would deal with any potential invader before he reached the British coast. Despite their outward confidence and the apparent complacency that victory in the Napoleonic Wars had given them, Victorians did not see themselves as living in a climate of international calm. France had indeed been defeated but was still rich and powerful, and it was taken for granted that she would seek revenge at a moment of her own choosing, probably with an attack upon Britain's shores. The country's defence relied upon the Royal Navy, and the strength of the Navy had lain in the skill of its sailors. They were unmatched in the world at the speed and accuracy of their gunnery and in their ability to handle a sailing ship. With the advent of steam, this latter skill, however, was suddenly rendered worthless and redundant. Their advantage was nullified by new technology, for now it was no longer necessary to wait for winds and tides before launching an invasion. The French navy had converted to steam while the Admiralty in London was still only considering the idea. France was therefore in a position to attack at any time.

The Duke of Wellington, commander-in-chief of the British Army and living in old age at Walmer Castle on the Kent coast (he was created Lord Warden of the Cinque Ports in 1829 and held the post until his death in 1852), looked out on the English Channel from his windows. Nearby was a pleasant beach on which he could walk, but he did not like to do so. The conqueror of Napoleon expected at any time to see the tell-tale black smoke on the horizon that would signal an approaching enemy fleet. If this was the view of the country's senior military officer, it must have been shared by many others below him in the hierarchy. This fear continued in spite of improving relations with France. In the 1840s King Louis-Philippe visited England, as did his successor, Napoléon III. France and Britain were allies in the Crimea, but Napoleon was a military adventurer (he involved France in four major wars during twenty-two years in power), and if his people wanted war with Britain it was unlikely that he would allow personal friendship to prevent it.

By the late fifties, paranoia on the subject of an expected invasion had reached fever pitch. The signs of this climate of fear can still be seen in and around Portsmouth. The immense, round stone fortresses that dominate the Solent, nicknamed 'Palmerston Forts' after the Prime Minister whose government had them built, and the equally impressive defences on the heights at the back of the city, would have made this important naval base impregnable, though they were never used. They remain as evidence that the 'mid-Victorian calm' was not as serene as we may think. These measures were not undertaken lightly, for naturally the need for them had to be accepted by Parliament. The signs were there that invasion was more than a possibility. Odo Russell, a Foreign Office official, was told by Pope Pius IX in 1859: 'Prepare and take care of yourselves in England, for I am quite certain the French Emperor intends sooner or later to attack you.'[13]

Panic

A generation later, in 1882, it was suggested that a railway tunnel be built under the Channel by a British company. Instead of greeting this with the enthusiasm that such 'wonders of the age' usually generated, there was considerable concern in Parliament and the press regarding the risk of invasion that it would bring. It was argued in the House of Commons that the only way of ensuring the safety of such a venture would be to build the tunnel so that the English end of it was *inside* a major fortress, with gun barrels pointing at the arriving trains. This might well have been stipulated – if the scheme had been allowed to go that far. The whole notion of a tunnel link with France created a climate of such invasion hysteria that politicians scrambled to dissociate themselves from a scheme that was seen as 'unpatriotic', and public opinion became so hostile that a London crowd broke the company's windows. The project was shelved.

Among Britain's rivals, none was in a position to challenge British hegemony until the end of the era. Prussia, which became the strongest power on the Continent, was preoccupied with the creation of a united German Empire. France, defeated by this same empire in 1870–1, was preoccupied with national recovery and revenge. The United States was preoccupied with civil war and with westward expansion (though, in spite of ties between Britain and America, there was almost war between the two in 1895, over opposing interests in Venezuela). Russia, which Britain had fought more or less successfully in the Crimea, remained a likely opponent, for the interests of both countries clashed in Central Asia. No pretext for outright war presented itself, however, and the backward Russian state could not have sustained a major conflict.

Modernization

The Navy, gradually but successfully, adapted to the needs of the age, building steam-powered, ironclad, screw-driven vessels that kept British maritime supremacy unchallenged until the twentieth century. The evidence of this might was put on show, on 26 June 1897, at the Diamond Jubilee Review at Spithead. Though other nations sent ships to participate in this tribute to the Queen, the Royal Navy effortlessly outshone its guests. Anchored in lines that were seven miles long (the total length of the fleet was thirty miles) were one hundred and seventy ships, including fifty-three ironclads (the French navy had only thirty-two). It was the Admiralty's boast that not one ship had had to be withdrawn from a foreign station to take part in the spectacle. It was by far the largest navy in history and the British public, gazing on the rows of masts and funnels from Southsea Common or Gosport, could surely not imagine that this power would ever fade. As a children's alphabet book of the time put it:

N is the Navy we keep at Spithead. It's a sight that makes
foreigners wish they were dead.

Volunteers

For home defence, Britain traditionally relied on the goodwill
of part-time volunteers. In the wars against France from the
1790s to 1815, counties had raised units of militia (infantry)
and yeomanry (cavalry), but the militia was disbanded in
1814, before the war had ended. In the year 1859, when
there was a sudden fear of invasion by the French, there was
a surge of recruiting for part-time rifle units, and the Volunteer officer, usually gorgeously attired but militarily inept,
became a stock character in music hall and in the pages of
satirical papers. Many present-day Territorial Army regiments were first raised as a direct result of this fear. The
Artists' Rifles is today an SAS unit, but its origins were very
different. Founded in 1859 by painters and sculptors, its
commanding officer throughout the late nineteenth century
was Lord Leighton, one of the country's most eminent artists,
and President of the Royal Academy.

Such amateur bodies were expected only to defend the
homeland in time of emergency and were not allowed to serve
overseas. This situation changed only with the outbreak of the
Boer War in 1899. Short of manpower, the War Office
accepted contributions of troops from Canada, Australia,
New Zealand and other parts of Greater Britain (even West
Indian soldiers were used for guarding Boer prisoners), and
also used short-term volunteers from the United Kingdom.
This was the first time that civilians had been able to enlist for
military service for the duration of a campaign, setting a
precedent that would be followed on a vastly greater scale
in the two World Wars.

The Yeomanries of many counties were deployed, and – most famously – the City of London raised a regiment (the CIV or City Imperial Volunteers) to serve in South Africa. These formations did much to foster respect for the Army on the part of the public, for previously soldiering had been a despised profession attracting misfits and petty criminals. The Army was sceptical and reluctant to invite civilians into its ranks, and many members of the public shared the view that amateurs would be of little value. Galsworthy's character Timothy Forsyte expresses this attitude when he exclaims: 'Volunteer-in', indeed! What have we kept the Army up for – to eat their heads off in time of peace! They ought to be ashamed of themselves, comin' on the country to help them like this! Let every man stick to his business, and we shall get on.'[14]

Britain's army would never catch up in size with those of its Continental counterparts until, in the middle of the First World War, conscription was introduced for the first time in the nation's history. What it lacked in size, however, it made up in the breadth of its experience. When conflict broke out in 1914 and the British Expeditionary Force was dispatched to France to halt the German drive on the Channel coast, it was the army of Queen Victoria that succeeded in doing so, for many officers and men who took part in the fighting were veterans of the Boer War or the North-West Frontier. Their enemy paid grudging tribute to the accuracy of their fire and to their ability to fight effectively in small units – traits learned in numerous small-scale colonial conflicts.

The Victorian Empire was maintained – in more or less equal measure – by the pound sterling and the Martini-Henry rifle. While the entrepreneurial drive of British merchants can easily be seen by critics as 'exploitation', and the wielding of military might as 'imperialism', there was, of course, a positive aspect to British power. It created a prosperous worldwide community of countries that preserves – as the Commonwealth of Nations – a strong sense of mutual empathy. It brought vast benefits – transport and engineering, medicine, Christianity, education – to large areas of the world, and these things are more appreciated in the countries that received them than perhaps critics of Empire are aware. Whatever the excesses of the Victorian age, and whatever the faults – individually or collectively – of Victorians, their era was one of progress, enterprise, compassion and civilization. Their achievement deserves our pride and our gratitude.

NOTES

Introduction

1 John Galsworthy, *The Forsyte Saga*. William Heinemann, 1950, pp. 546–9.
2 Walter Besant, in *Illustrated London News*, Diamond Jubilee number, June 1897, p. 1.
3 Carolly Erickson, *Her Little Majesty*. Simon & Schuster, 1997, p. 98.
4 George Gissing, *In the Year of Jubilee*. J. M. Dent, 1994, p.50.
5 W. R. Inge, *The Victorian Age*. Cambridge University Press, 1922, p. 9.
6 Talbot Baines Reed, *Parkhurst Sketches*. Religious Tract Society, n.d., p. 116.
7 Quoted in Randolph S. Churchill, *Winston S. Churchill*, vol. I, *Youth, 1874–1900*. Heinemann, 1966, p. 321.
8 Ibid., p. 378.
9 Quoted in John Montgomery, *1900. The End of an Era*. George Allen & Unwin, 1968, p. 133.
10 Bernard Fergusson, *Eton Portrait*. John Miles, 1938, p.44.

Chapter 1: Symbol of an Age

1 Richard Hough, *Victoria and Albert*. Richard Cohen Books, 1996, p.32.
2 Alan Hardy, *Queen Victoria Was Amused*. John Murray, 1976, p.10.
3 Carolly Erickson, *Her Little Majesty*. Simon & Schuster, 1997, p. 62.

4 Quoted in Dormer Creston, *The Youthful Queen Victoria, A Discursive Narrative*. Macmillan, 1952, p. 347.

5 Erickson, *Little Majesty*, p. 276.

6 Quoted in Hardy, *Queen Victoria Was Amused*, p. 97.

7 Quoted in Hough, *Victoria and Albert*, p. 52.

8 Quoted ibid., p. 30.

9 Quoted ibid., p. 11.

10 Quoted ibid., p. 56.

11 Quoted in Hardy, *Queen Victoria Was Amused*, p. 37.

12 Erickson, *Little Majesty*, p. 276.

13 Quoted in Godfrey Scheele and Margaret Scheele, *The Prince Consort*. Oresko Books, 1977, p. 51.

14 Laurence Housman, *Victoria Regina*. Jonathan Cape, 1937, p. 12.

15 Scheele, *The Prince Consort*, p. 95.

16 Quoted in John Matson, *Dear Osborne*. Hamish Hamilton, 1978, p.53.

17 Quoted in Hough, *Victoria and Albert*, p. 92.

18 Quoted in Elizabeth Longford, *Victoria R.I.* Weidenfeld & Nicolson, 1973, p. 134.

19 Quoted in Michael Paterson, *Churchill, His Military Life*. David & Charles, 2005, p. 116.

20 Hardy, *Queen Victoria Was Amused*, p. 184.

21 Quoted in James Montgomery, *1900*. George Allen & Unwin, 1968, p.188.

22 Giles St Aubyn, *Queen Victoria: A Portrait*. Sinclair-Stevenson, 1991, p. 340.

23 Housman, *Victoria Regina*, p. 12.

24 Quoted in St Aubyn, *Queen Victoria*, pp. 482–3.

25 Quoted in Hardy, *Queen Victoria Was Amused*, p. 186.

26 Quoted in Erickson, *Little Majesty*, p. 255.

27 Quoted in Hardy, *Queen Victoria Was Amused*, p. 186.

28 *Daily Telegraph*, 23 January 1901, quoted in Montgomery, *1900*, p. 239.

29 Housman, *Victoria Regina*, programme notes, Lyric Theatre, London, 1937, p. 2.

Chapter 2: The Masses

1 James Greenwood, *The Seven Curses of London*. Stanley Rivers & Co., 1869.

2 James Grant, *Sketches in London*, W. S. Orr, 1838, p. 225.

3 Both extracts quoted in E. Royston Pike (ed.), *Human Documents of the Age of the Forsytes*. Victorian Book Club, 1972, p. 260.

4 Quoted ibid.

5 Clara Collett, quoted ibid., pp. 78–9.

6 General William Booth, *In Darkest England and the Way Out*. Charles Knight & Co., 1970, p. 20.

7 Quoted in Geoffrey Pearson, *Hooligan. A History of Respectable Fears*. Macmillan, 1983, p. 129.

8 Quoted ibid., p. 94.

9 Steve Jones, *Capital Punishments: Crime and Prison Conditions in the Victorian Capital*. Wicked Publications, 1992, p. 46.

Chapter 3: What They Ate

1 Quoted in Reay Tannahill, *Food in History*. Eyre Methuen, 1973, p. 329.
2 Quoted in E. Royston Pike (ed.), *Human Documents of the Age of the Forsytes*. Victorian Book Club, 1972, p. 156.
3 Author's collection.
4 'A Member of the Aristocracy', *Manners and Rules of Good Society*. Frederick Warne & Co., 1908 (thirty-fifth edition; originally published 1888), p. 108.
5 William Thackeray, *The Book of Snobs*. Smith Elder, 1894, pp. 213–14.
6 Quoted in Jennifer Brennan, *Curries and Bugles: A Memoir and Cookbook of the British Raj*. Penguin Books, 1990, p. 24.
7 Ibid., p. 24.
8 Ibid., p. 25.
9 Quoted in Judy Spours, *Cakes and Ale. The Golden Age of British Feasting*. The National Archives, 2006, p. 93.
10 Kate Colquhoun, *Taste: The Story of Britain through its Cooking*. Bloomsbury, 2007, pp. 305–6.

Chapter 4: Taste

1 Arthur Schlesinger, *Saunterings in and about London*. Nathaniel Cook, 1853, pp. 3–4.
2 E. T. Cook and Alexander Wedderburn (eds), *The Works of John Ruskin*. Longmans, Green, 1904, p. 459.
3 George Augustus Sala, *Twice Round the Clock*. Richard Marsh, London, 1862, p. 188.
4 Schlesinger, *Saunterings*, p. 6.
5 Ibid.
6 Ibid., p. 7.
7 Ibid., p.10.
8 Sala, *Twice Round the Clock*, p. 81.
9 Quoted in E. Royston Pike (ed.), *Human Documents of the Age of the Forsytes*. Victorian Book Club, 1972, p. 222.
10 George Grossmith and Weedon Grossmith, *Diary of a Nobody*. Collins, 1955, p. 27.
11 Quoted in Shirley Nicholson, *A Victorian Household*. Barrie and Jenkins, 1988, p. 24.
12 Charles Dickens, *Our Mutual Friend*, The Educational Book Company, 1910.
13 Sir Hugh Casson, 'Red House, Bexleyheath, Kent, 1859', in Edward Hollamby (ed.), *Arts and Crafts Houses*. Phaidon, 1990, vol. I, p. 4.
14 Ibid.

Chapter 5: Getting About

1 Walter Besant, in *Illustrated London News*, Diamond Jubilee number, June 1897, p. 50.

2 *Illustrated London News*, quoted in Christian Wolmar, *The Subterranean Railway*. Atlantic Books, 2004, p. 27.

3 John Woodforde, *The Story of the Bicycle*. Routledge & Kegan Paul, 1970, p. 19.

4 Augustus Muir, *Scotland's Road of Romance*. Methuen, 1934, pp. 195–6.

5 Quoted in Woodforde, *The Story of the Bicycle*, pp. 112–13.

6 Quoted ibid.

7 Mrs F. Harcourt Williamson, 'The Cycle in Society', in A. C. Pemberton, *The Complete Cyclist*. A. D. Innes, 1897, pp. 47–8.

8 Earl of Albemarle and G. Lucy Hillier, *Cycling*. Badminton Library, Longmans, Green, 1896, pp. 183–210.

9 Albemarle and Hillier, *Cycling*, pp. 183–210.

10 Williamson, 'The Cycle in Society', pp. 47–8.

11 Ibid.

12 Lord Montagu of Beaulieu, 'The Utility of Motor Cars', in Lord Northcliffe (ed.) *Motors and Motor-Driving*. Badminton Library, Longmans, Green, 1902, pp. 25–7.

13 Alan Hardy, *Queen Victoria Was Amused*. John Murray, 1976, p. 131.

Chapter 6: Religion

1 R. W. Church, *The Oxford Movement*, 1891, quoted in Clive Dewey, *The Passing of Barchester*. Hambledon Press, 1991, p. xi.

2 Quoted in Alan Warwick, *The Phoenix Suburb*. The Norwood Society, 1972, p. 129.

3 L. C. B. Seaman, *Victorian England*. Methuen, 1973, p. 13.

4 Charles Dickens, *Sketches by Boz*. Chapman & Hall, n.d., p. 20.

5 Ibid., p. 21.

6 Ernest H. Shepard, *Drawn from Memory*. Methuen, 1957, pp. 45–6.

7 Charles Dickens, *Little Dorrit*. Educational Book Company, 1910, p. 29.

8 Geoffrey Best, *Mid-Victorian Britain, 1851–75*. Fontana, 1985, p. 185.

9 Dorothy Wise (ed.), *The Diary of William Tayler, Footman, 1837*. Westminster City Archives/St Marylebone Society, 1998, p. 16.

10 Wise, *The Diary of William Tayler*, p. 20.

11 Best, *Mid-Victorian Britain*, p. 197.

12 Charles Dickens, *Sketches by Boz*. Chapman & Hall, n.d., p. 27.

13 Molly Hughes, *A Victorian Family*. Sidgwick & Jackson, 1990, p. 59.

14 Quoted in Warwick, *The Phoenix Suburb*, p. 129.

15 Mrs Ellis, *The Daughters of England, Their Position in Society, Character and Responsibilities*. Fisher, Son & Co., 1845, pp. 162–3.

16 Hughes, *A Victorian Family*, pp. 58–9.

17 Ibid.

18 A. K. H. Boyd, *Twenty-five Years of St Andrews*, Longman's Green & Co., 1892, vol. I, p. 32.

19 Ibid., p. 165.

20 Ibid., p. 303.

21 Ibid., p. 32.

22 Ibid., p.178.

23 Shepard, *Drawn from Memory*, p. 45–6.

24 Hughes, *A Victorian Family*, pp. 59–61.

25 Seaman, *Victorian England*, p. 21.

26 Wise, *The Diary of William Tayler*, p. 27.

27 Zuzanna Schonfeld, *The Precariously Privileged*. Oxford University Press, 1987, pp. 50–1.

28 Edith Buxton, *Reluctant Missionary*. Lutterworth Press, 1968, p. 34.

29 George Augustus Sala, *Twice Round the Clock*. Richard Marsh, London, 1862, pp. 80–1.

30 Norman Grubb, *C. T. Studd. Cricketer and Pioneer*. Religious Tract Society, 1933, pp. 11–12.

31 Ibid., p. 15.

32 Buxton, *Reluctant Missionary*, p. 25.

33 Ibid., p. 29.

Chapter 7: Etiquette and Fashion

1 'A Member of the Aristocracy', *Manners and Rules of Good Society*. Frederick Warne & Co., 1908 (thirty-fifth edition; originally published 1888), p. 111.

2 Ibid., p. 19.

3 Ibid.

4 Quoted in E. A. Laborde, *Harrow School, Yesterday and Today*. Winchester Publications, 1948, p. 88.

5 Leila von Meister, *Gathered Yesterdays*. Geoffrey Bles, 1963, p. 139.

6 Ernest H. Shepard, *Drawn from Memory*. Methuen, 1957, p. 46.

7 'A Member of the Aristocracy', *Manners and Rules*, p. 20.

8 Ibid., p. 22.

9 Ibid., p. 35.

10 Ibid., p. 34.

11 Mrs Humphrey ('Madge' of *Truth*), *Manners for Men*. James Bowden, 1898, p. 94.

12 *Punch*, 23 January 1892, p. 42.

13 Florence Howe Hall, *Social Customs*. Estes & Lauriat, 1897, p. 178.

14 Hall, *Social Customs*, p. 175.

15 'A Member of the Aristocracy', *Manners and Rules*, p. 228.

16 Hall, *Social Customs*, p. 179.

17 Ibid., p. 181.

18 Dorothy Wise (ed.), *The Diary of William Tayler, Footman, 1837*. Westminster City Archives/St Marylebone Society, 1998, p. 72.

19 George Augustus Sala, *Twice Round the Clock*. Richard Marsh, London, 1862, pp. 113–14.

Chapter 8: The Office

1 George Augustus Sala, *Twice Round the Clock*. Richard Marsh, London, 1862, p. 83.

2 Shaw Desmond, *London Nights of Long Ago*. Duckworth, 1927, pp. 50–1.

3 Ibid.

4 Ibid.

5 Ibid.

6 Quoted in Trevor Fisher, 'Britain's Unpermissive Society'. *History Today*, vol. 42, August 1992, p. 40.

7 Walter Besant, in *Illustrated London News*, Diamond Jubilee number, June 1897, p. 45.
8 L. H. Grindon, *Manchester Banks and Bankers*. David Bogue, 1878, p. 174.
9 Charles Dickens, *Sketches by Boz*. Chapman & Hall, n.d., pp. 123–4.
10 Quoted in Alan Delgado, *The Enormous File: A Social History of the Office*. John Murray, 1979, p. 21.
11 Quoted ibid., p. 43.
12 Quoted ibid., p. 40.
13 Quoted ibid., p. 39.
14 Desmond, *London Nights*, pp.51–3.
15 Ibid.
16 Ibid.

Chapter 9: Leisure

1 Author's collection.
2 Jerome K. Jerome, *Three Men in a Boat*. J. W. Arrowsmith, 1889, p. 197.
3 The Revd Sabine Baring-Gould, quoted in Charles Quest-Ritson, *The English Garden Abroad*. Viking, 1992, p. 14.
4 Author's collection.

Chapter 10: The Press and Literature

1 Alan Lee, *The Origins of the Popular Press, 1855–1914*. Croom Helm, 1976, p. 88.
2 Quoted in the *Daily Telegraph*, 10 May 1998.

Chapter 11: Arms and the World

1 Quoted in H. V. Morton, *A Traveller in Rome*. Methuen & Co., 1957, p. 238.
2 Charles Dickens, *Great Expectations*. The Educational Book Company, 1910, p. 152.
3 Shaw Desmond, *London Nights of Long Ago*. Duckworth, 1927, p. 59.
4 Quoted in David Newsome, *The Victorian World Picture*. John Murray, 1997, p. 117.
5 Quoted ibid., p. 116.
6 *Letters from B.A.C.*, privately printed, London, 1880, pages un-numbered.
7 Walter Besant, in *Illustrated London News*, Diamond Jubilee number, June 1897, p. 41.
8 *Punch*, 17 February 1854.
9 Quoted in Henri Troyat, *Tolstoy*, Penguin Books, 1970, p. 165.
10 John Galsworthy, *The Forsyte Saga*, William Heinemann, 1950, p. 486.
11 Winston Churchill, *My Early Life*. Thornton Butterworth, 1930, pp. 88–9.
12 John Whitehead (ed.), *The Barrack-Room Ballads of Rudyard Kipling*. Hearthstone Publications, 1995, p. 34.
13 Quoted in Newsome, *The Victorian World Picture*, p. 110.
14 Galsworthy, *The Forsyte Saga*, p. 486.

FURTHER READING

Ames, Winslow, *Prince Albert and Victorian Taste*. Methuen, 1967.

Anderson, Gregory, *Victorian Clerks*. Manchester University Press, 1975.

Bennett, Will, *Absent-Minded Beggars*. Leo Cooper, 1999.

Best, Geoffrey, *Mid-Victorian Britain, 1851–75*. Fontana Press, 1985.

Bolland, R. R., *Victorians on the Thames*. Midas Books, 1974.

Calder, Jenny, *The Victorian Home*. Book Club Associates, 1977.

Davidoff, Leonore, *The Best Circles. Society, Etiquette and the Season*. Croom Helm, 1973.

Delgado, Alan, *The Enormous File. A Social History of the Office*. John Murray, 1979.

Dewey, Clive, *The Passing of Barchester*. Hambledon Press, 1991.

Dutton, Ralph, *The Victorian Home*. Bracken Books, 1964.

Erickson, Carolly, *Her Little Majesty*. Simon & Schuster, 1997.

Flanders, Judith, *Consuming Passions. Leisure and Pleasure in Victorian Britain*. Harper Press, 2006.

———, *The Victorian House*. HarperCollins, 2003.

Hardy, Alan, *Queen Victoria Was Amused*. John Murray, 1976.

Hart-Davis, Adam, *What the Victorians Did for Us*. Headline, 2001.

Heasman, Kathleen, *Evangelicals in Action*. Geoffrey Bles, 1962.

Hitchmough, Wendy, *The Arts and Crafts Home*. Pavilion, 2000.

Horn, Pamela, *High Society. The English Social Elite, 1880–1914*. Sutton Publishing, 1992.

———, *The Rise and Fall of the Victorian Servant*. Sutton Publishing, 1975.

Hough, Richard, *Victoria and Albert*. Richard Cohen Books, 1996.

Housman, Laurence, *Victoria Regina*. Jonathan Cape, 1937.

Hughes, Molly, *A Victorian Family, 1870–1900*. Sidgwick & Jackson, 1990.

Inge, W. R., *The Victorian Age*. Cambridge University Press, 1922.

Marples, Maurice, *A History of Football*. Secker & Warburg, 1954.

Massie, Alastair (ed.), *A Most Desperate Undertaking. The British Army in the Crimea 1854–56*. National Army Museum, 2003.

Metcalf, Priscilla, *Victorian London*. Cassell, 1972.

Money, Tony, *Manly and Muscular Diversions*. Duckworth, 1997.

Montgomery, John, *1900. The End of an Era*. George Allen & Unwin, 1968.

Newsome, David, *The Victorian World Picture*. John Murray, 1997.

Newton, Charles, *Victorian Designs for the Home*. V & A Publications, 1999.

Nicholson, Shirley, *A Victorian Household*. Barrie and Jenkins, 1988.

Pearson, Geoffrey, *Hooligan: A History of Respectable Fears*. Macmillan, 1983.

Price, R. G. G., *A History of Punch*. Collins, 1957.

St Aubyn, Giles, *Queen Victoria*. Sinclair-Stevenson, 1991.

Steinbach, Susie, *Women in England 1760–1914: A Social History*. Weidenfeld & Nicolson, 2004.

Weintraub, Stanley, *Uncrowned King. The Life of Prince Albert*. The Free Press, 1997.

Wise, Dorothy (ed.), *The Diary of William Tayler, Footman, 1837*. Westminster City Archives/St Marylebone Society, 1998.

Wolmar, Christian, *Fire and Steam*. Atlantic Books, 2007.

———, *The Subterranean Railway*. Atlantic Books, 2004.

INDEX